THE ART OF DEMOSTHENES

AMERICAN PHILOLOGICAL ASSOCIATION

SPECIAL PUBLICATIONS

Roger S. Bagnall, Editor

Number 4

THE ART OF DEMOSTHENES

by
Lionel Pearson

THE ART OF DEMOSTHENES

by
LIONEL PEARSON

SCHOLARS PRESS

Distributed by
Scholars Press
101 Salem St.
P. O. Box 2268
Chico, CA, 95927

THE ART OF DEMOSTHENES

Lionel Pearson

Reprinted with the permission of Verlag Anton Hain

Library of Congress Cataloging in Publication Data

Pearson, Lionel Ignacius Cusack.
  The art of Demosthenes.

  (Special publications / American Philological
Association ; no. 4)
  Reprint. Originally published: Meisenheim am Glan :
A. Hain, 1976.
  Bibliography: p.
  Includes index.
  1. Demosthenes—Technique. 2. Oratory, Ancient.
I. Title. II. Series.
PA3964.P4   1981   885'.01   81-16752
ISBN 0-89130-551-3 (pbk.)   AACR2

Printed in the United States of America
1 2 3 4 5
Edwards Brothers, Inc.
Ann Arbor, Michigan 48106

Preface

This book has been written in an effort to discover and explain the artistry of Demosthenes. It contains no narrative or interpretation of his life and career, and it has not been my particular concern to decide whether he was right or wrong in his political judgment, whether he was justified in his attitude towards Philip, whether he was a better man than his political opponents in Athens, or whether his clients in the courts had justice on their side. It is not necessarily a greater work of art to reveal the truth than to conceal or distort it, but Demosthenes deserves our respect and our special attention because he seems so often to have found himself faced with whichever one of these tasks happened to be the more difficult at the moment.

The art of Demosthenes is his command of persuasive argument and his skill in presenting a case in such a way as to give pleasure even to those who refuse to be persuaded. It cannot be understood without reference to the history of his times and the law and customs and social institutions of contemporary Athens. We learn much of these things from him, but (unlike his political rivals) we should not complain if he sometimes misrepresents fact or law in order to achieve his particular purpose. We should learn to appreciate his skill even when we know or suspect that he is being unfair to his opponents. But we cannot always be sure that the persons that he slanders or the causes which he misrepresents deserve more respect than he does.

Some modern critics who admire Philip have never forgiven Demosthenes for resisting him, and they consider that he was guilty of misleading the Athenians because their resistance was unsuccessful. No attempt will be made to dispute the point, just as no serious attempt will be made to decide how we should have voted if we had been members of the political assemblies or the juries that he addressed. He failed in the greatest contest of his life, the struggle with Philip, and he was successful, after initial failure, in the greatest personal contest, with his political rival Aeschines. Our task is to investigate how skilfully he fought these two opponents (as well as other opponents), using every weapon at his disposal, including the political ideals and prejudices of democratic Athens.

Our concern is with Demosthenes the orator, not Demosthenes the statesman, with the defender of Athenian liberty and autonomy and the defender of his clients, not the defender of truth and justice. If we are to understand why Demosthenes was considered the greatest orator of antiquity, we must be prepared to face the disapproval of Plato, while recognizing that Aristotle may sympathize with us and help us in our search.

Another distinction that must be made is between the art of Demosthenes as orator and advocate and his proficiency in the technique of rhetoric. We have not proved that he is the master of Attic oratory if we show that he has mastered the technique of his trade. The distinction between art and technique is familiar in all the arts, and it is a necessary distinction in an orator just as in a painter or poet or musician. The technical vocabulary of rhetoric was highly developed in antiquity, but the existence of this ready-made apparatus of criticism does not excuse us from seeking our own criteria of artistic excellence. Some readers will want more attention paid to the figures and devices of rhetoric, just as others will want more attention paid to political and legal controversy. These readers are entitled to their opinions, but I have found it a difficult enough task to examine the art of Demosthenes, without also examining his rhetorical technique, his political judgment, and his legal learning. My intention has been to discover an approach to his oratory, which will make it possible for students to read him with pleasure and understanding, instead of finding themselves repelled by technical detail or accepting the current prejudice that he is neither interesting nor important.

I have not attempted in this book any systematic discussion of such technical aspects of his art as the range of his vocabulary, and the cadence and structure of his sentences, but I hope to make some small contribution, in another place, towards understanding the demands he made of himself as an orator and the degree of virtuosity in his climactic passages, and also (a smaller detail) to study his use, not his avoidance, of hiatus. The proper place for such detailed linguistic studies is in the pages of a professional journal, though an occasional hint may be found in the notes here.

A word may also be necessary about the form, or apparent lack of form, in the arrangement of this book. It has been difficult for me to keep the themes that I want to pursue separate from one another. I want to discuss the development of the orator's style, how it differs from that of his predecessors and how his early addresses to the Assembly are different from the later speeches, and how he learns to adapt his forensic style so that it becomes the style of the *Philippics*. This obliges me first to examine his forensic style, where the special features which attract attention are his narrative and his devastating ability to characterize his opponents. This leads to chapters on Narrative and Characterization, illustrated from both private and public forensic speeches. An orthodox critic of rhetorical art might want to continue with a discussion of other elements in these speeches — methods of proof and refutation, recapitulation, summing up, and epilogue. But I found myself unable to follow this line of inquiry with any success, and so I turned my back on the law courts in the next chapter, "leaping from the courts to the bema," in order to return to my main theme. I wanted to show how, as Demosthenes developed his own style of political oratory, he learnt, among other things, how to introduce narrative into political speeches and how best to draw the attention of the public to what had happened and was likely to happen again, if they were not careful and if they were not willing to recognize the kind of people (like Philip) with whom they had to contend.

It also seemed to me that the political speeches, unlike the forensic, were best treated in chronological order, because they formed a coherent series. Once the *Philippics* are started we see Demosthenes treating the same topic and employing the same arguments in a variety of different ways; it is like a series of prosecutor's speeches against the same defendant, Philip.

The two great speeches in his contest with Aeschines have been treated separately in the final chapter, because they need and deserve special treatment. Almost every aspect of the art of Demosthenes could be illustrated from *On the Embassy* and *On the Crown*; they show what he has learnt on the Pnyx as well as in the courts; *On the Crown* represents not only the climax of his career, but his final artistic achievement.

Demosthenes has been out of favour for many years with students of the classics, both in Europe and America, and the volume of critical literature in the past thirty years is not as great as might be expected. There is no need for me to offer a formal bibliography, since D. F. Jackson and G. O. Rowe have recently published their report on "Demosthenes 1915—1965" in *Lustrum* 14 (1969). It should be enough to give the reader a brief bibliographical note, with abbreviated titles of works which are frequently cited.

I am grateful to Stanford University for granting me the privilege of sabbatical leave in 1965, when progress was made on the early chapters of this book. I enjoyed the advantage of a change of scene in 1968, when I was visiting professor at the University of Sydney, and the critical interest shown by my Australian colleagues spurred me on. But the book could never have been finished if it had not been for the loyal encouragement and support of my friends and colleagues at Stanford.

Los Altos Hills, California. 1973

Contents

Bibliographical Note

The Greek text of Demosthenes is quoted from the Budé edition (Collection des Universités de France, Paris, Les belles Lettres), in ten volumes:

Harangues I, II, ed. M. Croiset (1924–25, repr. 1955).
Plaidoyers politiques I, ed. O. Navarre and P. Orsini (1954). II, ed. J. Humbert and L. Gernet (1959). III, IV, ed. G. Mathieu (ed. 2, 1956, 1958).
Plaidoyers civils I, II, III, IV, ed. L. Gernet (1954–60).

Other texts, commentaries, and translations:

H. WEIL, Les Harangues de Démosthène (ed. 2, Paris 1881).
–   Les Plaidoyers politiques de Démosthène (ed. 2, Paris 1883).
J. E. SANDYS, Demosthenes, On the Peace, Second Philippic, On the Chersonesus, and Third Philippic (London 1900, repr. 1962).
P. TREVES, Demostene, L'Orazione per la Corona (Milan 1955).
J. E. SANDYS and F. A. PALEY, Select Private Orations of Demosthenes I (ed. 2, Cambridge 1886), II (ed. 3, Cambridge 1896).
F. C. DOHERTY, Three private speeches of Demosthenes (Oxford 1927, repr. 1961).
L. PEARSON, Demosthenes, Six private speeches (Norman, Oklahoma 1972).
DEMOSTHENES, Public Orations, translated by A. W. Pickard-Cambridge, 2 volumes (Oxford 1912).
–   Private and other orations, translated with notes and appendices by C. R. Kennedy (London 1882).
W. WYSE, The speeches of Isaeus (Cambridge 1904, repr. Olms, Hildesheim 1967).

General Works:

BLASS, Friedrich, Die attische Beredsamkeit (Att. Bered.), 3 volumes in 4 (Leipzig 1893, repr. Olms, Hildesheim 1962).
BONNER, R. J., and Gertrude SMITH, The Administration of Justice from Homer to Aristotle, 2 volumes (Chicago 1930–38).
BUSOLT, G., and H. SWOBODA, Griechische Staatskunde, 2 volumes (Munich 1920–26).
CLOCHÉ, Paul, Démosthènes et la fin de la démocratie athénienne (Paris 1937).
HARRISON, A. R. W., The Law of Athens I, The Family and Property (Oxford 1968).
JAEGER, Werner, Demosthenes, The Origin and Growth of his Policy (Berkeley 1938, repr. Octagon Books, New York 1963).
JEBB, R. C., The Attic Orators, 2 volumes (Cambridge 1876).
JONES, A. H. M., Athenian Democracy (Oxford 1960).
KENNEDY, George, The Art of Persuasion in Greece (Princeton 1963).
LACEY, W. K., The Family in classical Greece (London 1968).
LIPSIUS, J. H., Das attische Recht und Rechtsverfahren (Att. Recht), 3 volumes in 4 (Leipzig 1905–15).

PICKARD-CAMBRIDGE, A. W., Demosthenes and the last days of Greek freedom (London and New York 1914).

Special Studies – a selection (for further bibliography see the report on "Demosthenes 1915–1965," in Lustrum 14 (1969)).

ADAMS, C. D., "Are the speeches of Demosthenes to be regarded as political pamphlets?" TAPA 43 (1912) 5–22.
–   "Speeches VIII and X of the Demosthenic Corpus," CP 33 (1938) 129–44.
d'AGOSTINO, V., "Gli esercizi giovanili di Demostene," Riv. stud. class. 4 (1956) 145–50.
CALHOUN, G. M., "Demosthenes' Second Philippic," TAPA 64 (1933) 1–17.
CAWKWELL, G. L., "Eubulus," JHS 83 (1965) 47–67.
–   "Aeschines and the ruin of Phocis," REG 75 (1962) 453–59.
–   "Aeschines and the Peace of Philocrates," REG 73 (1960) 416–38.
–   "The Defence of Olynthus," CQ N.S.12 (1962) 122–40.
CHEVALLIER, R., "L'art oratoire de Démosthène dans le discours sur la couronne," Bull. de l'Assoc. Budé (1960) 200–216.
CLOCHÉ, P., "La politique de Démosthènes de 354 à 346," BCH 47 (1923) 97–162.
–   "Athènes et Kersebleptès de 357-6 à 353-2," Mélanges Gustave Glotz I 215–26 (Paris 1932).
–   "Le traité athéno-thrace de 357," Rev. de Phil. 46 (1922) 5–13.
DAITZ, S. G., "The relationship of the De Chersoneso and the Philippica Quarta of Demosthenes," CP 52 (1957) 145–60.
DELAUNOIS, M., "Du plan logique au plan psychologique chez Démosthène," Les études classiques 19 (1951) 177–89.
DORJAHN, A. P., "Anticipation of arguments in Athenian oratory," TAPA 66 (1935) 274–95.
ERBSE, H., "Zu den olynthischen Reden des Demosthenes," Rh. Mus. 99 (1956) 364–80.
–   "Über die Midiana des Demosthenes," Hermes 84 (1956) 135–51.
FINLEY, M. I., Studies in Land and Credit in Ancient Athens (Rutgers University Press 1951).
GRONINGEN, B. A. van, "Mantithée contre Mantithée," Symbolae ad ius et historiam antiquitatis I. C. von Oven dedicatae (Leiden 1946) 92–110.
KORVER, J., "Demosthenes gegen Aphobos," Mnemosyne, ser. 3, 10 (1941) 8–22.
MILES, J., "The Marriage of Plangon (Dolly)," Hermathena 77 (1951) 38–46.
MORFORD, M., "Ethopoiia and character-assassination in the Conon of Demosthenes," Mnemosyne 19 (1966) 231–48.
MURPHY, J. J. (editor), Demosthenes, On the Crown. A Critical Case Study (New York 1967).
OERTEL, F., "Zur Frage der attischen Großindustrie," Rh. Mus. 79 (1930) 230–52.
PEARSON, L., "The Development of Demosthenes as a political orator," Phoenix 18 (1964) 95–109.
–   "Cicero's debt to Demosthenes in the Verrines," Pacific Coast Philology 3 (1968) 49–54.

– "Apollodorus, the eleventh Attic orator," The Classical Tradition, Studies in Honor of Harry Caplan (Cornell Univ. Press 1966), 347–59.

– "Demosthenes (or Pseudo-Demosthenes) XLV," Antichthon 3 (1969) 18–26.

PUECH, A., Les Philippiques de Démosthène (Paris 1952).

RADERMACHER, L., "Anfänge der Charakterkunde bei den Griechen," Symbolae Osloenses 27 (1949) 19–24.

ROME, A., "La vitesse de parole dans les orateurs attiques," Bull. de la classe des lettres, Acad. royale de Belgique, 38 (1952) 596–609.

RONNET, Gilberte, Étude sur le style de Démosthène dans les discours politiques (Paris 1951).

ROWE, G. O., "Demosthenes, First Philippic: the satiric mode," TAPA 99 (1968) 361–74.

RUDHARDT, J., "La reconnaissance de la paternité dans la société athénienne," Mus. Helveticum 19 (1962) 39–64.

RUEHLING, R., "Der junge Demosthenes als Verfasser der Rede gegen Spudias," Hermes 71 (1936) 441–51.

SAINTE-CROIX, G. E. M. de, "The alleged secret pact between Athens and Philip," CQ 13 (1963) 110–19.

SAMPAIX, J., "Quelques notes pour l'étude littéraire de la 1ère. Philippique de Démosthène," Nova et Vetera (Revue d'enseignement et de pédagogique belge) 19 (1937) 23–30.

SCHWAHN, W., Demosthenes gegen Aphobos (Leipzig 1929).

SCHWARTZ, E., "Demosthenes' erste Philippika," Festschrift für Th. Mommsen (Marburg 1893).

TRAMONTANA, A., "Gli ἐπιτροπικοί demostenici," Stud. Ital. 25 (1951) 169–87.

TREVES, P., "La composition de la 3me. Philippique," REA 42 (1940) 354–64.

USHER, S., "Individual characterization in Lysias," Eranos 63 (1965) 99–119.

VENERONI, Bruna, "Démosthène logographe," REG 79 (1966) 640–54.

WENDLAND, P., "Beiträge zu athenischer Politik und Publicistik, II. Isokrates und Demosthenes," Götting. gelehrte Nachrichten, ph. hist. Klasse, 1910, 289–323.

WOLFF, H. J., "Demosthenes als Advokat," Schriftenreihe der juristischen Gesellschaft e.V., 30 (1968).

– Die attische Paragraphe (Weimar 1966).

ZIEBARTH, E., Eine Handelsrede aus der Zeit des Demosthenes (1936).

Chapter I

Demosthenes and his Predecessors

Ancient critics do not explain very successfully why they considered Demosthenes the greatest of the orators. Their admiration seems genuine enough, particularly when it is based on careful reading of the speeches, but they do not describe his artistic supremacy in terms that satisfy a modern reader. They are not very helpful to the critic who is trying to analyze it. They show how well his speeches exemplified the rules and principles of rhetoric and how he was master of rhetorical technique. But their highest praise is reserved for the power of his oratory and its emotional impact on an audience. Dionysius of Halicarnassus says: "When I pick up a speech of Demosthenes, I feel like a person possessed, carried in this direction and that, as one emotion after another takes possession of me—distrust, agonized uncertainty, terror, contempt, hate, pity, admiration, anger, envy—all the different feelings to which the human heart is subject."[1] And yet none of these critics had heard him speak. They were dependent for information on the traditional praise handed down from one generation to another. Any comparison that they make between their own contemporaries and "the great orators of old" is artificial so far as the effect on an audience is concerned. They are using their romantic imagination, like people who try to describe how great singers of the past held their audiences spellbound—without any records to guide them.

Writers of modern times have been quick to notice how highly practising orators admired him—Lord Brougham[2] as well as Cicero. Cicero knew how much he could learn from him, and a search for Demosthenic imitation or influence in his speeches is a rewarding occupation.[3] His observable debt to Demosthenes is a better testimonial than any formal acknowledgment in his rhetorical works.[4] It is more difficult to guess how

1 Dion. Hal. Dem. 22.
2 Cf. Blass, Att. Bered. III 75–78.
3 For a preliminary experiment, cf. L. Pearson, "Cicero's Debt to Demosthenes in the Verrines," Pacific Coast Philology 3 (1968), 49–54.
4 Cicero leaves us in no doubt about his opinion, e.g., Brutus 9. 35: Nam plane quidem perfectum et quoi nihil admodum desit Demosthenem facile dixeris. Nihil acute inveniri potuit in eis causis quas scripsit, nihil, ut ita dicam, subdole, nihil versute, quod ille non viderit; nihil subtiliter dici, nihil presse, nihil enucleate, quo fieri posset aliquid limatius; nihil contra grande, nihil incitatum, nihil ornatum vel verborum gravitate vel sententiarum, quo quicquam esset elatius; 84. 289: 'Demosthenem igitur imitemur.' O di boni, quid, quaeso, nos aliud agimus aut quid aliud

much he owed to earlier Roman orators or even to men like Hortensius. His critical remarks in the *Brutus* about orators before his time must be largely repetition of what others had told him, traditional criticism handed down from men who had actually heard them speak.

He is more interesting when he writes about his own apprenticeship, telling us what he learned from his eminent elders and how Apollonius Molo in Rhodes taught him to change his style.[5] It is useful to be reminded that distinguished orators recognized their debt to their teachers. Demosthenes is supposed to have received instruction from Isaeus.[6] It would be a pity to discredit or reject this tradition, but the few passages in Demosthenes which appear to be modelled on parallel passages in Isaeus or to use the kind of arguments that Isaeus preferred[7] prove only that he was familiar with the older man's written work. They do not oblige us to believe that the two men knew one another personally. Nor does the tradition tell us what Isaeus taught him, as Cicero describes his experience with Molo. All the tales of Demosthenes' private training and rigid self-discipline—the pebbles in the mouth and so on—are concerned with the technique of delivery and emphasize his difficulty in mastering it.[8] The proof that he did master it can be found in the *Olynthiacs* and the *Philippics*, where there are passages that no one would write for himself unless he had confidence in his advanced technique;[9] but the ancient critics do not think it worth while to cite these passages as illustration of his virtuosity or artistic mastery.

optamus? At non assequimur; Orator 6. 23: Hoc nec gravior exstitit quisquam nec callidior nec temperatior. Cf. 26. 90, 29. 104, 38. 133. For his mastery of rhetorical figures and his supposed insistence on *actio*, cf. Brutus 37. 140—142; Orator 39. 136.

5 Brutus 91. 316.

6 Dion. Hal. Isaeus 1, Plut. Dem. 5, X Orat. Vit. 839F, 844B.

7 The insistence on the value of evidence given by slaves under torture (a regular *topos*) in 30. 37 seems to be borrowed from Isaeus 8. 12. The Argument to Oration 31 notes that some critics regarded both 30 and 31 as written by Isaeus. For discussion of this whole tradition, see Blass, Att. Bered. II 489—91, who quotes earlier literature.

8 Plut. Dem. 6—7.

9 Cf. Chap. IV, below, pp. 115 — 16. If a passage can be called "difficult" when it requires a high standard of breath and voice control and the ability to interpose parentheses, at a fast pace, without losing the flow of the paragraph's movement or losing the thread of the argument, some good examples can easily be found. The reader might experiment with 2. 21, 3. 24, 4. 38—39. The matter deserves further investigation. Ancient teachers of rhetoric, like modern teachers of music, must have been well aware what passages in the classic works were "easy" or "difficult." Many modern critics are inclined to be content, when admiring a particular passage, to speak of the effect instead of searching for the means by which it is produced; it is not enough to say that a passage is moving, unless one is ready to explain how the writer has led the way to this effect. Critics like Blass regularly mention the di-

Demosthenes delivered his *Philippics* with an eye to the prevailing opinion in the Assembly and the effect on the audience of remarks made by previous speakers; that setting is part of his speeches. It might be argued that the Areopagus crisis is part of the *Eumenides* or the memory of the plague in Athens part of the *Oedipus Tyrannus*,[10] or that we cannot appreciate the *Trojan Women* properly unless we recreate the political setting of 415 B.C., with the memory of the Melian massacre fresh in our minds. But the setting is not so essential for our appreciation of a play's dramatic quality, unless we believe its principal value lies in its political message; and in that case we are treating the play as though it was the work of an orator, an attempt to influence public opinion.[11]

In order to appreciate the quality of a speech we must determine how well its argument and its style suit the occasion. A play may come to be regarded as a masterpiece though it was not well received at its first performance. When a fine play is poorly received, we can blame the poor taste of the audience or the poor performance of the actors, and remind ourselves that it was not the duty of the playwright to write for this particular audience or this particular theatrical company. But when a speaker, who has written his own speech, makes a poor impression on his audience, it is not easy to absolve him of all blame, since his task was to meet that particular occasion. There can be extenuating circumstances. The task that he faces may be very difficult, even impossible. No one would call the *First Philippic* a poor speech because it failed to make the Athenians take appropriate action, or think that Aeschines' reply to Demosthenes' speech *On the Embassy* was the better speech just because he was acquitted; and there are other reasons besides the acquittal of Ctesiphon for thinking that *On the Crown* is a better speech than *Against Ctesiphon.*

visions of a speech into its rhetorical elements, the variation in tone and emotional tension, the ability to express anger, bitterness, or enthusiasm, the use of commonplace and metaphor and other familiar figures of rhetoric, the clarity of exposition or the logical connection and flow of the argument. This is all part of a speaker's basic technique. It describes the craftsman, not the artist.

10 Cf. B. W. Knox, Oedipus at Thebes (New Haven 1957).
11 Critics have often found fault with the Trojan Women because of its episodic construction and its supposed lack of dramatic coherence, and it has been restored to favour in more recent years only because it has become usual to regard it as a powerful anti-war play or a protest against the proposed Athenian expedition to Sicily. Cf. e.g. H. Steiger, "Warum schrieb Euripides seine Troerinnen?" Philologus 13 (1900), 326–99; H. Grégoire, "Euripide – Ulysse et Alcibiade," Bull. de la classe des lettres, Acad. r. de Belgique 19 (1933), 83–106; E. Délébecque, Euripide et la Guerre du Peloponnèse (Paris 1951), chap. XI; and Gilbert Murray, The Trojan Women, translated, Introductory note (London 1905).

It is not a simple task to set down the principles by which the forensic or political speeches of an Attic orator should be judged. We must take account of the setting, but it is not strictly our business to inquire if he is recommending the best policy to the Assembly or if the client whom he represents in court is in the right. The historian cannot ignore the first question, and it must be answered if we are to pass judgment on Demosthenes as a politician. The jurist cannot resist attempting to answer the second, but the answer does not affect Demosthenes' merits as a legal counsel. Sometimes, when he seems to have a hard case, we have too little information to be quite sure that he has handled it wisely. If we had the speech of the opposing party, we might be in a better position to pass judgment. And yet, when we have the opposing speech in the contest with Aeschines, we are easily able to decide that Demosthenes' speech is the better of the two, although (especially in the *Embassy* case) this decision does not help us to decide judicially how we should have cast our vote if we had been on the jury.

If we are to pass judgment on a forensic speech, we must first master the relevant facts of the case as well as we can and decide what are the points at issue; then we must ask if a strong and convincing case has been presented and how difficult it would be to counter (we can only guess when it would be tactically possible to protest that the speaker is lying or misrepresenting facts).[12] The procedure will be similar for a political speech, though we must remember that here the audience may be much better informed about the relevant facts than the members of a jury before the trial starts. But we cannot with any confidence estimate the actual emotional impact of a speech when delivered. We cannot even be sure how closely the written version resembles the original spoken version. We must be content to pass judgment on the written version that we have.

Demosthenes had ten years' experience in civil cases before he started on his political career, "leaping from the law-courts to the bema," as Aeschines says (3.171), and the private speeches will be examined first, since they provide evidence of the stages by which he learned his craft. He started very young, as soon as he came of age, at eighteen; either because of poverty or from independence of spirit he decided to handle his own case against his guardians. His speeches as they are preserved show that his self-confidence was amply justified. Already in these first attempts we find characteristics that he retains throughout his career. His narrative is economical and he avoids unnecessary or irrelevant detail; he knows what can be left out and what must be included. Also, more noticeably in the speeches *Against Onetor* than in those *Against Aphobus*, he shows his

12 As in Aesch. 2. 8—10 and Dem. De Cor. 10.

ability to pick out the weak points in his opponent's story which give him the best chance of discrediting his claim.

In Athenian litigation the plaintiff frequently wants to do more than establish the fact that he has been treated unjustly or that the defendant has committed certain acts. He wants to establish the worst possible motive on the defendant's part, so as to convince the jury that his guilt is even more serious than the evidence seems to demand. The argument is essentially the same when directed against Aphobus as when directed against Aeschines. A criminal intention on the defendant's part is presented as the only explanation of his behaviour.

This was the method of attack that was used against Socrates at his trial. Socrates might have tried to save his life by offering the jury a penitent explanation that would cause them to modify their sentence, if not their verdict. The accusers had insisted on his criminal intentions, and he might have attempted (though it would not have been easy) to convince people that he was unaware of what he was doing and was not as intelligent as they said. But he refused to play the game that was expected of him; he declined to propose an acceptable alternative to the death sentence or give an explanation that might make his "guilt" seem less serious, and the jury supposed themselves forced to pass the severe sentence.

Just as a prosecutor presented the guilt of the defendant in the blackest terms, so he regularly asked for a severer penalty than he expected the jury to vote; and in civil cases a plaintiff asked for a larger sum of money than he expected to receive, because he would be lucky if he succeeded in collecting even half of the sum to which the jury's verdict entitled him. Demosthenes asked for and obtained a judgment of ten talents against Aphobus, but he did not expect to recover more than half that amount, and with a less severe sentence his chances would have been further decreased. It is not necessarily foolish to demand more money than the other party can produce. A political opponent, who is unwilling or unable to pay more than a fraction of what the court orders, can be forced into exile, and this should satisfy his prosecutor, whose real aim is to drive him out of politics.

In the cases *Against Aphobus* and *For Phormio* we are able to follow developments after the trial and to see what difficulties a litigant faced in actually securing the object for which he went to court. All these considerations should have some bearing on our judgment of the speeches of Demosthenes. He must be well aware that he often overstates his case, and his object will then be to force his opponents to suggest to the jury the kind of judgment that they will be willing to pass. Recognition of his tactics may lead us to a fairer appreciation and interpretation than any attempt to discover the true facts and the strict demands of the law.

The case against Meidias is supposed never to have come into court. Demosthenes is reported to have accepted an offer of money and to have settled the matter privately, and he has been criticized for doing so in both ancient and modern times.[13] The object in bringing suit was, of course, to ruin the public career of Meidias and eliminate him from politics. But if Demosthenes failed to secure a favourable verdict, it would ruin his own career. With strong feelings on both sides the result was very uncertain, and Meidias was likely to be no less brutal in his defence than Demosthenes in his attack. And since we never hear of Meidias causing him trouble afterwards, this may be an instance when the threat of prosecution was effective. The threat of prosecution evidently meant the careful preparation of a prosecutor's speech, perhaps also a deliberate "leaking" of information about its contents.[14]

It is easier to pass judgment on a speech when one is in no doubt about the object that it has in view. In political trials, when one politician is trying to discredit the character of another and to wreck his good name, the technique may not be the same as in a regular civil suit, where he will be content to prove his opponent in the wrong and recover money from him. When Demosthenes wrote his first speech for a political prosecution, *Against Androtion*, he had nearly ten years' successful experience in civil suits behind him, and it must have been on the basis of that experience that Diodorus engaged him to write a speech for him. In this kind of case (as the speech *On the Crown* makes very clear), though the formal basis for prosecution is a legal technicality, it is not so important to prove that the proposal made by the defendant in the Assembly was unconstitutional as to present evidence or supposed evidence of the defendant's character. The precise legal issue becomes less important in a struggle for power between rival politicians, and the jury's verdict may depend, in great part, on larger and not strictly relevant questions. Furthermore, the greater length of time allowed for speaking[15] does not enforce the same kind of

---

13 Plut. Dem. 12, Aesch. 3. 52 and 212.
14 Aeschines accuses him of letting his adversary know about his speech in advance in the dispute between Phormio and Apollodorus; this is meant as an accusation of disloyalty to his client, and we need not take it seriously, 2. 165 ἔγραψας λόγον Φορμίωνι τῷ τραπεζίτῃ χρήματα λαβών· τοῦτον ἐξήνεγκας Ἀπολλοδώρῳ, τῷ περὶ τοῦ σώματος κρίνοντι Φορμίωνα. Cf. 3. 173.
15 For an estimate of the time taken by speeches, see A. Rome, "La vitesse de parole des orateurs attiques," Bull. de la classe des lettres, ʿAcad. r. de Belgique, 38 (1952), 596−609. For private cases involving an amount of over 5000 drachmas Aristotle, Resp. Ath. 67, says speakers were allowed ten choenices of water in the clepsydra. Now that a clepsydra and a presumed choenix measure have been found

economy that is required in private cases. A different manner of introduction and a different style of narrative can be used.

In private cases, when certain facts are in dispute and there is conflict between the evidence offered by plaintiff and defendant, Demosthenes may begin the plaintiff's speech by presenting the defendant as a dishonest and unsavoury character, as the kind of man likely to have wronged the plaintiff and with no scruples about perjuring himself in the story that he tells. He will present the man's alleged bad character as though it were evidence of his wrongdoing, as though his character were known and only his particular acts in dispute. In political trials the situation is different. The jury will be more familiar with the defendant's career, and some of his acts will be beyond dispute—his activities in the Assembly, the results of a diplomatic mission or military expedition when he has been in charge. This supposedly familiar material can be used as the basis for conclusions about his general character and his eligibility for public office; if an unfavourable conclusion can be sustained, the jury can be invited to remove him from public life by their verdict and the actual legal question at issue loses most of its importance.

In a political trial the current version of his opponent's career may be so firmly established that the speaker cannot call it into question, even though it is unfavourable to him. Or he may decide that these "facts" will be favourable or damaging to his case according to the manner in which they are presented. The first point of view seems to be reflected in Cicero's youthful treatise *De Inventione*. A narrative, he says, will not help your case if the facts have been set forth by your opponents and there is nothing to be gained by telling the story again or in a different way.[16] In his later practice it is doubtful whether Cicero thought such a

---

in the Athenian Agora (T.L. Shear, Hesperia 4 [1935], 347; S. Young, Hesperia 8 [1939], 274), it is possible for Rome to argue that a choenix of water lasts only three minutes, so that a speech like the first oration Against Aphobus would have to be completed in thirty minutes. In important public cases Aristotle (loc. cit.) appears to say that equal amounts of water were allowed for plaintiff and defendant and that the time available for the case was the length of the shortest day in the year (in the month of Poseideion), i.e., rather more than nine hours. If time is set aside for supporting speeches and speeches in rebuttal, Rome takes this to mean that each chief speaker had about three hours at his disposal, and that a speech like On the Crown would have to be delivered at a rate of about 150 words a minute.

16 De Inv. 1. 21. 30. The entire passage is worth quoting: Illud autem praeterea considerare oportebit, ne aut cum obsit narratio aut cum nihil prosit, tamen interponatur; aut non loco aut non quemadmodum causa postulet narretur. Obest tum, cum ipsius rei gestae expositio magnam excipit offensionem quam argumentando et causam agendo leniri oportebit. Quod cum accidet, membratim oportebit partes rei gestae dispergere in causam et ad unam quamque confestim rationem accomodare, ut vulneri praesto medicamentum sit et odium statim defensio

12

situation ever occurred. He certainly did not think he could do without narrative in *Pro Milone*, though the Greek treatises which he had studied may have recommended a very scanty use of narrative in such a situation.

Demosthenes certainly seems to have recognized that narrative was the heart of any speech in the courts and that no inconvenient version of the "facts," the current version or his opponent's version, need ever be accepted. He clearly believes that the "facts" can and must be presented in such a way that the desired conclusion will seem to follow naturally from his narrative. Quintilian puts this point of view very well when he says that the purpose of narrative is not merely to put the judge in possession of the facts, but to make him share our opinion.[17]

On the other hand, there are occasions when a new narrative will serve only to confirm the unfortunate conclusions which the opposing speaker has presented. In such a situation it will suit the orator's purpose better to confine himself to selected details of the story.[18] In the duels between Demosthenes and Aeschines, the one usually avoids describing an event which the other can exploit more effectively. Aeschines does not describe or attempt to explain the delays of the second embassy's journey to Macedonia, which Demosthenes attributes to criminal negligence (Dem. *F. L.* 155–164). Nor does Demosthenes mention the unhappy occasion on the first mission to Philip when, according to Aeschines (2. 34–35), he broke down in the middle of his speech and was unable to continue. Aeschines has nothing to say about the famous evening in Athens when the news arrived that Philip was at Elatea or about the following day when Demosthenes took command in the Assembly. The ἑσπέρα μὲν γὰρ ἦν

mitiget. Nihil prodest narratio tum, cum ab adversariis re exposita nostra nihil interest iterum aut alio modo narrare; aut ab eis qui audiunt ita tenetur negotium ut nostra nihil intersit eos alio pa ·to docere.

17 Inst. Or. 4.2. 20–21. Ne hoc quidem simpliciter accipiendum quod est a me positum, esse supervacuam narrationem rei, quam iudex noverit; quod sic intellegi volo, si non modo quid factum sit sciet, sed ita factum etiam ut nobis expedit opinabitur. Neque enim narratio in hoc reperta est ut tantum cognoscat iudex, sed aliquanto magis ut consentiat.

18 The point is put very clearly by Cicero: Non quemadmodum causa postulat narratur, cum aut id quod adversario prodest dilucide et ornate exponitur aut id quod ipsum adiuvat obscure dicitur et neglegenter. Quare, ut hoc vitium vitetur, omnia torquenda sunt ad commodum suae causae, contraria quae praeteriri poterunt praetereundo, quae dicenda erunt leviter attingendo, sua diligenter et enodate narrando.

Quintilian, more shrewdly, sees that the term "narrative" must not be taken in too narrow a sense: Duas esse in iudiciis narrationum species existimo, alteram ipsius causae, alteram rerum ad causam pertinentium (4.2. 11). And he notes that there may indeed be a great deal of "relevant material": Quare ambitus quoque causae et repetundarum hoc etiam plures huiusmodi narrationes habere poterunt quo plura crimina (4.2. 14).

passage in *On the Crown* (169–174) has no parallel in Aeschines' speech *Against Ctesiphon*. Even when Aeschines (3. 141) is trying to show that Demosthenes deserves no credit for the alliance with Thebes, because it is the product of circumstance (καιρὸς καὶ φόβος καὶ χρεία συμμαχίας, ἀλλ' οὐ Δημοσθένης), he finds it better to dispense with narrative.

Aeschines, however, made one serious mistake in choosing an incident to describe. He was very proud of his angry speech before the Amphictyonic meeting at Delphi, which fired the assembled *hieromnemones* with indignation at the desecration of the Sacred Plain by the Locrians of Amphissa, and he describes this speech at some length in *Against Ctesiphon* (118–122), as though it was an oratorical triumph. But Demosthenes (18. 149) presents the speech not as a triumph but as a political disaster, because the *hieromnemones* were "men unaccustomed to oratory and without suspicion of what was likely to result" when, in response to Aeschines' eloquence, they took action which led to an Amphictyonic war and provided Philip with the opportunity he needed to bring an army into central Greece. By crediting Aeschines with foresight that he surely did not possess, Demosthenes represents this well-meant speech as a traitor's master stroke. This technique had not succeeded in the earlier trial, when he was trying to prove Aeschines a dangerous man, if not an actual traitor. But here he will be satisfied if he convinces the jury that his own actions showed more political wisdom and served the interests of Athens better. His purpose will be served if Aeschines is considered guilty of bad judgment.

In a *graphe paranomon*, where the formal charge is that of making an unconstitutional proposal in the Assembly, the object is almost always to discredit a politician or the policy which he represents. This formal charge gives the jury an opportunity to register a vote for or against him, but an experienced speaker will not ask the direct question: "Will you discredit the defendant and put an end to his political career?" It is hardly a legal question, and one would expect a speaker to avoid formulating it directly. But in *Against Androtion*, Demosthenes' first speech in this kind of prosecution, the true intention is not masked with any great care. Technically, it seems, the defendant was guilty of an illegal act if he had proposed a crown for an outgoing Boule which had not built any triremes. But his proposal is presented as a dangerous precedent which will result in a shortage of ships (if members of the Boule take it as an invitation to find a plausible excuse for not building ships, instead of meeting their obligations) and as an example of the defendant's tendency to think he can say or propose anything he pleases. He is said to have broken other laws (though no proof is offered) and represented as a man without regard for Athenian interests, high-handed, and with no respect for established law.

With this sketch outlined of a man who regularly breaks laws, the way is prepared for a fuller narrative of "this fine fellow's political life" (47). The rest of the speech is devoted to narrative, so as to show what a totally undesirable person Androtion is.

Against Androtion is hardly one of the most admirable of Demosthenes' speeches,[19] and one need feel little regret that the accusation was unsuccessful. But it is a most interesting example of the way in which the *graphe paranomon* was exploited against political rivals. It seems to say, with quite shameless frankness, to the jury: "Here is a legal technicality which can be used to ruin the defendant's career; but if you don't find it a sufficiently good reason, here are some other details (not actionable, of course) which you may find more convincing." In their later speeches Demosthenes and Aeschines take more trouble to make their detailed narrative appear relevant to the formal charge. Important issues are at stake, their complaints may often be genuine, though the impertinence and irrelevance of much that they say is evident to the modern reader.

Some resemblances can be observed between Demosthenes' style of argument in political prosecutions and the manner in which Isaeus treats some of his inheritance cases.[20] When his client is claiming an inheritance, he quite frequently bases his claim not on strict law but on equity and on the ground that he is a more worthy heir and a man of excellent character, while his adversary has shown himself an undesirable person in various ways—dishonest, ungrateful, not deserving of any sympathy.

Like Demosthenes he presents his case with a skilful and abundant use of narrative, and he often has an astonishing tale to tell, in which some remarkable characters appear. When he wants the jury to disregard the letter of the law in favour of his client's personal merits, he will concentrate his attention on trying to convince them that his client is a better man than his adversary and he will blacken his opponent's character by presenting his family life as totally disgraceful. Like Demosthenes he knows when to interrupt his story with a comment or explanation which

---

19 Androtion can be identified with the historian of that name, author of an Atthis, and some Attic inscriptions give evidence of his public spirited activity (Jacoby, F. Gr. Hist., III B, No. 324, T. 4, 5, 7, 12). Jacoby has protested vigorously at the injustice of the accusations made in this speech (F. Gr. Hist., III B, Supp. I, pp. 93—102) and done his best to represent Androtion as a "patriot and an idealist" and a member of the party of "decent and honourable men" (p. 95). His defence is perhaps somewhat exaggerated; there may be some, though not much, truth in what Demosthenes writes.
20 Cf. A. Tramontana, "Gli ἐπιτροπικοί demostenici," Stud. Ital. 25 (1951), 169—87, who finds many examples of stylistic mannerisms that could be borrowed from Isaeus. Cf., also, V. d'Agostino, "Gli esercizi giovanili di Demostene," Riv. stud. class. 4 (1956), 145—50.

can turn an incident into a powerful argument. Demosthenes' speech *For Phormio* is a particularly successful example of narrative combined with argument,[21] but some of Isaeus' speeches also offer good examples of the same technique.

Demosthenes was familiar with Isaeus' eighth oration, *On the Estate of Ciron*, from which he borrowed some turns of phrase and the *topos* in praise of the Athenian custom of taking evidence from slaves under torture.[22] The whole strength of the speaker's case here depends on the story he tells. Ciron's estate is being claimed by a nephew (his two sons are apparently no longer alive), but the speaker claims a closer relationship, saying that he and his brother are Ciron's grandchildren, that their mother is Ciron's daughter by his first wife, who died when her child was still an infant (7). Apparently he has no formal evidence or documentation of Ciron's first marriage, and he therefore takes great trouble to show how kindly the girl was treated by Ciron and his second wife—how they brought her up in the household with their own two sons, how her marriage was arranged, and a second marriage when her first husband died. He explains how he and his brother (her children) were treated with great kindness and affection by Ciron and invited to family gatherings, and when Ciron died their stepmother made no objection to their making arrangements for his funeral.

Every detail is used as an indication, a *tekmerion*, that Ciron considered them his legitimate grandchildren, so as to make up for the lack of direct evidence about the marriage. The witnesses whom he actually calls are relying on hearsay. The rival claimant has in his possession some slaves who have spent their lives in Ciron's service and might be expected to know the facts, but he has refused to release them for interrogation, and this is represented as a strong indication that they know more than is convenient for him to have revealed (10—11).[23]

The story is cleverly told in such a way as to make it seem evident that these young men are Ciron's grandsons and that he intended to leave his property to them, since he was clearly very fond of them. Some information about Diocles, the rival claimant, is brought in at the end, to

21 Cf., e.g., Blass, Att. Bered., III 465—66.
22 Isaeus 8. 12; Dem. 30. 37.
23 Wyse (Speeches of Isaeus, p. 595) finds this argument very feeble, "an attempt to cover his weakness by raising a false issue. Even if the slaves possessed the knowledge attributed to them, the opponents could not be fairly required to give assistance to a fishing inquiry. Their rejection of the challenge is no sign of a bad conscience." This may be fair legal comment, but it is doubtful whether the reasoning would convince an Athenian jury. So also in Dem. 54. 27 one wonders how damaging or dangerous it was for Ariston to refuse the challenge of interrogating slaves (see below, Chapter II, p. 60, n. 32).

show that he is not a person of good character, and (as a final touch) that he has been "caught in adultery" (μοιχὸς ληφθείς, 44). By emphasizing the dire consequences that will follow for them if their claim is disallowed, the speech invites the conclusion that Diocles is as heartless a scoundrel as they are honest and scrupulous.

It is not recorded how Diocles presented his case in reply (an effective reply, which did not antagonize the jury would be difficult), but Isaeus' third oration, *On the Estate of Pyrrhus*, shows us the kind of speech he could write for a client in this sort of position—this time it is his client who refuses to admit that the deceased, Pyrrhus, had a legitimate daughter. Instead of a long narrative, there is a short statement at the start of the speech:[24] "My maternal uncle Pyrrhus had no legitimate children; he adopted my brother Endius, who inherited the property, and for twenty years, up to the time of his death, his claim was never disputed." It is only after Endius' death that a certain Phile appears, saying that she is Pyrrhus' legitimate daughter. She is represented by her husband, Xenocles.[25] "We fought his claim, sued Xenocles for false witness, and won our case; in the course of the trial we discredited the statement of Nicodemus, who said that he had given his sister in marriage to Pyrrhus and that Phile was their child" (1—6).

A great part of the speech is devoted to reinforcing the prejudice established against Xenocles and Nicodemus in this earlier trial. Phile's mother is said to have been a notorious *hetaira*, who was not in the habit of marrying the men with whom she consorted (13—16); there had been, at the earlier trial, one witness to her marriage with Pyrrhus, but he has not repeated his evidence now (18). There is even some doubt if Phile was the correct name of her daughter—a strange thing if Xenocles, after eight years of marriage, did not know his wife's legal name! (30—31). The only way to counter this kind of argument would be a long narrative which explained everything, including the reason for Phile's silence over so many years. As in the dispute about Ciron's estate, it may be to the advantage of one side to present a detailed consecutive narrative, while the other concentrates attention on a limited number of details and the supposed character of certain persons.

Isaeus' first and second orations also present an interesting contrast, and the speaker in the first case (for reasons that we can only guess) seems to be concealing the sort of detail that is revealed in the second. For example, he refuses to tell the story of the quarrel between his two uncles,

---

24 What follows is a summarized version of his statement.
25 Endius, as an adopted son, who has no children of his own, has not the legal right to dispose by will of the property that he received from his adoptive father. Cf. Wyse, op. cit. (n.23, above), p. 276; Lipsius, Att. Recht II, 566—67.

because it was not very creditable to his uncle Cleonymus and might suggest that he was unbalanced or actually afflicted with *paranoia*.[26] In Oration II the narrative is much fuller and more circumstantial and every detail has its weight. The speaker's "uncle" is shown as spiteful and ill-natured in contrast with the even-tempered, kindly, and totally unselfish Menecles, to whom the speaker is proud to declare his loyalty. It will be difficult for the opposition to maintain that it is Menecles who has been dishonest and perverse, unless they can discredit the accuracy of the narrative. We never know all the facts, of course, and not knowing what went on in the speech -writer's interview with his client, we cannot tell how much has been invented or judiciously manipulated.

The contrast between Isaeus' cleverly composed speeches and the cruder methods of Antiphon in *On the Murder of Herodes* is interesting to observe. Antiphon's client has been accused of murder, but his accusers have not followed the proper procedure for a homicide charge; they should have taken care not to bring a person suspected of blood-guilt into a building where he might contaminate other people; but instead of summoning him to stand trial in an open-air court, they have brought him into the Agora, into a heliastic court, which is concerned with misdemeanours (κακουργήματα): "They have made an assessment of damage, though the law is that a killer must pay with his own life, and they have done this not to help me, but because of the monetary advantage to themselves. They have put a lower valuation on the dead man's life than the law does" (10). The speaker also complains that they have refused bail and kept him in prison (17). Such special care to prevent his escape does not suggest that their motives are dishonest, but (if Isaeus or Demosthenes had written the speech) one would expect the conclusion to be drawn that they are brutal and contemptuous of the law, as well as motivated purely by αἰσχροκέρδεια, with each detail of their irregular procedure contributing to the sketch of their character.

The defendant must surely want the jury to draw this inference, because he explains his tactics with alarming candour: "I want you to take the violent and irregular behavion of these men as an indication of their attitude, towards me and towards everyone" (8).[27] He seems to be explaining his tactics without carrying them out very effectively.

---

26 In Oration VI (On the Estate of Philoctemon) the *paranoia* of old Euctemon is well illustrated by the complicated story which the speaker unfolds; the opponents were apparently less careful in their narrative, and the speaker finds some serious flaws and inconsistencies (14–15). The strange story of the spell exercised over Euctemon by Alce and her two sons is very cleverly told, with an eye to members of the jury who will be ready to believe that "there is no fool like an old fool."

27 ἵνα ἦ τεκμήρια ὑμῖν καὶ τῶν ἄλλων πραγμάτων καὶ τῶν εἰς ἐμὲ ἡ τούτων βιαιότης καὶ παρανομία. I prefer to retain the second καί which editors generally delete.

The narrative itself is startlingly brief. And it lacks circumstantial detail. The speaker and Herodes were passengers on a ship sailing from Mytilene to Aenos, and were forced by bad weather to put in "at a place in the territory of Methymna"—he does not even mention the name of the anchorage. He explains that he and Herodes had perfectly good independent reasons for sailing in this ship, but the narrative contains no reply to the inevitable charge that "of course a man planning a murder would find or contrive some explanation for being on the ship." He gives no names for the other passengers, though he knows what their business was; nor does he describe what they did or said to one another; he simply says that after reaching the anchorage they transferred to another ship, which gave better protection against the weather, and "we started drinking."

The story is told in the fewest possible words: "When we had transferred to the other ship, we started drinking; as all agree, he left the ship and never returned; but I never left the ship that night. Next day, when there was no sign of him, I took part in the search for him just as vigorously as the others; I was just as deeply distressed at what had happened as anybody; and I was the one responsible for having a messenger sent to Mytilene; it was done at my suggestion."[28] But that is all. When the man simply could not be found, they put to sea again. "That is what happened"—τὰ μὲν γενόμενα ταῦτ᾽ ἐστίν (25).

The long argumentative section that follows shows how the charges rest·on very flimsy evidence and is put together with much greater skill. But the narrative is too short to suggest any conclusions about the speaker's behaviour that night. What went on at the drinking party? Who started it? Who provided the wine? How many were there in the party, and were they friendly or quarrelsome? And how much did the speaker drink, and is he clear about all that happened on that fateful evening? One is left wondering what questions the speech-writer asked his client and what answers he received.

Defendants accused of serious offences can help their case enormously by a detailed narrative which reveals their good character. Lysias' first oration, *On the Murder of Eratosthenes*, offers an admirable example of this kind of narrative.[29] The speaker, Euphiletus, readily admits killing his wife's lover, Eratosthenes, in his own house before witnesses, as the law of

---

28 ἐπειδὴ δὲ μετεξέβημεν εἰς τὸ ἕτερον πλοῖον, ἐπίνομεν. καὶ ὁ μέν ἐστι φανερὸς ἐκβὰς ἐκ τοῦ πλοίου καὶ οὐκ εἰσβὰς πάλιν· ἐγὼ δὲ τὸ παράπαν οὐκ ἐξέβην ἐκ τοῦ πλοίου τῆς νυκτὸς ἐκείνης. τῇ δ᾽ ὑστεραίᾳ, ἐπειδὴ ἀφανὴς ἦν ὁ ἀνήρ, ἐζητεῖτο οὐδέν τι μᾶλλον ὑπὸ τῶν ἄλλων ἢ καὶ ὑπ᾽ ἐμοῦ· καὶ εἴ τῳ τῶν ἄλλων ἐδόκει δεινὸν εἶναι, καὶ ἐμοὶ ὁμοίως (23).

29 Cf. S. Usher, "Individual Characterization in Lysias," Eranos 63 (1965), esp. 101–05.

Athens permitted; all that is required of him in law is to show that this is exactly what he did, that he had caught the man with his wife and not attacked him outside or craftily enticed him inside. But by a shrewd choice of detail he does better than this. He expects the jury to understand the trust he had in a wife who looked after him well and took good care of their child; all that needs explanation is the arrangement of their house, perhaps unusual at Athens, with their bedroom upstairs and the "women's quarters," where the baby was left with the servants, downstairs; this avoided the risk of taking him down the ladder to wash him, and often his wife spent a good part of the night downstairs, so as to be with the baby (9—10). He is therefore not in the least suspicious when the baby starts crying in the night, and she goes down apparently to look after him, but really to meet her lover; she locks the door to the upstairs room as she goes, saying that if she leaves it open for him he will probably entice the servant girl up there; the incident is made to appear like a good-humoured jest, which amused him, and she seemed quite reluctant to leave him: "I laughed, and she got up and closed the door as she left, making a joke of it and taking the key with her" (13).

He finally learns the truth from the elderly servant of a woman whom this "professional seducer" Eratosthenes has abandoned. He repeats the actual words that she used, always a good sign of authenticity, and also describes how he took his own servant girl to the Agora and, in the presence of witnesses, questioned her and made her admit that she acted as a go-between (16—20). Then he comes to the final scene, when he called in the neighbours to witness the death of the man who had dishonoured him (33—37). His story provides all the explanation and justification of his actions that is necessary.

Lysias at his best has the reputation of providing a narrative which seems obviously accurate and in keeping with the speaker's character. The speeches *Against Eratosthenes* and *Against Agoratus* provide the best known examples of this apparently "guileless" story-telling. But even accomplished masters of the art cannot produce a convincing narrative that looks like winning the case on its own merits, if the speaker is not fully in command of the facts.

In Isaeus' fourth oration, *On the Estate of Nicostratus*, the speaker has no witnesses to support him in his contention that his opponents are lying. Nicostratus was a professional soldier who died in service overseas, and the lack of real information about events makes it impossible to offer a coherent narrative; the opposing side is therefore challenged to produce a credible story. Isaeus' fifth oration, *On the Estate of Dicaeogenes*, also concerns the estate of an unmarried man killed on war service, but in this instance the speaker can illustrate the dishonest character of the rival claimant and his assistants by a complicated story of litigation that has been going on over the years.

Demosthenes was no mere imitator of Lysias and Isaeus, but the following chapter will show how much he learned from them about introducing, presenting, and exploiting a well-designed narrative. When he turned from civil cases to *graphai paranomon*, his clients were evidently satisfied that he could put his earlier experience to good use and that he was wise to use a similar technique in their cases. Before long he is speaking in the Assembly, and once again we must ask what use he is making of his previous experience. Deliberative oratory, according to orthodox teaching, was different from forensic, but the more successful speeches of Demosthenes, which are designed to influence public policy, are written in the forensic manner. They are worked out in terms of attack and defence; his task as he sees it, in the Philippic orations, is to convince his hearers that Philip is guilty and that Athens has been shamefully treated and should take action against him.

Demosthenes is often characterized as a man who could not have remained content with composing speeches for others and was bound to enter politics before long.[30] But how did he first present himself to the Assembly and what was the occasion of his first speech?

No ancient writer actually describes for us the procedure of obtaining permission to speak in the Assembly.[31] It is easy to say that every citizen had the right to make his voice heard. The herald declared the debate open with his question τίς ἀγορεύειν βούλεται; and in describing the famous special meeting of 339 Demosthenes can say: "If it was the duty of men to come forward who had the safety of the state at heart, every Athenian would have risen to his feet and made for the bema" (18. 170−171). People were not always so reluctant to speak as at that critical moment. Who received preference when several men rose to their feet at the same time, and how difficult was it for an unknown person, with no previous reputation as a speaker, to obtain the floor? Did he make some arrangement before the meeting, approaching the presiding officer

30 Cf., e.g., Jaeger, Demosthenes, Chap. II, p. 41.
31 Aeschines, In Ctes. 2−4, complains how regular procedure was being violated and the old orderly ways abandoned because of the *akosmia* of politicians, and he would like to see proper Solonian procedure restored, ἵνα ἐξῆν πρῶτον μὲν τῷ πρεσβυτάτῳ τῶν πολιτῶν, ὥσπερ οἱ νόμοι προστάττουσιν, σωφρόνως ἐπὶ τὸ βῆμα παρελθόντι ἄνευ θορύβου καὶ ταραχῆς ἐξ ἐμπειρίας τὰ βέλτιστα τῇ πόλει συμβουλεύειν, δεύτερον δ'ἤδη καὶ τῶν ἄλλων πολιτῶν τὸν βουλόμενον καθ' ἡλικίαν χωρὶς καὶ ἐν μέρει περὶ ἑκάστου γνώμην ἀποφαίνεσθαι. We may doubt if such procedure was ever followed in the lifetime of Aeschines, and we are under no obligation to believe that it was ever so simple a matter to gain a hearing as in the opening scene of the Acharnians.

perhaps with the assistance of influential friends?[32] Was a show of loyalty to a political group or party or to some particular policy expected of a young man if he wanted notice to be taken of him? Ancient writers are remarkably uncommunicative on such matters, and dogmatic statements in modern handbooks must be treated with caution.[33]

We need not take too seriously the famous descriptions in Aristophanes of citizens without any interest in the meetings, unwilling to climb the Pnyx unless compelled.[34] But there is no positive evidence that numerous citizens were often anxious to exert their prerogative of speaking.[35]

32 The procedure of submitting proposals in writing is known from Aeschines 2. 68 and 83 (cf. Aristoph., Thesmo., 432). Xenophon (Mem. 3.6. 1) describes the incident when young Glaucon tried to mount the bema and had to be forcibly removed, because he was under the legal age of twenty. Various rules of the order of procedure, known from Aristotle, Resp. Ath., and other sources, are collected in Busolt-Swoboda, Gr.Staatskunde, II 986–1019. But the details are not always as explicit as we should like. For example (p. 999) we are told that, after a speech in which a formal proposal is made, the debate is thrown open and every citizen has the right either to move the adoption of the *probouleuma* as presented or to propose additions or alterations or to bring in a complete counter-proposal. The procedure sounds like a nightmare to anyone who has ever presided at a meeting. Who is in order and who is not, and what happens if all three proposals are made? And if A. is clamouring to speak from this corner and B. from another, how does the chairman justify giving preference to one over the other? And if B. is a complete stranger, what chance has he of being called upon?

33 Jaeger, Demosthenes,Chap.IV, writes quite confidently, as though there were no problem: "His progress from the writing-desk to the orator's tribune was made easier by close contacts with a group of like-minded associates who, drawn together by the unanimity of their criticism, must soon have been forced to work out certain basic features of a common political program" (68). Or again: "The isolation and poverty of Athens made foreign politics an extremely difficult sphere of activity. It was a great mark of confidence when despite his youth Demosthenes was given a chance to speak on such occasions. This was obviously because his political friends had recognized his special bent and aptitude for this kind of work" (71). Our understanding of the procedure in the Assembly is not greatly advanced by the constant derogatory allusions to "the orators," who are accused of controlling the Assembly. Cf., e.g., Aesch. 3. 4.

34 Cf. Ach. 17–22, and Ecc. 299–310, Plut. 329–30, for the contrast between the crowds that attended when the *triobelia* was introduced and the old days; no one came for the sake of one obol, but there had been a time when they came willingly for nothing. Cf. V. Ehrenberg, The People of Aristophanes (Oxford 1951), p. 349.

35 In Busolt-Swoboda, Gr. Staatskunde II.999, it is stated categorically: "Es pflegten nur verhältnismäßig wenige Männer zu reden." There is no real authority for believing that the speakers were few in number. It is unwise to give too much weight to remarks by Demosthenes and Aeschines, when they contrast "ordinary private individuals" with professional politicians who expect to have things all their own way in the Assembly. Cf. Aesch. 1. 7 and 195; 3. 3; Dem. 4. 1; 22. 37; and especially 10. 70: οὐ τὸν αὐτὸν δὲ τρόπον περὶ θ᾽ ὑμῶν καὶ περὶ αὐτῶν ἐνίους τῶν λεγόντων ὁρῶ βουλευομένους· ὑμᾶς γὰρ ἡσυχίαν ἄγειν φασὶ δεῖν, κἄν τις ὑμᾶς ἀδικῇ, αὐτοὶ δ᾽ οὐ δύνανται παρ᾽ ὑμῖν ἡσυχίαν ἄγειν οὐδενὸς αὐτοὺς ἀδικοῦντος. Such remarks cannot be taken as strictly accurate; but one cannot altogether ignore Isocrates 8. 3: ὁρῶ δ᾽ ὑμᾶς οὐκ ἐξ ἴσου τῶν λεγόντων τὴν ἀκρόασιν ποιου-

Even the Funeral Oration of Pericles, which tries to show how generally and how dutifully citizens actually participated in government, emphasizes only their readiness to think out issues and vote on them.[36] It says nothing about taking an active part in debate as part of their service to Athens.

Plutarch (*Dem.* 6) tells us that Demosthenes' first speech before the people was a dismal failure. But he does not say what the occasion was. Was *On the Symmories* the first speech that he delivered, or was there an earlier, less successful venture? and had he linked himself with any political group or pledged himself to support its policy? Some writers of modern times have maintained that he allied himself with Eubulus and his presumed policy, believing that it was necessary to build up a financial reserve and avoid war or expensive rearmament. They argue that his early speeches support these conclusions. But though he advises against any conflict with Persia in *On the Symmories*, he makes quite explicit proposals for rearmament, and in *For the Megalopolitans* he is ready to risk a conflict with Sparta. One can hardly maintain that his first speech favours a reduction of expenditure on armament, unless one argues that he does not mean what he says; and even if we are prepared to believe this, we still cannot be sure that Eubulus' policy was categorically isolationist and pacifist.[37]

μένους, ἀλλὰ τοῖς μὲν προσέχοντας τὸν νοῦν, τῶν δ'οὐδὲ τὴν φωνὴν ἀνεχομένους. καὶ θαυμαστὸν οὐδὲν ποιεῖτε· καὶ γὰρ τὸν ἄλλον χρόνον εἰώθατε πάντας τοὺς ἄλλους ἐκβάλλειν, πλὴν τοὺς συναγορεύοντας ταῖς ὑμετέραις ἐπιθυμίαις. Cf. 121, where certain speakers are said to have established a *dynasteia* of the bema. Whether strictly true or not, these remarks should be remembered in considering the initial difficulties of Demosthenes in facing the Assembly, since De Pace was written about this time and contains many complaints about the popularity of speakers who recommended war.

36 Thuc. 2.40. 2, καὶ οἱ αὐτοὶ ἤτοι κρίνομέν γε ἢ ἐνθυμούμεθα ὀρθῶς τὰ πράγματα, οὐ τοὺς λόγους τοῖς ἔργοις βλάβην ἡγούμενοι, ἀλλὰ μὴ προδιδαχθῆναι μᾶλλον λόγῳ πρότερον ἢ ἐπὶ ἃ δεῖ ἔργῳ ἐλθεῖν.

37 A very careful statement of the question will be found in Pickard-Cambridge, Demosthenes 110–13. The difficulties of linking Demosthenes with Eubulus are stated in stronger terms by Cloché, "La politique de Démosthènes de 354 à 346," BCH 47 (1923), 97–162, esp. Part I. He concludes in Démosthènes, 44: "Les textes nous défendent donc formellement de ranger sans réserve l'auteur de la harangue Sur les Symmories dans ce qu'on a appelé le 'parti d'Eubule.' " Cf. M. Croiset, Démosthène, Harangues I, xvii, n. 3.

Jaeger, however (see n. 33, above), following the lead of E. Schwartz, "Demosthenes' erste Philippika," Festschrift für Th. Mommsen (Marburg 1893), is still convinced that Demosthenes was acting in the interests of Eubulus and his party; he argues that the proposals for rearmament were not seriously intended and not expected to be approved. In [Dion. Hal.] Ars Rhet. 8. 7, 9. 10, the speech is presented as an example of the orator's skill in "concealing his true wishes"; but

Perhaps we should be content to notice how deeply concerned Demosthenes was over Athenian foreign policy, and how important he thought it was for Athens to recover and maintain its reputation as a great power and a predominating influence in panhellenic affairs. He may have regarded Philip as a dangerous enemy from the very beginning of his political career, since already in *On the Symmories* he warns against the folly of seeking new enemies in addition to those that already exist: "Let us make our preparations against our existing enemies, and we shall be able to face the Persian king, if he attempts to move against us" (14.11). Philip's aggressive intentions might have been feared in Athens as early as 354, but it was not until three years later that Demosthenes developed his own method of countering them.[38]

It is also only in 351 (in the *First Philippic*) that we find him using in a political speech the style and method of argument characteristic of his forensic speeches. The earlier political orations, *On the Symmories, For the Megalopolitans, On the Freedom of the Rhodians*, reveal a quite different manner, of which there is no trace after 351. Ancient critics are aware of this, but they offer no explanation of the special style that distinguishes the earliest political speeches.[39] Plutarch tells us that his first speech in the Assembly was neither well received nor well delivered, and how he took the advice given him by the actor Satyrus and had to train himself intensively before he achieved success (*Dem.* 7—8). But all the stories about his difficulties and his training are concerned with his delivery, not his manner of writing or composition.

Since no speeches given before the Assembly in these years have been preserved except those of Demosthenes, we cannot tell how far his early political style conformed to the fashion of the day. We are no better informed about the style that was in fashion when Demosthenes started his political career than about the style which prevailed in the Roman senate and comitia when Cicero was very young. Cicero tells us about the exuberant style of Hortensius, which he tried to copy until he realized that he was making a mistake, but we should be on much surer ground if we had some actual samples of the work of Cicero's elder contemporaries.[40] For Attic oratory we have the conventional classifications of

what pseudo-Dionysius meant was concealing his concern about Philip and understating his opposition to war against Persia.
For a full discussion of Eubulus and his policies, see G. L. Cawkwell, "Eubulus," JHS 83 (1965), 47—67.
38 Cf. Blass, Att. Bered. III 278.
39 For an attempt to analyze this style, see L. Pearson, "The Development of Demosthenes as a political orator," Phoenix 18 (1964), 95—109.
40 Cic. Brutus 101—147, 301—303, 317—327 (Antonius, Crassus, Hortensius). For further references. see A. S. Wilkins, Cicero, De Oratore I, Introduction.

"grand," "simple," and "middle," and enough Attic oratory has been preserved so that these classifications are more than mere names. But the only non-forensic speeches, apart from Demosthenes' political orations, are those of Isocrates, which were not written to be delivered and cannot readily be taken as evidence of prevailing fashion, and one solitary speech from earlier days, Andocides' *On Peace with Sparta*. Otherwise, for the fifth century as well as the fourth, we are dependent for our information on the historians. Thucydides warns us that he is not giving us faithful examples or copies of actual speeches, and we cannot feel any confidence that Herodotus or Xenophon is more trustworthy in reproducing the authentic style. What Plutarch tells us about Pericles' oratory is not much more helpful than what he and Cicero tell us about Roman orators of an earlier generation, like the Gracchi. [41]

We might suppose that when Demosthenes changes his style, as he moves from the courts to the Assembly, he is making the change out of deference to the current fashion of political oratory, or because he thinks the style which had been successful in the courts would be unacceptable to the Assembly. But not only do we lack the evidence to support this opinion, but we find his early political speeches reminiscent of Thucydides (as ancient critics point out[42]), and it is very hard to believe that the Thucydidean style was fashionable in the mid-fourth century. It is more likely that he had been reading Thucydides and admired his work and took the speeches in his history as a model. There was in fact no collection of political oratory available anywhere except in the historians, since politicians of his generation did not apparently, like professional speech-writers, revise and publish the orations of which they were proud. There were other historians, but he might not think them fit to be compared with Thucydides. And there was also Isocrates, whose "speeches," even if not delivered, could at least be read; traces of Isocratean influence can be found in these early political speeches, as well as echoes of Thucydides.

Demosthenes begins *On the Symmories* not by describing his own situation or difficulty or the problem which he proposes to discuss, but with a general statement, the relevance of which is not immediately clear: "It seems to me that speakers who praise your ancestors are adopting a manner of speaking that flatters you, but is not really advantageous to the persons whom they are praising." He is speaking in general terms, as though he were criticizing a literary or rhetorical fashion and about to introduce a new style or a topic more suitable for the occasion, just as Pericles, after

41 Plut. Pericles 8, Ti. Gracchus 2; Cic. Brutus 103–04, 125.
42 See the passages listed by Blass, Att. Bered. III 19.

explaining why it is difficult to praise adequately the deeds of the fallen, proceeds to do it in his own way by describing the Athenian ideals for which they have given their lives.

Demosthenes, however, soon drops the topic of praise, and says: "I propose to discuss what seems to me the best way of rearming ourselves." This seems to re-echo the opening remarks of Isocrates in the *Areopagiticus* (a product of this very year, 354, or the preceding one). Isocrates complained of orators who gave the false impression that Athens was strong and well enough supplied with allies to fear no enemy.[43] Demosthenes shared his feelings and may have read his pamphlet, so it is not surprising that he should reflect its way of thinking.

The Thucydidean influence on Demosthenes has attracted more attention than the Isocratean. Dionysius of Halicarnassus finishes his essay on Thucydides by remarking that Demosthenes was the only one of the Attic orators who rivalled or copied the best features of Thucydidean style, notably its speed and conciseness and tension, "its bitter astringent quality and its astonishing power of rousing strong feeling"; he did not take over its oddities and perversities, but like the historian he avoided symmetry and liked variety and the use of rhetorical figures; he tended to express his meaning in a complex and involved form, so as to suggest several things at the same time, demanding continuous attention from the reader if he was to be understood properly (*De Thuc.* 53, cf. 55). Modern critics generally have approved this verdict,[44] and one of the passages which Dionysius quotes as an illustration is from *On the Symmories* (13).

It is hardly likely that Demosthenes analyzed Thucydides like Dionysius and picked out particular mannerisms and tendencies of style for imitation, but one can well believe that he paid special attention to passages that seemed to him particularly apt for certain situations, and expressed himself in a similar manner when he thought he was faced by a similar problem or situation. Longinus reminds us that a writer should ask himself: "How would one of the great masters have expressed what I am trying to say?" (*De Sub.* 14). He can hardly be the first to have thought along these lines.

If Demosthenes in 354 was afraid that appeals to the aggressive spirit of Salamis and Eurymedon might stir the Athenians to provoke Persian

43 Isocrates begins the Areopagiticus by listing the apparent reasons for Athenian confidence and complacency (1–2), ἐγὼ δὲ δι'αὐτὰ ταῦτα τυγχάνω δεδιώς (3). He recalls how quickly in the past Athens lost its commanding position (4–7) and therefore must not be over-confident now:
ἄλλως τε καὶ τῆς μὲν πόλεως ἡμῶν πολὺ καταδεέστερον νῦν πραττούσης ἢ κατ' ἐκεῖνον τὸν χρόνον, τοῦ δὲ μίσους τοῦ τῶν Ἑλλήνων καὶ τῆς ἔχθρας τῆς πρὸς βασιλέα πάλιν ἀνακεκαινισμένης (8).

44 Cf., e.g., Blass, Att. Bered. III 87, 96, 150–151, 220.

intervention, he needed a safe reason for deprecating "praise of the olden days." The words in the Funeral Oration gave him the reason that he wanted—it was impossible to praise them adequately, because certain deeds were beyond praise.[45] The Funeral Oration could not teach him how to urge caution in provoking or starting a war with Persia, but there were plenty of good arguments against starting a war to be found elsewhere in Thucydides, for example in Archidamus' speech at the Congress of Sparta (1. 80—85) or Nicias' speech warning the Athenians not to be carried away by Alcibiades' enthusiasm for the Sicilian expedition (6. 9—14). Demosthenes was certainly familiar with these passages, since he repeats several turns of phrase from the Thucydidean text.

Archidamus did not contradict what the Corinthians had said about the aggressive policy of Athens, nor did Demosthenes deny that the Persian king was "the common enemy of all Greeks" (14. 3). He had to make it clear that he was no friend of Persia, just as Archidamus could not appear pro-Athenian. But it is Archidamus' first sentence in 1.82 that gives Demosthenes exactly what he wants: "I am not of course suggesting that we should be callous about letting the Athenians maltreat our allies or that we should stupidly fail to notice their aggressive policies, but I maintain that the time for taking up arms against them has not yet come. We should send representatives to complain to them, not positively threatening war, but not letting them think that we shall allow them to have their way. And meanwhile we must see to the business of building up our armament and securing allies."

This argument and the somewhat evasive way of stating it can be found very closely reproduced in *On the Symmories*. Like Archidamus, Demosthenes finds no real justification for going to war, and he is not in favour of war at all if it can be avoided, but neither of them is willing to say so categorically; they say instead that the time for war has not yet come, using a form and order of words which will suggest that the time is not far off and they must be ready for it when it comes: κελεύω ... ὅπλα μὲν μήπω κινεῖν, πέμπειν δὲ καὶ αἰτιᾶσθαι ... καὶ τὰ ἡμέτερ᾽ αὐτῶν ἐξαρτύεσθαι (Thuc. 1.82.1), τὸν μὲν δὴ πόλεμον διὰ ταῦτα παραινῶ μηδ᾽ ἐξ ἑνὸς τρόπου προτέρους ἀνελέσθαι, ἐπὶ δὲ τὸν ἀγῶνα ὀρθῶς φημὶ παρεσκευασμένους ὑπάρχειν χρῆναι (Dem. 14.10). They do not say "I am against war," but "As for the war, I don't think we should start it yet, but let us be sure we have a good cause and are well prepared when we do." And in the later stages of their speeches they shift the emphasis from war to "preparedness." The constant repetition of noun and verb (παρασκευή,

---

45 χαλεπὸν γὰρ τὸ μετρίως εἰπεῖν ἐν ᾧ μόλις καὶ ἡ δόκησις τῆς ἀληθείας βεβαιοῦται (2. 35).

παρασκευάζεσθαι) is notable in both speeches.[46] And both use the same word (ἐπιβουλεύειν) to describe the "hostile intentions" of the supposed enemy.[47]

Archidamus finishes by reminding his audience that caution and hesitation about making important decisions represent a good Spartan tradition (85.1). The Corinthians had insisted that they must abandon this tradition, if they are to be a match for the adventurous Athenians (1.71), and Demosthenes cannot appeal to an Athenian tradition of caution. But he can remind the Athenians of their traditional obligations toward the rest of the Greek world, which they have inherited from the great days of Themistocles and Aristides and which impose a special caution upon them. Just as Pericles, in the Funeral Oration, claimed that for Athenians "the contest was not on the same terms, the issues were not the same as for men who had no share in the privileges of Athenians" (Thuc. 2.41), so Demosthenes can now say:

For other Greeks, as I see it, discussion of relations with Persia does not involve the same issues as for us. So long as they are likely to gain some advantage for their own city, many of them are prepared to ignore what happens to the rest of the Greeks, whereas you, even when you have real grounds for complaint, cannot think it right to go so far in punishing offenders as to let any of them become subject to barbarian rule (14.6).

Demosthenes warns the Athenians that they have "existing enemies" who demand their attention as well as the Persian king (14.11), and when Nicias was opposing the plan for a Sicilian expedition one of the strongest arguments that Thucydides attributed to him was the danger of taking on a new enemy when the Athenians had enough "admitted enemies" nearer home. Like Archidamus at Sparta, he pointed out the folly of "making a quick decision on important matters" and said they should not be "persuaded by foreigners to undertake a war that they could not justify" (Thuc. 6.9). As though remembering what Archidamus and the Corinthians had said, he admitted that, in view of the Athenian character, it would be a losing battle to try and persuade them to "conserve their assets," and he looked for arguments that would have a stronger appeal: "I must point out that you are leaving many enemies behind you here" (6.10.1). And in his second speech, when the Athenians are still determined to go to Sicily, he falls back on the need for more extensive "preparation" (6.20–23).

At the time when Demosthenes is speaking the Athenians have not the same confidence in their military and naval power, and he is prepared

46 Dem. 14. 2, 3, 11, 13, 14, 21, 41; Thuc. 1. 80. 4; 82. 3; 84. 4; 85. 2. Cf. the adjective ἀπαράσκευος in 80. 4; 82. 5; 84. 1.
47 Dem. 14. 7 and 12; Thuc. 1. 82. 1.

to urge them openly to "help their existing allies and preserve the advantages that they have." "Why," he asks, "when we have enemies that we recognize as enemies, do we seek out others?" (14.11).[48]

It must be admitted that the thought and language which Demosthenes shares with Thucydides are neither unusual nor striking. But the Thucydidean style of *On the Symmories* is very different from that of Isocrates' *On Peace,* written about the same time and concerned with the same problems, and a work which Demosthenes is likely to have consulted.[49] Like Demosthenes Isocrates begins by complaining that speakers who favour war are more favourably received than those who want to preserve peace. But he writes in a severe, rebuking style, quite unsuitable for a politician at the start of his career, and he lacks the conciseness and the *brevitas*, which is as noticeable in *On the Symmories* as in Thucydides' work. He uses examples and analogies to explain what a more practical orator (with his eye on the clock) would expect the audience to see for themselves, and he is not "enthymematic" to the degree that Aristotle would recommend.[50] A successful orator avoids using a full syllogism, when the major premiss is a familiar truism; rather than waste time by stating a principle that no one would contradict, he prefers to take the major premiss for granted and present his argument in the form of an enthymeme. Isocrates' work, however, is full of commonplace *gnomae* like "War and peace are questions of prime importance in the life of man" and "Good advice must inevitably produce good results" (*On Peace* 2). If

48 καὶ πρὸς μὲν τοὺς τρόπους τοὺς ὑμετέρους ἀσθενὴς ἄν μου ὁ λόγος εἴη, εἰ τά τε ὑπάρχοντα σῴζειν παραινοίην καὶ μὴ τοῖς ἑτοίμοις περὶ τῶν ἀφανῶν καὶ μελλόντων κινδυνεύειν (Thuc. 6.9. 3); φημὶ γὰρ ὑμᾶς πολεμίους πολλοὺς ἐνθάδε ὑπολιπόντας καὶ ἑτέρους ἐπιθυμεῖν ἐκεῖσε πλεύσαντας δεῦρο ἐπαγαγέσθαι (6.10. 1). Cf. Dem. 14. 11: ἐπεὶ δὲ πάσης ἐστὶ παρασκευῆς ὁ αὐτὸς τρόπος καὶ δεῖ ταῦτ' εἶναι κεφαλαῖα τῆς δυνάμεως, τοὺς ἐχθροὺς ἀμύνασθαι δύνασθαι, τοῖς οὖσι συμμάχοις βοηθεῖν, τὰ ὑπάρχοντ' ἀγαθὰ σῴζειν, τί τοὺς ὁμολογουμένους ἐχθροὺς ἔχοντες ἑτέρους ζητοῦμεν;

49 The precise date of composition of "On Peace" is hard to establish. Ed. Meyer, Gesch. d. Altertums 5. 494, was inclined to put it later than "On the Symmories", but it is more commonly assigned to spring or summer 356. Cf. G. Mathieu, Isocrate (Budé ed.) III, 3—6; M. L. W. Laistner, Isocrates: De Pace and Philippus (New York/London 1927), pp. 17—18.

50 One might think Aristotle was thinking of Isocrates when he wrote: καὶ ῥήτορες ὁμοίως οἱ μὲν παραδειγματώδεις, οἱ δὲ ἐνθυμηματικοί. πιθανοὶ μὲν οὖν οὐχ ἧττον οἱ λόγοι οἱ διὰ τῶν παραδειγμάτων, θορυβοῦνται δὲ μᾶλλον οἱ ἐνθυμηματικοί (Rhet. 1. 1356b). Cf. also his conclusion on the nature of enthymematic argument: φανερὸν ὅτι ἐξ ὧν τὰ ἐνθυμήματα λέγεται, τὰ μὲν ἀναγκαῖα ἔσται, τὰ δὲ πλεῖστα ὡς ἐπὶ τὸ πολύ (1357a). Only a pedantic orator, like Isocrates, takes time to argue the strict accuracy of premisses granted to be "generally or for the most part true." Was Aristotle perhaps a little old-fashioned in remarking that in general paradigm was particularly suited to deliberative oratory, enthymeme to forensic (Rhet. 1. 1368a)? The remark of course is offered only as a generalization (ὅλως).

Demosthenes had followed the Isocratean manner in *On the Symmories*, the argument of his opening sentences would have been expanded to three times its present length.

It may satisfy some critics to point out the influence of Thucydides and (to a lesser degree) that of Isocrates in these early speeches, but we still have to ask, in more precise terms, in what respects Demosthenes altered the style which he had found successful in the courts and what changes he thought he was making. Though he was very probably aware that he was "borrowing" arguments from these authors, it does not follow that he thought of himself as imitating one style or another. But he must have known that this was a change from his forensic manner. And he may have thought that his forensic manner was not suitable for the Assembly.

He must have known that he was providing hardly any narrative, giving his hearers less information, and assuming that their command of "the facts" (τὰ πράγματα) was as good as his. Even when he ventures a comparison with events or situations in the past, he assumes (or at least pretends) that he is reminding them of things that they all know and contents himself with saying why he thinks the comparison useful or relevant.[51] This means that he has time to spare for argument, so as to explain what has been done wrong and why it is wrong, and what ought to be done and why and how it can be done. He also expresses his own opinion and takes responsibility for it. The first person singular ("I think," "it seems to me") appears as frequently in these early political speeches as in Isocrates or the Thucydidean speeches; it is much less common in the later speeches.[52]

On the other hand discussion of persons and their qualities is not common in his political speeches until he starts on the Philippic series. We learn much more history from them than from *On the Symmories* or *For the Megalopolitans*. The *Philippics* give us information, as the forensic speeches did; and the speaker seems to think of himself as facing a rival, not another Athenian politician, but Philip. He offers information without necessarily asking, perhaps, whether or not it may all be familiar to his hearers, without always insisting that it has been misrepresented by others. He also speaks constantly like a pleader in the courts who is concerned to show that someone is a dangerous and untrustworthy criminal, against whom the people must pass sentence by declaring war. If this is a fair way of describing his more mature political oratory, we have answered the second question that had to be asked. When Demosthenes

51 Dem. 14. 15, 30, 34, 36, 40.
52 Cf. L. Pearson, Phoenix 18 (1964), 103–04.

abandoned the style of his first political speeches and wrote the *First Philippic*, he was returning to his forensic style.[53]

This question will be discussed, with fuller illustration, in a later chapter, but there are some points which should be clarified at the start. Should we believe that it was normal for speakers making "demegoric" speeches in the Assembly to dispense with narrative? Aristotle says that narrative had no place in deliberative oratory, but he has a way of not distinguishing between current practice and what he regards as proper practice. It is true, however, that the speeches in the historians and the deliberative speeches of Isocrates (as opposed to the epideictic and forensic) contain no narrative, but only allusions and *paradeigmata*. In many Thucydidean speeches a narrative section, setting forth the exact situation and the events leading up to it, would be most welcome to us; but it is not there when we want it. The Corcyreans and Corinthians, in their speeches at Athens, discuss the principles which should govern the behaviour of colonists towards the metropolis, but tell us hardly anything of their quarrels and how they started (1.32–43). Narrative detail is equally lacking in the speech of the Mytilenians at Olympia, when they are asking for Spartan support of their revolt (3.9–14), and in the speeches of Cleon and Diodotus in Athens (3.37–48), when they are debating how to treat the Mytilenian rebels.

On the other hand, when the Plataeans and Thebans address the Spartans after the surrender of Plataea (3.53–67), they are defendants and prosecutors arguing their case before a Spartan jury (3.52), and the Plataeans recognize that they are on trial for their lives (3.53). In these speeches the speakers supply the relevant detail themselves. The Plataeans cannot defend themselves without appealing to "the facts," just as previously, when the Spartans first approached the city, they told them exactly what sort of pledge Pausanias had given them (2.71). The anonymous Athenian speaker at the conference at Sparta before the outbreak of war supplies an interesting contrast. He is represented as having no intention of "defending himself" or "replying to the charges against Athens" (1.72), and in consequence we learn very little from him about actual relations between Athenians and their tributary allies.

---

53 Aristotle wants to distinguish deliberative from forensic oratory by suggesting that the juryman has to decide about the past, the political assembly about the future (1. 1358b). This appears to mean that, in his view, all members of the Assembly are presumed to know the facts of the past as well as the speaker knows them; and on this basis the Philippics would not properly be classed as deliberative oratory, if they are speeches designed to make the Assembly change their ideas about the past as well as the future.

Thucydides does not use speeches as a substitute for narrative. He describes events on his own authority, explaining when necessary why he believes that his account is correct. He prefers to give it as his own opinion that the Peloponnesians were driven into war by their fear of Athenian expansion, rather than let Spartan or Corinthian speakers document their motives fully and present their narrative of the development of the Athenian empire. His speeches do not inform us about "facts," but they help us to see how people thought and they allow general reflections on war and politics to emerge, which we suspect are the historian's opinions and not really an essential part of the speaker's argument.[54] It is useless to ask how exactly or completely Thucydides records "what was actually said." But we can reasonably ask whether he gives the kind of argument that was likely to have been used, and seek an answer by comparing his speeches with those of Xenophon or Isocrates or the one political speech from the fifth century that we may call "real," the third oration of Andocides.

It is manners and methods of argument that are in question, not literary styles. A litigant usually begins by explaining why he is in court, and whether he is plaintiff or defendant he cannot explain his grievance without a narrative. It would be helpful to the modern reader if speakers in political assemblies began in comparable fashion, explaining how a crisis has arisen and who is to blame for it before finding fault with solutions already proposed or proposing a new solution. It would, for example, be much easier to establish a definite date for Isocrates' *On Peace* or *Areopagiticus*, if he had started in this fashion. But he does nothing of the kind, and his failure to do so may be evidence of contemporary fashion. These are the only speeches in which he supposes himself to be addressing the Athenian Assembly.

Andocides in his third oration is equally uncommunicative. He says nothing about the course of the war and how it has come about that the Spartans are offering peace terms, but begins at once by claiming to prove that making peace with Sparta has led the way to prosperity and never resulted in overthrow of the democracy. This lack of detail about the immediate situation makes his speech seem just as unpractical as those of Isocrates. He offers more detail in his historical illustrations, when he "reminds" his audience of what is supposed to be familiar to them. But even here he is often vague, so that we are uncertain how well he knows his history. Isocrates is often no more precise or convincing in his historical detail, but it is not easy to believe that he is ignorant or unintelligent about the history of the fifth century.

---

54 Cf. J. de Romilly, Histoire et Raison chez Thucydide (Paris 1956), esp. Chap. III.

One might expect to find more conclusive and reliable evidence in Xenophon's *Hellenica*, since there is no reason why he should misrepresent the character of debates in the Assembly. There are quite a number of speeches before various legislative assemblies in the *Hellenica*, as well as informal speeches and passages of dialogue in the narrative, but strictly deliberative addresses by Athenian speakers in the Athenian Assembly or Boule are not easily found. The famous speeches of Critias and Theramenes before the Boule are more of a forensic nature, with Critias prosecuting and Theramenes speaking in his own defence (2.3.24—49). And when Euryptolemus rises to speak in the debate about the commanders in the battle of Arginusae, who were charged with neglect in not recovering the bodies of the dead from the sea, he begins by saying that his speech will be a mixture of attack, defence, and recommendation of what he thinks best for the city (1.7.16); and it has its fair share of narrative (1.7.29—31).[55]

A number of speeches in the *Hellenica* are delivered by foreign envoys at Athens or Sparta, and it is their business to acquaint their audience with "the facts." Cleigenes the Acanthian, speaking at Sparta, makes this quite clear and presents a careful statement of the situation (5.2.12—19). When he and his colleagues speak a second time, Xenophon points out himself that they "gave information" (ἀναστάντες οἱ Ἀκάνθιοι πάλιν ἐδίδασκον, 5.2.23). Likewise when the Thessalian Polydamas speaks at Sparta, he has a long story to tell about the aggressive methods of Jason of Pherae (6.1.2—16).[56]

Speeches by foreign envoys are not always as full of information as we might expect. A Spartan delegation at Athens reminds the Athenians how Athens and Sparta have helped each other in the past, offering familiar *paradeigmata*; and Procles of Phlius delivers an argumentative speech, quite in the manner of Demosthenes' early addresses to the Assembly.[57]

Since Xenophon gives no examples of symbouleutic speeches by Athenians in their own Assembly, he does not provide us with the evidence that we need. He does not help us to decide whether speakers in

---

55 Likewise Callicratidas, in his brief address to the Assembly at Miletus, is defending himself against anticipated accusation when he explains his difficulties in getting what he wants out of Cyrus (1.6. 8—11). Xenophon also gives the speech of accusation against the supposed murderers of Euphron delivered before the Theban Boule (7.3. 6).

56 Cf. the Demosthenic manner of Autocles in his speech at Sparta: ὅτι μὲν ἃ μέλλω λέγειν οὐ πρὸς χάρω ὑμῖν ῥηθήσεται οὐκ ἀγνοῶ, ἀλλὰ δοκεῖ μοι, οἵτινες βούλονται, ἢν ἂν ποιήσωνται φιλίαν, ταύτην ὡς πλεῖστον χρόνον διαμένειν, διδακτέον εἶναι ἀλλήλους τὰ αἴτια τῶν πολέμων (6.3. 7).

57 6. 5. 33 & 38.

the Assembly really withheld the kind of information that the members needed if they were to vote intelligently. There was no need to repeat what a previous speaker had said, if he had given the information correctly, and references to earlier speakers can be found in Andocides and Isocrates. It is only in the *First Philippic* that Demosthenes announces himself as the first speaker of the day. This may perhaps in part explain why he describes the problem that faces them. The general public, when called upon to vote in favour of a resolution of the Boule, would need to have the information on which this resolution was based, and one would expect the first speaker to give it to them.

In a famous passage in *On the Crown* (167 ff.) Demosthenes describes how the news reached Athens that Philip was at Elatea and was given to the members of the prytany as they were having dinner in the *tholos*. Since he was not himself a member of the Boule, Demosthenes cannot describe what was done in their meetings; but when a meeting of the Assembly was called next morning, he rose to speak when no one else came forward. He complained that many people had been confused and baffled by the news, but instead of describing what had actually happened he was content to give his opinion of Philip's purpose in advancing to Elatea, and he interpreted the situation in such a way as to calm their fears and make them accept his proposals. The members of the Boule presumably were in possession of whatever information could be obtained, and so no doubt was Demosthenes, thanks to private sources of intelligence. But at no point in his narrative does he tell us how and when the news was given publicly and officially to the general public. We can imagine individuals finding out things for themselves, questioning the messenger's servants as they waited outside the *tholos* for their master and spreading rumours through the city. But this is not the same thing as receiving an official report, on the strength of which the voters will have to make their decisions.

In the speeches which Demosthenes delivered in the Assembly in the years following 354 B.C., we can see him gradually abandoning the habit of offering arguments without information. He adapts the technique of courtroom argument to political speeches. In *For the Megalopolitans* he begins, as before, by criticizing other speakers and then defines the problem in very general terms. He notes the danger of being unable to weaken Thebes without strengthening Sparta or to weaken Sparta without strengthening Thebes, whereas Athenian interest demands that both should be kept weak, so far as possible (4—5). He does not explain why support of Megalopolis, which will weaken Sparta, will not seriously strengthen Thebes, but starts instead to reply to other speakers, who have appealed to sentiment and tradition. A modern reader feels no better qualified to make a decision about Megalopolis after reading the speech than before he looked at it; he learns nothing from it about the importance or significance of Megalopolis or what its existence means in the whole context of Peloponnesian politics. There is not a word about any of its inhabitants.[58]

Demosthenes begins *On the Freedom of the Rhodians* by telling the Assembly there is no difficulty about explaining to them what they should do, "because I think all of you generally know what that is perfectly well; what is difficult is to induce you to do it."[59] He "explains" the situation by arguing that, if they take his advice, they have a wonderful opportunity of winning new prestige for Athens. Rhodes, their recent enemy in the Social War, is now threatened by a foreign enemy, Mausolus, and cannot expect any help from her former allies, Chios and Byzantium. What an opportunity for Athens to show pure good will, to help someone to whom she owes nothing, offering assistance gratuitously to people who must be expecting hostility—an opportunity to "heap coals of fire," as a conventional modern speaker would be tempted to say.

So far this is the same perverse manner as *For the Megalopolitans*. But with section 5 there is a remarkable change, and the approach to the question now recalls the manner of a litigant: "Other speakers are absurdly inconsistent, urging you to oppose the Persian king in defence of the Egyptians, but too frightened of 'this fellow' to urge defence of the Rhodians" (5). It is not quite clear whether 'this fellow' (ὁ ἀνὴρ οὗτος) means the Persian king or Mausolus,[60] but this is the phrase that a litigant commonly uses in mentioning his opponent. It is also normal procedure to accuse one's adversary of inconsistency in speech and to remind the jury of any previous judgment connected with the question at issue. Demosthenes now reminds his hearers that his present speech is in conformi-

---

58 The speech has been praised by some modern critics as showing a statesmanlike approach to the problem. Blass, Att. Bered. III 291, calls it "ein Denkmal großer Staatsklugheit und Voraussicht," and quotes Brougham's approval of it as "a calm and judicious statement of the sound principle of foreign policy, on which the modern doctrine of the balance of power rests." But Blass admits that it is not well designed and the application of the principles not adequately argued.

59 Aristotle says that in the Assembly ὁ κρίτης περὶ οἰκείων κρίνει, ὥστ᾽ οὐδὲν ἄλλο δεῖ πλὴν ἀποδεῖξαι ὅτι οὕτως ἔχει ὡς φησιν ὁ συμβουλεύων (Rhet. 1. 1354b). Demosthenes thinks he knows better; he would surely also disagree with Aristotle's remark on the purpose of rhetoric, ὅτι οὐ τὸ πεῖσαι ἔργον αὐτῆς, ἀλλὰ ἰδεῖν τὰ ὑπάρχοντα πιθανὰ περὶ ἕκαστον (1355b), at this stage of his career at least, when he does seem more concerned to convince his listeners than to gather all the evidence in his favour. What Aristotle surely means is that it is not the task of rhetoric to convince people of what cannot be demonstrated except by fraudulent argument.

60 Pickard-Cambridge, in his translation (Demosthenes, Public Orations I 58), takes it to mean the Persian king, as does Croiset in the Budé edition.

ty with what he had said before (in *On the Symmories*), that he had urged a programme of rearmament, that might come in useful against the Persian king. He declares boldly that "this recommendation was found acceptable" (6), but we need not believe that this is strictly true; there is no positive evidence that his advice was taken in 354.[61]

The logic of his argument is much clearer here than in earlier speeches.[62] He argues that they are no more likely to invite Persian reprisals by helping the Rhodians than by the armament programme that he had previously recommended. And he offers evidence in support of his contention by recalling what happened when Timotheus was sent out to support the rebel satrap Ariobarzanes, "on condition that he did not violate the Athenian peace treaty with Persia." Timotheus decided he could not have anything to do with Ariobarzanes, but when he liberated Samos his act was not regarded as a serious provocation by the Persian king (9–10).

There is much greater attention paid to personalities than in the earlier speeches. Demosthenes invites his audience to put themselves in the king's place, to try to understand his reasoning; he even tells them what advice he would give the king if he were his minister (7). And what of Artemisia? Is it really more in her interest to let Persia control Rhodes than to allow Athens to do so? (11–13) And what of the Rhodian oligarchs, who have taken over the government, after expelling the democratic party with foreign aid? Are they to be trusted? (14) The democrats, who have not been faithful allies of Athens in the past, will now have learnt their lesson, they will recognize that only Athens can ensure Rhodian freedom (16). Demosthenes is not yet using his technique of characterization with the same deadly effect as in his later attacks on Philip. But there has been nothing like this in earlier speeches. The contrast can be seen with even greater clarity when he returns to his older pattern in the latter part of this speech, offering arguments based on principles and appealing to historical examples, like the Peace of Callias, "a familiar example to all of you" (29).

The *First Philippic*, which is earlier in date than this speech, offers more striking examples of the new style, and it will appear to many readers that *On the Freedom of the Rhodians* represents a return to the older manner. It is more accurate to say that both these speeches show a

---

61 The accuracy of his declaration is, rather curiously, not questioned by Pickard-Cambridge (Demosthenes, p. 122) or Jaeger (Demosthenes, p. 80). Croiset (Budé ed., Harangues I 4) and Cloché (Démosthènes, p. 46) are more cautious. Certainly war was not declared on Persia; but the influence of Demosthenes in securing this result must not be exaggerated.

62 Cf. Blass, Att. Bered. III 306.

mixture of the old and the new. Demosthenes begins the *First Philippic* by pleading for a renewal of national confidence, and he offers an example from the past to show how Athenians could succeed against apparently heavy odds, when they knew their cause was just and took the steps which they knew to be necessary (2—3). This is conventional enough, and he goes on to compare their attitude with Philip's:

"There was a time, men of Athens, when we held Pydna and Potidaea and Methone and all that area, and when many of the peoples now united with him were autonomous and free and more inclined to friendship with us than with him. If Philip at that time had made up his mind that, with no allies to help him, it was a hard task to fight the Athenians when they held so many strong points threatening his territory, he would not have done any of the things which he has in fact accomplished; he would never have become so powerful as he is now. But he had clear vision, men of Athens, he recognized that all these places were lying there to be won as prizes of war; and he knew the law of nature that anyone who is on the spot takes what belonged to the absent and anyone who is willing to work and take risks comes into the property of the negligent" (4—5).

This warns the Athenians that Philip is a man of strong character and the only way to deal with him is to learn from him. But they must not be allowed to think that he is admirable in any way, and his "outrageous behaviour" (ἀσέλγεια) is soon pointed out (9), with the warning that it is Athenian weakness which is responsible for his success; even if Philip dies, unless the Athenians mend their ways, they will "create another Philip" (11). Harsh words are used to describe Athenian ineptness: "like barbarians who do not know how to box," they let their hands fly to where they are hit, instead of putting up a proper guard (40). But to atone for his severity Demosthenes reminds them what kind of man Philip is, a man who cannot rest content with his victories but is always trying something new (42); in fact he seems to be drunk from his great successes (49). There is no need to underline the conclusion. If the speech shows that Philip is both guilty and vulnerable, it will have achieved his purpose.

Hardly any time is taken up with replies to other speakers or appeals to tradition or principle. It does no harm to remember what was accomplished by men like Iphicrates and Chabrias (24), but the main object is to show that Philip presents Athens with a special problem which demands special measures; Demosthenes wants the Athenians to understand the problem that faces them, and this is what makes the *First Philippic* different from his earlier efforts.

A brief analysis of the *Third Philippic* will show that his general plan of argument is still the same ten years later. He reproves the Athenians for their failure to take things properly in hand and says he cannot understand why they are unwilling to listen to unpalatable truths (1—3). This leads him into a criticism of other speakers, who are giving a patently false account of relations between Athens and Philip when they refuse to admit that a state of war exists. This, he says, is exactly what Philip wants, since it is his policy to pretend benevolence when he really intends conquest (10–14). Without any delay Demosthenes can now return to his familiar theme of Philip's character, his cleverness and uncanny ability to win points by trickery without resort to violence until the right moment for it arrives. The point is made clearer by some reference to his past successes (15–17). These are not conventional "historical examples," but evidence of Philip's methods which should have been noticed and understood long ago. The evidence indicates that he has consistently followed the method of a "cold war," technically perhaps not war at all, though anyone who calls it peace "is simply out of his mind" (19). Athenians, therefore, must recognize the true state of affairs, that Philip is a threat to "all Greeks," and plan action accordingly (20).[63]

The argument is reinforced by a more detailed narrative which occupies most of the rest of the speech. After the general description of Philip's character and behaviour, the details can serve as confirmation rather than proof of the speaker's contention. Even a slight acquaintance with Demosthenes' forensic speeches will show that this is the technique which he normally practises in prosecution. He argues that the defendant is dishonest and has a clever system which he has been practising for several years; unless he is stopped soon, it may be too late; a more detailed account of his activities will remove all doubt from the minds of the jury—thus the fuller narrative is introduced.

The Athenians listening to the *Third Philippic* are themselves part of the narrative, because they have been Philip's victims. In contrast with the "extreme *hybris*" of Philip, their behaviour has been correct (32), but it is hardly admirable and shows a sorry decadence from the heroic days of the fifth century: "You can see for yourselves the way things are now; you have no need of me to bear witness to them; but I shall show you that they were very different in times gone by" (41). And there are certain politicians who must be held responsible: "Not only is it necessary to recognize all this and take action to stop Philip by force of arms; you must also use your reason and intelligence in detesting the men who speak here in Athens on his behalf" (53). The recommendations—a verdict of guilty and a severe sentence—follow immediately from the narrative.

63 Would Aristotle think that Demosthenes was attempting to present "what is immediately persuasive by itself"? Cf. Rhet. 1.2. 1356b, ἐπεὶ γὰρ τὸ πιθανὸν τινὶ πιθανόν ἐστι, καὶ τὸ μὲν εὐθὺς ὑπάρχει δι' αὐτὸ πιθανὸν καὶ πιστόν, τὸ δὲ τῷ δείκνυσθαι δοκεῖ διὰ τοιούτων, οὐδεμία δὲ τέχνη σκοπεῖ τὸ καθ' ἔκαστον. The task of rhetoric, as Aristotle understands it, should be to prove by enthymeme and example that Philip is at war with Athens and must be actively resisted. Would he regard this direct method of presenting a situation as rhetoric at all?

When Demosthenes prosecuted Aeschines in 343 (three years before the *Third Philippic*), one of his most serious charges was that Aeschines had given an inadequate and misleading report of his diplomatic mission to Philip.[64] It might be unwise and dangerous for a speaker in the Assembly to make a comparable charge against any individual politician, but the accusation is implied here; no names are mentioned, but a narrative is presented and political opponents are challenged to prove it wrong, as though they were defendants in a trial. Once Demosthenes has decided what the main purpose of his oratory should be, he is able to adapt the method which he has followed in the courts. His oratory might have developed on quite different lines if he had been faced by a different political emergency. But his fame as a political orator depends on the Philippic orations, and they are unanswerable unless the narrative can be proved false.

In modern times admirers of Philip may be ready to admit (with certain reservations) the accuracy of the narrative and still maintain that Athens was wrong to take Demosthenes' advice in resisting him. Even if opponents of Demosthenes had held this opinion, they could not possibly have maintained it in public debate. They could not escape his conclusions, if they could not question the truth of his narrative—because the narrative demanded these conclusions. Thus it was almost impossible for them to explain to the Assembly why they were opposed to Demosthenes' plans of resistance. Subterfuge was the method they had to use, they had to make sure that none of the drastic measures recommended and voted were actually carried out. Such tactics, of course, made Demosthenes all the more insistent on the urgency of the danger; he constantly repeated his narrative and challenged anyone to answer it. Everything now depended on his ability to tell his story in such a way that the right conclusion seemed to follow from it inevitably. This called for art as well as knowledge and determination. The art of narrative is a very important part of Demosthenes' oratory, and it deserves closer investigation.

64 19. 19—24.

Chapter II

Narrative

A narrative skilfully presented and supported by convincing evidence can win a case in court without the need of much supplementary argument. The speaker may say that he is simply "presenting the facts as they happened," so as to give the impression that there is no other way to tell the story. But narrative can do more than "present the facts." A plaintiff must not only set forth his sufferings, but tell his story in such a way that the defendant is shown responsible for them, with no other explanation possible except his deliberate and malicious purpose. Rhetorical handbooks give the orthodox advice that a narrative should be as brief and uncomplicated as possible,[1] but Longinus shows a finer sense of the art, when he says that great writers can pick out the most relevant details and create something unified by combining them. As examples of this art he cites Sappho's poem φαίνεταί μοι κῆνος ἴσος θεοῖσιν and the ἑσπέρα μὲν γὰρ ἦν passage from *On the Crown*. He has the same comment to make on them both, that the authors have chosen the high points and the most significant details, eliminating what is superficial and trivial.[2]

The experience which a poet describes may be fictitious and a historian can use his imagination to supplement meagre sources, knowing that his readers are no better informed than he is. But a litigant in his narrative often has to remember what the jury will or will not already know, and what his adversary knows that is unknown to him and what he knows that is unknown to his adversary. A plaintiff may be very well informed about recent events and about his own personal sufferings, but much less certain about earlier stages of the story; and he may not trust his imagination to reconstruct the past behaviour or intentions of his adversary. Or he may know the beginning and the end of the story, while the middle is known only to his adversary. In such a situation he has to decide whether he will supply the missing details by conjecture or leave the other side free to present its version, in the hope that it will be unconvincing.[3]

---

1 Cf. e.g., Quintilian 4.2.31, 40–51.
2 De Sublim. 10.
3 Aristotle, Rhet. 2.1396a, remarks that we cannot argue on any subject unless we have some of the necessary information: πρῶτον μὲν οὖν δεῖ λαβεῖν ὅτι περὶ οὗ δεῖ λέγειν καὶ συλλογίζεσθαι εἴτε πολιτικῷ συλλογισμῷ εἴθ᾽ ὁποιῳοῦν, ἀναγκαῖον καὶ τὰ τούτῳ ἔχειν ὑπάρχοντα, ἢ πάντα ἢ ἔνια. μηδὲν γὰρ ἔχων ἐξ οὐδενὸς ἂν ἔχοις

Demosthenes' first speeches, in the case against his guardians, show him facing this question at the very start of his career in the courts. His father had died ten years ago, and by the terms of his will the estate was left in trust for Demosthenes until he came of age. None of this was in dispute, but now that it is time for him to receive the principal the trustees offer him a sum which seems to him absurdly small. He cannot explain exactly what has happened, how the estate has shrunk from fourteen talents (as he reckons it) to little more than a talent. His guardians' administration might be dishonest or incompetent or merely unlucky. He has no direct evidence that it was dishonest, and if he attempted a purely conjectural restoration of their operations, he might expose himself to charges of irresponsible lying and the charges might be substantiated. So he chooses the safer course. He omits the doubtful details, and describes the part of the story which he thinks he knows and understands, in such a way that it will be easiest to supply the missing details by assuming dishonest conduct on the defendant's part.[4] This challenges the defendant to offer a better explanation; he will have to deny or modify numerous details in the plaintiff's story if he is to fill the gaps in the narrative with a version that suits his purpose.

There are some resemblances between the incomplete narratives that Demosthenes devises and the prologues of Attic tragedy, particularly those of Euripides. The prologues not only outline the background and the past history of a family, but present a situation and a problem that has to be solved, a setting for a tragic plot and an *agon*. Just as a litigant explains why he is in court, why he is suing his adversary, and how the jury can repair the wrong that he has suffered, so the Nurse, in the *Medea* of Euripides, gives a brief account of Medea's grievance against Jason. And just as Demosthenes in prosecuting Aphobus makes no attempt to explain how a good relationship deteriorated, so the Nurse does not try to describe what went wrong with Medea's marriage:

νῦν δ'ἐχθρὰ πάντα καὶ νοσεῖ τὰ φίλτατα (16).

συνάγειν. Thus it is impossible to discuss whether Athens should go to war without knowing the military and economic resources available. Likewise, he adds, in forensic oratory one must use the information that is available and appropriate: ὡς δ' αὔτως καὶ οἱ κατηγοροῦντες καὶ οἱ ἀπολογούμενοι ἐκ τῶν ὑπαρχόντων σκοπούμενοι κατηγοροῦσι καὶ ἀπολογοῦνται. But he is thinking of topics for argument, not material for narrative.

4 Cicero's remarks on narrative in De Inv. 1.20.28 are brief and generally obvious. Neither he nor Quintilian, in his fuller discussion of narrative, 4.4.1−132, takes any account of a situation where the speaker may lack exact knowledge; omission of detail or failure to follow chronological order is recommended only if the full story may seem prejudicial to the speaker or if it will not be *probabilis*. He might have cited [Dem.] 48 as an example of imprudent narrative which revealed too much.

Jason has betrayed her to marry a Corinthian princess. But why? We have to wait for Jason to appear and give his (the defendant's) version of the story;[5] and it is not a version which disposes us to give a verdict in his favour.

An orator's narrative can resemble a tragic prologue in form as well as in purpose. Demosthenes describes how he was seven and his sister five years old when their father died, leaving an estate of about fourteen talents; in order to provide for their future, he left the estate in trust for them until they came of age, appointing his nephews Aphobus and Demophon and his old friend Therippides as trustees and arranging for Demophon to marry the daughter and Aphobus the widow, who would receive her dowry and the family house. But now, after the trustees have managed the estate for ten years, "they have robbed me of everything except the house and fourteen slaves and thirty minas in cash; all that they have handed over to me amounts to about seventy minas" (27.6).

The actions of ten years ago are described in the aorist, and when Demosthenes shifts to present time he uses the perfect indicative, since he is presenting a situation, not describing action. And without giving further details of this situation he returns to the past and explains why the estate was worth fourteen talents when his father died. The trustees were classified, for purposes of *eisphora*, in the same category as the wealthiest men in Athens; there was therefore no attempt on their part to conceal their wealth or the size of the estate (7–8). It consisted of various items—a sword-factory or cutlery business, with thirty slaves, whose value Demosthenes estimates, a couch-factory or furniture business with twenty slaves, whose value can be substantiated since they were originally given to the elder Demosthenes as security for a loan;[6] and in addition to these

5 There is the same lack of comment or explanation in Apollo's narrative in the prologue to the Alcestis. He tells how he arranged for Admetus to offer a substitute to die in his place, and Admetus, after a long search, found no one willing except his wife, ἡ νῦν κατ' οἴκους ἐν χεροῖν βαστάζεται ψυχορραγοῦσα (19–20). There is no criticism of Admetus, no hint of Alcestis' love. The tale is as bare and the transition from past to present as abrupt as in the Medea. Likewise in the prologue to the Orestes Electra withholds explanation of the murders in the house of Atreus, no mention of Aegisthus or Cassandra, no discussion of Clytaemnestra, nor does she say whether Orestes was right or wrong to obey the oracle (25–31). She quickly moves to the present and tells of Orestes' sickness. A similar pattern can be found in the prologue to the Electra. One might also compare the speech of protest made by the Plataeans in Thuc. 2.71: "Pausanias promised us independence and protection and now the Spartans are attacking us." This is a kind of prologue to the tragedy of Plataea.

6 It is more accurate to translate *ergasterion* by "business" than by "factory" or "workshop," because, as M. I. Finley points out, "Studies in Land and Credit in Ancient Athens" (Rutgers University Press 1951), 67–68, there appears to have been no separate building, apart from the house, in which the work was carried on,

two establishments there was cash in hand and in banks, a certain amount of money invested, a house with furniture, and various valuable objects: "This was the total estate that he left. It is not possible, within the limited time allowed me, to tell you how much of it has been plundered, how much each individual has taken, and how much all three of them together are conspiring to keep out of my hands" (12). Now we have returned to the present, with two perfect indicatives followed by a present indicative (ὅποσα κοινῇ πάντες ἀποστεροῦσιν).

In the next section imperfect and historic present indicatives are used in the narrative, to show how Aphobus proceeded to act, to describe the past situation and the defendant's purpose, as well as simple disconnected events. At the same time argument is offered in support of details in the narrative. Already the jury is being invited to recognize the deliberate intention of Aphobus and to pass judgment before the whole story is told:

"Immediately after my father's death Aphobus started living [ᾤκει] in the house, after taking possession in accordance with the terms of the will. He takes over [λαμβάνει] my mother's gold ornaments and the drinking cups left in the house. With these items he had in his possession [εἶχεν] about fifty minas worth of property, and in addition, as the slaves began to be sold, he kept on receiving [ἐλάμβανεν] from Demophon and Therippides the prices that they fetched, until he made up [ἀνεπλη-ρώσατο] the full amount of the dowry. And when he was in possession of this amount [εἶχεν], before setting out for Corcyra as trierarch he made formal declaration to Therippides that he had it and proceeded to acknowledge [ὡμολόγει] his receipt of the dowry. As witnesses to these events we have first of all his fellow-trustees, Demophon and Therippides; and as to his personal acknowledgment that he had this amount in his possession we have the evidence of Demochares, of the deme of Leuconoe, my aunt's husband, and many other witnesses" (13–14).

Evidence follows to substantiate some details, and some argument, since Aphobus does not admit having received the dowry (16).

The switch from past to present and back again is quite characteristic of tragic prologues. In Euripides the speaker may begin with some statements about the past, perhaps to explain his ancestry or that of the principal character, and then turn abruptly to the present, as he explains his own presence or the scene and situation at the start of the play; then he will return to the past, to give further details, before finally setting the stage for the dramatic action to start. Good examples can be found in the

and in general "the word *ergasterion* does not necessarily indicate the existence of a workshop as a distinct building," but simply a group of organized workers. Cf. the use of the word to denote a criminal organization or "gang" in 32.10 and 39.2. A workshop, as Finley says, cannot "disappear into thin air." But a business, the assets of which, apart from the good will built up by good management, consist only of slaves and materials, can and will decline in value, if neglected, to the point when it will "disappear."

prologues of the *Heraclidae* and the *Hecuba*,[7] and in other dramatists also. In the choral opening of Aeschylus' *Persae* the tenses alternate, quite in the manner of Demosthenes: "All the might of Asia is gone [ᾤχωκε], no news is coming in [ἀφικνεῖται], they left [ἔβαν], some on horseback, some in ships" (13–18). And in the opening scene of the *Oedipus Tyrannus* Sophocles makes Oedipus demand an explanation of the scene that confronts him: "Why are you here as suppliants, what fear or need made you stand here?"

τίνι τρόπῳ καθέστατε
δείσαντες ἢ στέρξαντες; (9–10).

The play will show, by gradual unfolding of events, why Thebes is afflicted by a plague, and Oedipus is asking questions like those that a plaintiff answers in his opening words: "Why am I in court, what grievance has caused me to bring suit?"

A question of conduct is often argued in Attic tragedy, especially in Euripides, with protagonists making speeches of attack and defence. The audience might not expect to be convinced by a "defendant" like Jason, but their experience as jurors would give them a keener appreciation of the quality of his speech. We do not know whether many fourth-century dramatists continued the Euripidean style of tragic *agon* or continued to write prologues which resembled a litigant's speech in form. It is tempting to believe that Demosthenes learned this detail of his technique from the theatre, but the evidence scarcely justifies such a conclusion. It is equally difficult to be sure that he learned it from Isaeus or any other contemporary orator, since none of their extant speeches show a particular liking for this device of alternating between past and present tenses.[8] On the other hand, the contrast of the present situation with the past is often found in Isaeus. It is an effective device in a speaker's account of his

---

7 Cf. especially Heraclid. 7–15:

ἐξὸν κατ' "Αργος ἡσύχως ναίειν, πόνων
πλείστων μετέσχον εἰς ἀνὴρ ᾽ Ἡρακλέει,
ὅτ' ἦν μεθ' ἡμῶν· νῦν δ᾽, ἐπεὶ κατ' οὐρανὸν
ναίει, τὰ κείνου τέκν᾽ ἔχων ὑπὸ πτεροῖς
σῴζω τάδ᾽ αὐτὸς δεόμενος σωτηρίας.
ἐπεὶ γὰρ αὐτῶν γῆς ἀπηλλάχθη πατήρ,
πρῶτον μὲν ἡμᾶς ἤθελ' Εὐρυσθεὺς κτανεῖν,
ἀλλ' ἐξέδραμεν· καὶ πόλις μὲν οἴχεται,
ψυχὴ δ᾽ ἐσώθη. φεύγομεν δ᾽ ἀλώμενοι.

In the Hecuba the ghost of Polydorus shifts from present to past, then back to present and into future (42) and back into past (49) before finally returning to present.

8 Alternation between aorist, imperfect, and historic present is of course a common device of narrative. For its effective use by Lysias cf. S. Usher, "Individual Characterization in Lysias," Eranos 63 (1965), 99–119. But this is not the same thing as shifting from past to present in time.

disappointment, when he had expected to be named as heir to an estate; he can point out how, in the lifetime of the deceased, he was constantly treated with great kindness and it cannot have been the intention of the testator to leave him penniless and unhappy.[9] Isaeus also likes to combine argument with narrative, and since Demosthenes is ready to do this from the start of his career, it is likely enough that he learned this lesson from him. Isaeus is careful not to hurry ahead with his story before explaining the import of an incident that needs some commentary.

In the first speech *Against Aphobus* the alternation between detail of the past and detail of the present makes it hard to decide where narrative ends and proof begins; the speech cannot be divided neatly into sections devoted to narrative, proof, and refutation, as the formal rules of rhetoric are supposed to demand. Demosthenes cannot give a full narrative because he has not enough information at his disposal; what he has to do is to make Aphobus produce his version of "the facts." Aphobus will perhaps maintain that the estate has been over-valued, the so-called assets really liabilities and the business enterprises not profitable, and that he never received the dowry, just as he never married the widow. But Demosthenes will make his task very difficult if he can show clearly what his father's intentions were, prove the high value of the estate, convince the jury that the factories were capable of bringing in a good income, and that Aphobus behaved very shabbily towards the widow.

Some modern readers are disappointed that Demosthenes does not offer more precise details of accounting to show how the business of the sword- and furniture-factories was carried on. Does his lack of detail mean that his description is misleading? And if his account has the effect of concealing important or inconvenient business detail,[10] should we say that

---

9 The opening of Isaeus 1 provides a good example. The speaker laments the great change (πολλὴ μεταβολή) that has occurred with the death of Cleonymus: "In his lifetime he proposed to leave us (κατέλειπε) his property, but by his death he has put us in peril of losing it; and thanks to our strict upbringing, we never even entered a law-court, but now we are here to fight for life itself" (περὶ πάντων τῶν ὑπαρχόντων). And in 8.1 (after the preliminary outburst): τοῦ γὰρ ἡμετέρου πάππου Κίρωνος οὐκ ἄπαιδος τελευτήσαντος, ἀλλ᾽ ἡμᾶς ἐκ θυγατρὸς αὐτοῦ γνησίας παῖδας αὐτῷ καταλελοιπότος, οὗτοι τοῦ τε κλήρου λαγχάνουσιν ὡς ἐγγυτάτω γένους ὄντες, ἡμᾶς τε ὑβρίζουσιν ὡς οὐκ ἐξ ἐκείνου θυγατρὸς ὄντας, οὐδὲ γενομένης αὐτῷ πώποτε τὸ παράπαν.
Here the alternation of tenses (in participles as well as in indicatives the contrast is maintained) does represent the constant shifting between past and present and is reminiscent of Demosthenes' manner. And this is the speech that Demosthenes is supposed to have studied (cf. Chapter I, supra, pp. 15–16.

10 Cf. F. Oertel, "Zur Frage der attischen Großindustrie", Rh. Mus. 79 (1930), 230–52 (esp. 233–35), who tries to rationalize Demosthenes' figures and criticizes the earlier attempt of W. Schwahn, "Demosthenes gegen Aphobos" (Leipzig

his vagueness is deliberately assumed to deceive jurors who may not be experienced in business? or does it merely reveal his own inexperience or ignorance? It is hard to be sure of the right answer, particularly since he is so young. But there are quite a number of passages in the Attic orators where one can detect what seems like a deliberately non-technical or non-professional manner of reporting business detail; and there must be some reason for this apparently casual style. We can only guess how well Athenian jurors were expected to understand details of accounting or business procedure, just as we do not know what degree of exactness in accounting the law required of Athenian business. It is particularly surprising to a modern reader when a speaker thinks it necessary to explain to the jury how simple banking procedures are carried out.[11] One would expect him to take for granted that the jury understood such things. Equally remarkable is the absence of business documentation in the speeches. We never find anything like an annual report or statement presented in evidence.

In the Roman courts Cicero regularly takes it for granted that an educated Roman, certainly any senator or knight, will understand accounting and be competent to keep his own books.[12] But it is not clear whether an Athenian jury could be expected to have similar competence or to understand a financial statement. It is possible that Athenian orators could have told us much more about the business life of Athens, if they

<hr>

1929). See also J. Korver, "Demosthenes gegen Aphobos", Mnemosyne ser. 3, 10 (1941), 8–22.

11 There are two remarkable examples in Orations 49 and 52, speeches spoken and perhaps written by Apollodorus, certainly not by Demosthenes. The passages are written in very simple Greek, and it is quite difficult to translate them into language that does not sound insulting to a juror's intelligence: "It is usual banking practice, when an individual brings in a sum of money with the request that it be transferred to a certain person, first to record the name of the depositor and the amount, and then add the notification: 'To be paid to so-and-so.' If the person to whom it is to be paid is known to them by sight, all they do is write down his name; but if they don't know him, they add the name of whoever is to introduce and identify the person who is to receive the money" (52.4).
"No one should be surprised at my being so exact; the fact is that bankers regularly make records in writing of the money that they pay out and the purposes for which it is paid out, and likewise of all sums deposited with them; in this way they know what to enter as credits and debits in their statements" (49.5).

12 In addition to numerous passages in the Verrines, the opening remarks of Pro Roscio Comoedo are very clear in their implications: Is scilicet vir optimus et singulari fide praeditus in suo iudicio suis tabulis testibus uti conatur. Solent fere dicere qui per tabulas hominis honesti pecuniam expensam tulerunt: 'Egone talem virum corrumpere potui, ut mea causa falsum in codicem referret?' And later (1.2): Si tabulas C. Fannius accepti et expensi profert suas in suam rem suo arbitratu scriptas, quo minus secundum illum iudicetis non recuso.

had thought it would have helped their case; perhaps they deliberately withheld detail, thinking it would merely confuse the jurors.

Demosthenes tells the jury that in his father's time one of the factories produced an annual income of thirty minas. He draws the conclusion that when half the slaves were sold the income should be fifteen minas, and that when Therippides declares an income of eleven minas "he reckons four minas less than he should" (27—29). He is assuming, apparently as a matter of course, that the "normal income" was in fact produced, leaving it to persons with little knowledge of business to presume that the defendant pocketed the extra four minas. He is equally unreasonable in his valuation of the slaves in the furniture business. It will seem obvious enough that the value of slaves decreases as they grow older, until they become a liability when they can no longer work. But Demosthenes speaks as though Aphobus should owe him the capital value, as of ten years ago, plus the income that they should have produced during these ten years. Would the jury really suppose that he is entitled to receive both their original capital value and the income that they produced? (27—29).

It is hardly a satisfactory explanation to say that Demosthenes is speaking like a naive and inexperienced young man, because he had plenty of time to make revisions and corrections, if he wanted an improved corrected copy for publication or his own records. It is more likely that he is being deliberately inexact, forcing his adversary to contradict him and to produce detail which he had perhaps hoped to keep to himself. Alternatively he may have thought that precise detail was more likely to confuse the jury than to enlighten them, that it might even arouse their hostility; in that case, why not leave it for the defendant to produce, if he thinks it necessary?[13] Instead of any precise or professional explanation of financial detail, there is just enough to make a person with little knowledge of business suspect that Aphobus has been grossly dishonest. Instead

---

13 An interesting example of what may be a reply to a simple story can be found in Oration 34 (almost certainly a spurious speech). The speaker's adversary, Phormio, admits having borrowed 2000 drachmas, at 30 per cent interest, for a Black Sea voyage, and claims that in the Bosporan kingdom he borrowed 120 staters (3360 drachmas) at 16 2/3 per cent and gave it to a ship's captain to take back to Athens; but the captain denies receiving it. Told like this it sounds a reasonable story, but against the background of the more complicated tale which the speaker unfolds it can be shown as most unlikely and suspicious. Why in the world should he give the captain all that money, when all that he owed the speaker was 2600 drachmas? Phormio may have had an explanation for handing over the larger sum; but if he had been content to simplify matters further, and say that he gave the captain enough to cover his debt, he would have robbed the speaker of the opportunity to ridicule his story.

of complaining that Demosthenes has told us too little, we should notice that he has told the jury nothing that they will not be able to follow.

Though he omits many details, a speaker may none the less say that he is telling the whole story,[14] as in *For Phormio*, one of Demosthenes' most successful private orations, written about fifteen years later than *Against Aphobus*.[15] The story has some features which are reminiscent of the case against Aphobus, except that Phormio is the defendant, not the plaintiff. Apollodorus, Pasion's son, is suing him for a large sum of money, and it is for him to show that he owes nothing and has been faithful in carrying out the instructions in Pasion's will. He has countered Apollodorus' move by a *paragraphe*, an action to show that no grounds exist for bringing suit against him, and this gives him the advantage of speaking first. It is not Phormio who speaks, since he was apparently unable to present his case himself and "without experience in speaking," but an anonymous friend who acts as his *synegoros*. He explains the reason and purpose of the *paragraphe*; it is not in order to gain time, but to obtain final release from the systematic persecution to which Apollodorus has been subjecting Phormio. "I will therefore tell you, as briefly as I can, the whole story of the relationship between Phormio and Pasion and Apollodorus, after which, I am sure, it will be clear to you that Apollodorus is a *sycophantes* and that there is no basis for his suit" (36.3).

The speaker does not, however, offer a continuous narrative of events in chronological order, and there is a reason for this. He wants to begin by establishing the genuineness of two documents, and he explains a few details in their text, which Apollodorus is expected to misrepresent. First, the contract under which the elderly Pasion leased the bank and shield-factory to Phormio, his former slave, and secondly Pasion's will, which authorized Phormio to marry his widow and act as trustee for his younger son, Pasicles, until he came of age. His presentation of the documents is combined with a brief narrative, but he is careful to keep the story as simple as possible, with only such detail as is required for the moment.

There is one item in the contract which he thinks it particularly necessary to explain. It is formally stated there that Pasion "owes eleven talents to the bank," evidently because Pasion, as an Athenian citizen, preferred to leave himself in control of the foreign loan operations of the

---

14 But cf. 34.5: ἀναγκαῖον δ' ἐστὶν βραχέα τῶν ἐξ ἀρχῆς διηγήσασθαι ὑμῖν. Here (cf. previous note) the speaker perhaps feels he should apologize for the complications of his story and so says that he will tell some of it, briefly. Gernet (Budé ed.) curiously mistranslates: "Il est nécessaire de vous exposer brièvement les faits depuis le commencement."

15 The Phormio of Oration 36 is not the same man as the Phormio of Oration 34.

bank instead of handing them over to the newly liberated slave (5—6). A part of the bank's capital assets is therefore withheld from Phormio. This seems clear enough, but Apollodorus, as we learn later, will argue that it means something quite different and offer an explanation that seems somewhat absurd, though it might be believed by members of the jury who are not familiar with business language and procedure. He will maintain that Phormio is in fact responsible for this sum of eleven talents, and is fraudulently withholding it from him. He will thus try to obtain the same sum twice over, arguing that it was part of the capital assets of the bank as administered by Phormio and also part of Pasion's estate when he died. For the present, however, no hint is given that this will be Apollodorus' contention.

There are also a few points in the will which require an explanation. Since Apollodorus, the elder son, was already of age and had a bad name for extravagance, Phormio and his fellow trustees decided to protect the younger son's share of the estate by handing over to Apollodorus his share of the capital without further delay. This meant arranging for him to receive half of the income from the enterprises which had been leased to Phormio. It was important to establish that Apollodorus accepted this arrangement at the time it was made and that, when Pasicles came of age, both brothers expressed themselves satisfied with Phormio's administration and declared him free of all indebtedness when the lease was terminated (8—10). No actual sums of money are mentioned here; the story is kept as simple as possible.

When Pasicles comes of age and the two brothers gain full control of all their father's estate, Apollodorus agrees to take the shield-factory and lets Pasicles have the bank. The choice might seem unexpected, it is argued, if Apollodorus had really believed there were eleven talents more in the bank than were actually there. The real reason, according to the speaker, why he chose the factory must be because it was a safer enterprise, though it produced an annual income of only one talent and the bank normally produced a hundred minas. Here again, as in *Against Aphobus*, the "normal" income is brought into the argument (11).

In section 12 the argument switches to the present, and the jury is invited to conclude that Apollodorus is a *sycophantes* with no real case. It is argued that he must have understood perfectly well that Pasion withheld eleven talents of the bank's capital from Phormio, as recorded in the lease contract, because in subsequent leases of the bank, on the same terms as in the contract with Phormio, Apollodorus withheld a portion of the bank's capital just as Pasion had done (13). Even if this does not prove positively that the contract between Pasion and Phormio is a genuine document, it is an indication that Apollodorus is trying to deceive the jury. It is a detail that acquires special force because it has been held back until this point. Further details are now produced, from the period between the death of Pasion, in 370, and the date of the speech, 350–49, but there is no continuous narrative. Apollodorus raised no objections so long as his mother was alive, we are told; and after her death he gave Phormio a formal release from all claims for the second time. And so the conclusion comes out: "As you see, his present suit is based on totally unfounded complaints" (16).

The technique is similar to that which Demosthenes used against Aphobus. He is economical of details in the narrative, but insists that his adversary's claims are inconsistent with his attested behaviour in former years. Apollodorus would be expected, in his reply, to produce other details from these years, incidents that would serve to explain the apparent discrepancies and cast doubt on Phormio's narrative and the evidence that supported it. Demosthenes made no serious attempt to anticipate the resourcefulness of Aphobus, but he takes greater precautions here: "I expect Apollodorus will tell you that his mother, under Phormio's influence, destroyed certain documents; he will say that the loss of these documents makes it impossible to refute our contentions convincingly" (18). In fact, he continues, Apollodorus was in possession of all the papers relating to his father's affairs, and thanks to these papers he was able to bring actions against various persons for sums that they allegedly owed Pasion (20). Here is another detail cleverly held back until it serves a particular need. It is not until a later stage in the speech (36) that mention is made of the large sums in cash which Apollodorus acquired in the course of these twenty years; they are mentioned when the speaker wants to ridicule Apollodorus' complaint that he has been short of money: "If you add up the total, you will find that he got more than forty talents" (38). His contention that he spent all his money in the service of the state is made to appear ridiculous, and it is suggested that his younger brother received considerably less than his due.

Blass remarks (*Att. Bered.* III.i.465) that the real merit of this speech lies not in the narrative but in the arrangement and use of the available material. An important part of this skilful arrangement is the limitation of the opening narrative, which enables the speaker to avoid repetition and avoid confusing the jury with too much detail at any one time. A less skilful orator might have tried to give a continuous narrative of the twenty-year period, but anyone who tries to construct such a narrative will soon discover what difficulties it presents. He might begin, in orthodox fashion, by saying that Pasion had two sons and, as he grew older, entrusted the management of his business to his former slave, Phormio. But he cannot go any further without answering the question, Why not to his elder son? He will have to give some account of the youthful career and behaviour of Apollodorus. A digression of this sort will not only interrupt the continuity of the narrative, but will bring Apollodorus into the centre of the story and oblige the speaker to anticipate his direct attack on the character of Apollodorus, which is much more effective at the end of the speech, where it serves to corroborate all that has been said before.[16] Alternatively, instead of breaking off the narrative at Pasion's death, it would be possible to continue by describing Phormio's operations as manager of the bank (to show his skill and integrity in business). But this would mean introducing many details of banking and the names of numerous persons not directly connected with the case. By his present arrangement Demosthenes keeps the technicalities of business to a minimum and limits his cast of characters. Comparison with the drama is instructive here too. A dramatist could not bring more than three characters onto the stage at any one time, and was generally content with two. The orator who observed this rule made his story easier to follow.

A less skilful speech by an unknown orator, the spurious oration *Against Lacritus* (35), shows the difficulties that arise if one tries to describe everything in the order in which it happened. The speaker had lent money to Artemon to finance a voyage to the Black Sea; Artemon died without repaying the loan, and when the speaker tries to recover it from his brother Lacritus, Lacritus blocks his suit with a *paragraphe*, saying there is no case at all against him; this speech is the reply to the *paragraphe*. After introductory remarks and an initial statement of the case, there is a long sentence (written in such a way that it would leave anyone but an expert speaker breathless) in which more characters are introduced, Thrasymedes and Melanopus, "good friends of mine, who persuaded me to make the loan and who had no notion that they were dealing with dishonest men" (6—7). The text of the contract of loan is

---

16 It appears that some teachers of rhetoric had strict views about following chronological order. Aristotle says that diversion from chronological order is appropriate in epideictic oratory: διήγησις δ᾿ ἐν μὲν τοῖς ἐπιδεικτικοῖς ἐστιν οὐκ ἐφεξῆς ἀλλὰ κατὰ μέρος. δεῖ μὲν γὰρ τὰς πράξεις διελθεῖν ἐξ ὧν ὁ λόγος (Rhet. 3.1416b). He recommends the change because the ἐφεξῆς order is δυσμνημόνευτον—when the story is told continuously it is hard to keep the details straight in your mind. His remark seems quite as fully applicable to forensic oratory as to any other type. Quintilian, on the other hand, disagrees strongly with the advocates of chronological order on principle: Ne eis quidem accedo qui semper eo putant ordine, quo quid actum sit, esse narrandum, sed eo malo narrare quo expedit. Quod fieri plurimis figuris licet. Nam et aliquando nobis excidisse simulamus, cum quid utiliore loco reducimus (4.2.83). There will always be some listeners who will maintain that they want to be told of each event as it happens; the device of pretending that you "forgot to mention it before" will appease them.

then read, with statements of witnesses to show that it is an authentic document (10–14).

If the speaker were following the pattern of Demosthenes in *For Phormio*, he would now switch to the present, but he goes on to characterize Lacritus, a pupil of Isocrates, who behaved like an "important person" (μέγα πρᾶγμα, 15). It was he who made all the arrangements, his brothers being just young fellows, and he gave many assurances that the contract would be kept and that he would be in Athens while his brother was away. According to the contract they were supposed to carry a cargo of three thousand amphorae of wine, but they never bought anything like this quantity and spent the money on something else (evidently the speaker does not know what they did with it).[17] Witnesses are called to testify that no more than four hundred and fifty amphorae were put on board the ship (16–20).

From now on the story becomes more difficult to follow, partly because the speaker seems not to be sure enough about detail to give a coherent and continuous account. He knows that the brothers borrowed further money, which was illegal since their cargo was already fully pledged as security, and that they failed to secure a proper return cargo in the Black Sea. But there is much that he does not know, and in telling the story of their voyage and shipwreck he has to rely entirely on hearsay evidence. There is another part of the story, however, where he is telling his own experience, his conversations with Lacritus and some members of the ship's company, when they reappear in Athens and he starts finding out how dishonestly he has been treated. He is not very skilful at combining the two parts of the story without confusing them, and he also lacks skill at combining argument with narrative. Lacritus had maintained that he was free of all responsibility, that he was not the heir of Artemon, and that he could not be sued in a "trade case" (ἐμπορικὴ δίκη), because he had no contract with the speaker (42–49). The speaker is quite ineffective in countering these claims; indeed he does little more than protest that they are dishonest. Nor does he make it clear what has happened to the third brother, Apollodorus, who may be still alive but beyond the reach of prosecution.

His reticence on this point has roused the curiosity and suspicion of modern readers,[18] but we cannot fairly blame him for his lack of information and his consequent inability to tell the whole story "as it happened."

---

17 ἀντὶ τοῦ ἠγοράσθαι αὐτοῖς τὸν οἶνον ὅσον προσῆκεν, τοῖς χρήμασιν ἐχρῶντο ὅ τι ἐδόκει τούτοις (35.19).
18 For a discussion of these questions, with bibliography, see Gernet's introduction in the Budé edition, Plaidoyers civils I 169–80.

The most serious weakness of the speech is that it does not seriously attempt to achieve its purpose, which is to meet the argument of the *paragraphe*. Instead of countering the legal argument of Lacritus, he simply sets out to show that he is a dishonest man; in fact, if it were not for the information given in the *hypothesis,* we would not learn until the speech was half finished that it was delivered in answer to a *paragraphe*. It has been suggested, and it may be true, that the speaker adopted these tactics because his legal case was weak. But lack of skill supplies an equally good explanation.[19] He appears to think that all he has to do in court is to tell the truth, but this is not always such a simple task with inadequate information and evidence, and he has not exploited as well as he might the damaging information that he does possess.

Much greater skill in handling a story of a maritime loan and shipwreck is shown in another speech of doubtful authenticity – *Against Zenothemis*(32). Only the earlier part of the speech is preserved, but its narrative technique, so far as it goes, is admirable, reminiscent of the mature manner of *On the Embassy* and *On the Crown.*

Demon is bringing a *paragraphe* against Zenothemis, arguing that there is no case against him and that he is not liable to prosecution in a "trade suit" (ἐμπορικὴ δίκη), since he had no business contract with Zenothemis. But he is not content with proving his technical point, and undertakes to show that a criminal fraud has been attempted.[20] His narrative begins after a brief introduction: "This man Zenothemis was employed by the ship-owner Hegestratus, whose death at sea he mentioned in the text of his complaint without giving any details. I shall now give them to you; together they devised the following fraud" (4).

Demon tells the astonishing story with great economy of detail. Zenothemis and Hegestratus both borrowed money in Syracuse (he does not say how much or from whom or on what terms, not wasting time on

19 Libanius in the *hypothesis* maintains that the speech is by Demosthenes and excuses its weakness by saying: πρὸς δὲ τὴν παραγραφὴν ἀσθενέστερον ἀπήντηκε διὰ τοῦ πράγματος τὸ πονηρόν.

H. J. Wolff, Die attische Paragraphe (Weimar 1966), 74–81, suggests a different reason for the speaker's reticence about the question raised in the "paragraphe". He thinks there may have been no legal basis on which the issue could be decided, and that this is the reason why there is no argument about it. Another possibility is that the speech was originally written for an action against Lacritus, and was not adapted as much as it should have been to meet the new situation when the suit was blocked by the "paragraphe". Cf. T. Thalheim, "Der Prozeß des Androkles gegen Lakritos und seine Urkunden", Hermes 23 (1899), 333–45. We might even conjecture that the speaker had paid for the original text and did not care to go back to his speech-writer and pay an extra fee for a revised version.

20 Other speakers in support of *paragraphai* are content to protect themselves by blocking the prosecution. Cf. e.g. 37.1–2, πειράσασθαι σῴζειν ἐμαυτόν.

unnecessary details), each in his turn offering as security the cargo of grain on board the ship (which did not belong to either of them). They carefully did not take any of the money on board, but sent it off to Massalia. Their ship put to sea, and when it was two or three days out of port, Hegestratus went down into the hold and started to cut a hole in the bottom of the ship; but he was discovered, leapt overboard, failed to find the ship's boat ("missing the boat," διαμαρτὼν τοῦ λέμβου), and was drowned.

The implication is that the two of them had meant to escape in the boat, leaving the rest of the ship's company to drown; but time is not wasted in trying to prove that part of the plan, and no charge of attempted murder is made. Even now Zenothemis wants the ship to be abandoned, but it is saved and brought into port at Cephallenia, thanks to the insistence of "our man on board," who offers rewards to the crew if they can save the cargo. We do not learn this man's name and his connection with the case until later; but the speaker mentions him now to remind the jury that he has a witness who can support his story.

The ship was bound for Athens, to complete the round trip which had been financed there, and despite efforts of Zenothemis and others to have it directed to Massalia, the Cephallenian authorities insisted that it must continue its voyage to Athens. "And this man, whom no one would ever have expected to dare show his face here, has not only come to Athens but actually brought suit against us, claiming the grain that belongs to us" (9). In the familiar Demosthenic manner the narrative returns to the present with perfect tenses: οὐκ ἐλήλυθεν μόνον ἀλλὰ καὶ ... ἡμῖν δίκην προσείληχεν.

This is only the beginning of the story; new complications and new characters are now introduced, one at a time. There is a new villain in the person of Aristophon, a man whom the speaker sent out from Athens to Cephallenia, to represent his interests when the dispute with the local authorities was in progress. He turns out to be a far from reliable representative: "There is an organization of criminals in Piraeus whose faces will be familiar even to you when you see them. While Zenothemis was trying to stop the ship being directed to Athens, we engaged a member of this group as our representative, not knowing what kind of person he was; and this was an even greater disaster, if that is possible, than our becoming involved with dishonest men in the first place. This man's name was Aristophon; and, as we now learn, it was he who organized the Miccalion affair" (10—11).

The speaker takes pains to show that he is a simple innocent man, who does not recognize the faces of men in the criminal underworld. He is no match for Aristophon, who makes an offer to Zenothemis and they are soon working together: "Since the scheme to sink the ship had failed, and Zenothemis had no means of satisfying his creditors (how could he produce merchandise which he had never put on board?), he now claims the cargo which belongs to us. He maintains that he lent money to Hegestratus on the security of this grain which our man on board had bought" (12).

The creditors of Zenothemis and "our man on board" still remain nameless as the story continues: "His creditors finding that, instead of money, they had nothing but a dishonest debtor on their hands, conceived the hope that, if you could be misled, they might be able to recover their money at our expense. Their own interest has forced them to cooperate with this man, who (as they know quite well) is making fictitious charges against us. Here, in a nutshell, is the story of the case on which you will have to pass judgment" (12–13).

Witnesses are now called, and details are not repeated when the narrative is resumed.[21] The original plan must have been for Zenothemis or Hegestratus to claim ownership of the cargo after the ship was lost at sea, but since it went wrong it is not necessary to explain all its details. The speaker now concentrates his attention on describing the revised plan, as devised by Aristophon. When the ship reached Athens, it was immediately seized by the persons who had put up a loan that was covered by the ship; the cargo was claimed by its purchaser, "to whom we had lent money" (14). This man, whose name is Protus, now takes the centre of the stage with Zenothemis, and Aristophon becomes a non-speaking character in the background. We are given some scraps of dialogue: "Do you really mean," says Protus, "that you lent money to Hegestratus, the man with whose help you tricked others into making loans, the man who so often told you that people who put up money would never see it again? You mean that you were willing to put up money after hearing him talk in this way?" (15). Zenothemis sticks to his story, unmoved by remarks of some bystanders (members of the chorus, as it were). He will not recognize any of the legal moves of Protus and his partner Phertatus, when they try to dispossess him, and will not deal with anyone except the speaker, Demon.[22]

The subsequent course of events is far from clear, and possibly it is not intended to make it clear. The speaker combines argument with nar-

---

21 In 37.9 the speaker takes the chance of summarizing the story after presenting his witnesses.
22 For an explanation of this manoeuvre see L. Mitteis, "Romanistische Papyrusstudien", Zeitschr. d. Savigny Stiftung 23 (1902), 288–91. There is no reason why the speaker should explain the legal manoeuvre; the story as he tells it is quite sufficient to make the jury suspicious of Zenothemis' motive.

rative, and it is in a protest to the jury that one remarkable detail is revealed: "No member of our partnership ever supposed that you would rule that the grain belonged to Zenothemis—the grain which he tried to persuade the crew to abandon, so that it would go down with the ship when it sank" (21). This verdict—a totally unexpected one, if the facts as hitherto presented are correct—is best explained on the presumption that Protus and Zenothemis are now acting in collusion, and that Protus allowed Zenothemis to win his case by default. But the speaker first tells the story as it appeared to him at the time: "Nor did we think that you would recognize his right to bring suit in regard to merchandise which he had worked so hard to prevent coming to Athens" (22). Then Aristophon returns to play a further part in the story. He and Zenothemis, we are told, persuaded Protus to cooperate with them, leaving Demon and his partners in a very difficult situation: "So long as Protus thought he could gain something out of the grain cargo, he maintained his claim to it and preferred to combine his own profit with meeting his obligations to us, instead of making them partners in his profit and failing in his obligations to us. But after he returned to Athens and became involved in this business, the price of grain fell—and then he soon changed his mind" (25).

The true facts of the case are beyond our recall. It has been conjectured that Protus behaved dishonestly from the start, that he never bought the grain which his contract with Demon obliged him to buy, and that he therefore had no claim to the cargo. Alternatively it has been suggested that perhaps Demon never really had any contract with him.[23] But we have nothing except our own ingenuity to guide us in solving the problem, and we have even less information than the jury, since the second half of the speech has been lost.

Just before the text breaks off, Demon describes how he approached Demosthenes and asked him for help in the case, and received this answer:

---

23 Cf. Gernet, Démosthène, Plaidoyers civils (Budé ed.) I 114—15. But in that case who actually bought the grain? Is there another party whose name never comes up? It is hard to believe that it actually belonged to Hegestratus; it would certainly not be in keeping with the scheme (as it is described) for him and Zenothemis to put a cargo of their own in a ship which they intended to scuttle. Admittedly the text of Demon's contract with Protus is not presented in evidence in the portion of the speech that survives; it may of course have been produced at a later stage in the argument, and Blass (Att. Bered. III 495) points out quite correctly that we are not entitled to suspect Demon because he does not produce it at the start of the narrative. The moneylenders in Syracuse, always unnamed, must have been shown some papers to convince them that the grain belonged first to Hegestratus and then to Zenothemis, but Zenothemis will not be anxious to have these questionable documents produced, nor does Protus (once he has deserted Demon) really intend to go to Syracuse to look for them; his challenge to Zenothemis (19—21) is not meant to be accepted.

56

"Demon, I will do as you ask, it would be shameful for me to refuse. But we have to consider your position and mine. Since I started to take an active part in public affairs I have never involved myself in any private litigation . . ." (32). The sentence that follows is not completed in the text and its meaning is very uncertain. Perhaps Demosthenes' remark is meant to be ambiguous, perhaps he did write the speech, but was not prepared to admit having done so. But its evident late date (about 340)[24] makes it unlikely that he is the author, and we have no right to insist that he must have written it because it is a good speech.

The speech presents a complex story with considerable skill and its narrative style is not unlike the Demosthenic manner of *On the Embassy* and *On the Crown.*[25] It is economical of detail, the characters of the drama are kept distinct, with only two or three of them in action at any one time, and adopts the plan of telling the story from two separate points of view—sometimes the speaker tells what he saw himself, sometimes he is dependent on the observation of another character. A less skilful speaker might concentrate too much on his own personal experience, and leave the other side a freer hand in telling its version of the story. An interesting detail is the delay in revealing the dishonesty of Protus; it is not revealed until it is directly relevant to the story. A modern reader who attempts to summarize the case will perhaps want to begin with Demon and Protus and the contract to purchase grain in Syracuse. Does the author perhaps decide against this arrangement in order to concentrate attention from the beginning on Zenothemis and Hegestratus and their fraudulent devices? The jury are not being asked to pass judgment on Protus, and if he is introduced too early their attention may be distracted from Zenothemis.

The speech *Against Phormio* (34) is even later in date than *Against Zenothemis* (327 at the earliest)[26] and is quite definitely not the work of Demosthenes, but it presents a complicated story in a similar skilful manner. It is delivered in reply to a *paragraphe* brought in by Phormio

24 The late date is established by the age of Demon, who was much younger than Demosthenes and who refers to him as a prominent politician, too busy with public affairs to engage in forensic work (32); and by the trade with Syracuse, which would not have been possible before Timoleon came to power in 344 (cf. Gernet, Plaidoyers civils I 117).
25 Cf. the discussion of these speeches in Chapter V, infra.
26 The speaker refers to Alexander's march on Thebes (335) and then to two critical grain shortages in Athens, when he and his brother made useful contributions of money (34.38—39). These shortages must be connected with the general crisis in the grain supply between 330 and 326. Cf. Tod, Gk. Hist. Inscr. II 196, where references to relevant Attic inscriptions are given; cf. also Gernet's introduction to the speech, Plaidoyers civils I 150—51 and E. Ziebarth, Eine Handelsrede aus der Zeit des Demosthenes, and H. J. Wolff, Die attische Paragraphe, 63—74.

(who is no relation of Demosthenes' earlier client), and the speaker[27] therefore faces a different problem from Demon. He argues that the other party has had a contract with him, that he has not fulfilled it, and is therefore quite properly subject to legal action. He presents the text of his contract with Phormio, a loan covering a voyage to the Crimea and back, after making it clear that he has witnesses who know quite well what went on in the Crimea (2). His adversaries do not deny the contract, but deny having broken it in any way. Since in this kind of dispute a *paragraphe* is apparently not authorized unless it can be shown that there never was a contract, there is no need to take up much time with legal argument—περὶ μὲν οὖν τῆς παραγραφῆς βραχὺς ἐστιν ὁ λόγος. The speaker is much more interested in telling the story of Phormio's attempt to defraud him. He chooses his detail carefully, has only three main characters in his story, with the emphasis shifting to each of them in turn, while the scene shifts from Athens to the Crimea and back again.

Phormio is shown behaving in a suspicious manner from the start. He borrows more money in the Piraeus than is warranted by the cargo he can carry on the ship; indeed the merchandise on board is not even enough to cover his contract with the speaker. Lampis, the ship's captain, appears to back the speaker at first, but is in fact accused of being Phormio's partner in the fraud. He is the character who corresponds to Protus in the case against Zenothemis. But just as Demon was more anxious to prove Zenothemis guilty than Protus, so here the main target of attack is Phormio.

In both these cases if the speaker had adequate evidence to support his statements, nothing much more was required of the speech-writer than a lucid and well organized narrative. The same is true of *Against Dionysodorus* (56), which is certainly a spurious speech, where the story is quite simple and presents little that is of much interest. The speaker takes on no definite character in any of these speeches. He is allowed to appear as a rather colourless figure in contrast with the shameless dishonesty of his opponents.

There are in fact a number of speeches in which a great effort is made to prove the defendant's unworthy motives but no very clear-cut character is given to the plaintiff. In the first speech *Against Boeotus* (39), which appears to be the genuine work of Demosthenes, the speaker, Mantitheus, tells the jury nothing about himself and no more than is absolutely necessary about his father, Mantias. He is much more concerned to show that Boeotus is a most undesirable person and that it is

---

27 There are in fact two speakers, Chrysippus and his partner, as the opening sentence informs the jury; but it is not quite clear how the speech is divided between them. For an outline of the narrative see p. 46, note 13 above.

quite "impossible" to let him call himself Mantitheus; he is not the kind of person with whom one would want to be confused. Boeotus and his brother are claiming that their mother, Plangon, was the legitimate wife of Mantias. Despite his conventional declaration that he will tell "the whole truth" (3), the speaker has no intention of describing how his father treated her or regarded her.[28] He prefers to describe how badly she and her sons behaved. He says that she made a statement under oath that Mantias was the father of her two sons, having previously promised that she would refuse to swear if invited by him to do so; and after her statement the "father" had no choice but to register the boys in the phratry and adopt them formally as his sons: "At the Apaturia he registered the defendant under the name of Boeotus and his brother as Pamphilus. Then, when my father died before they could be registered in the deme, the defendant went to the demesmen and had himself registered as Mantitheus instead of Boeotus" (4).

This is as far as the narrative goes, and it is supported by evidence and no doubt accurate so far as it goes; but there is much more to be told and explained, if the speaker chose to reveal what he knew. He prefers to complain about the inconsistent and irrational arguments of his adversary and the grave wrong that he is committing by usurping the name of Mantitheus.

The second speech *Against Boeotus* (40), which is certainly not by Demosthenes, introduces more "facts," and some unnecessary and scarcely relevant detail in its rambling and untidy narrative. But despite the speaker's pose of frankness and apparent readiness to tell "the whole truth" (10), he is cautious and reticent about some things and when he says it is "not proper" for him to describe his father's "irregular relationship with Plangon" (8), there are other reasons that hold him back besides respect for his father's memory. He neither admits nor denies that Mantias was the father of her two sons, or that he married her or divorced her, and we never learn the date of Boeotus' birth. If he admitted the marriage of Plangon and the birth of Boeotus before his father's marriage to Polyaratus' daughter and his own birth, he would be admitting that Boeotus was a legitimate son and the eldest son. If he denied the marriage, it might be thought he was accusing his own father of illegally registering an illegiti-

---

28 He does not, on the other hand, disguise his opinion—the story that Boeotus told before the arbitrator, whether true or not, is quite inconsistent with his claim to be the son of Mantias (39.22—24). But he is studiously vague about details of his father's life and career, saying only that he was in politics and could not afford to be involved in any scandal (3) and expecting the jury to remember that he never succeeded in business; to imagine him keeping two wives and maintaining two households is preposterous (25—26).

mate son as his legitimate son. Hence the need for caution; better leave it for his adversary to present his story and face the difficulty of substantiating it (it will not be easy since both Mantias and Plangon are dead).[29]

The two speeches *Against Boeotus* raise some interesting problems in Athenian law and they show how Mantitheus (like Apollodorus in the two speeches *Against Stephanus*), after failing at his first attempt with a cautious and restrained speech, tries a different approach (and a different speech-writer) in his second attempt. He reveals further details and makes a greater effort to give an impression of candour or naiveté,[30] in a manner that is sometimes reminiscent of Lysias. The second speech *Against Boeotus*, like the second speech *Against Stephanus*, is unlikely to win a modern reader's admiration; but, for all we know, it may have won the case for the speaker.

The speech *Against Conon* (54) provides a more attractive example of the candid or "naive" style of narrative and shows that Demosthenes was fully capable of writing in this style when circumstances demanded it. This speech has often been admired for its form as well as its style, and is quoted by Dionysius of Halicarnassus as an example of clear, precise writing, after the manner of Lysias, convincing and appropriate to the speaker's character, which it reveals as natural and unsophisticated.[31] The

29 It is extremely difficult, if not impossible, for us to discover the true facts and their legal significance, when a speaker is not speaking with as much frankness as he pretends. The latest discussion of this case is by J. Rudhardt, "La reconnaissance de la paternité dans la société athénienne," Mus. Helveticum 19 (1962), 39–64 (with bibliography in note 2). See also B. A. van Groningen, "Mantithée contre Mantithée," Symbolae ad ius et historiam antiquitatis I. C. von Oven dedicatae (Leiden 1946), 92–110. J. Miles, "The Marriage of Plangon (Dolly)," Hermathena 77 (1951), 38–46, suggests boldly that Plangon was in fact Mantias' legal wife, and the speaker's mother, a wealthy woman of good family, only his mistress.
Part of our difficulty in discovering the right answer is that we do not know exactly what constituted legal marriage in fourth-century Athens. We know that husband and wife had to be citizens, if their children were to be "legitimate" Athenian citizens, and we often hear how marriages were (or ought to be) arranged in respectable families; but this is not the same thing as a definition of legal marriage. Cf. W. K. Lacey, The Family in Classical Greece (London 1968), Chap. V, and A. R. W. Harrison, The Law of Athens I (Oxford 1968), Chap. I.
30 Cf. Gernet, Plaidoyers civils II 31.
31 Dion. Hal. Dem. 13: ταῦτ' οὐ καθαρὰ καὶ ἀκριβῆ καὶ σαφῆ καὶ διὰ τῶν κυρίων τε καὶ κοινῶν ὀνομάτων κατεσκευασμένα ὥσπερ τὰ Λυσίου; ἐμοὶ μὲν γὰρ ὑπάρχειν δοκεῖ. τί δέ; οὐχὶ σύντομα καὶ στρογγύλα καὶ ἀληθείας μεστά, καὶ τὴν ἀφελῆ καὶ ἀκατάσκευον ἐπιφαίνοντα φύσιν, καθάπερ ἐκεῖνα; πάντων μὲν οὖν μάλιστα. οὐχὶ δὲ καὶ πιθανὰ καὶ ἐν ἤθει λεγόμενά τωι καὶ τὸ πρέπον τοῖς ὑποκειμένοις προσώποις τε καὶ πράγμασι φυλάττοντα; ἡδονῆς δὲ ἄρα καὶ πειθοῦς καὶ χαρίτων καιροῦ τε καὶ τῆς ἄλλης ἀπάσης τῆς τοῖς Λυσιακοῖς ἐπανθούσης ἀρετῆς οὐχὶ πολλὴ μοῖρα; οὐκ ἔνεστ' ἄλλως εἰπεῖν.

speaker Ariston is expected to win the jury's sympathy by his manner and appearance as well as by his story, which is simple, self-explanatory, and based entirely on his own experience. Its purpose is to show that he is a law-abiding young man, with many friends, and that he has been the innocent victim of a brutal attack made on him by the defendant and his companions in the Agora in Athens.

Whatever witnesses may say on either side,[32] there is one line of defence which the speaker cannot ignore. An Athenian jury was unlikely to be very severe towards a man who admitted an act of violence but defended it as an act of legitimate revenge against a personal enemy who had done him an injury. Conon might argue that his quarrel went back to the time when he and the speaker had served in the army, and the speaker had reported him and his friends to the commanding officer for their rowdy and drunken behaviour in camp. The speaker is careful to point out that he did not make the complaint as an individual, but in common with his messmates, when they found themselves unable to handle the situation; and he does not say that any particular disciplinary action was taken against the offenders, except that the *strategos* rebuked them severely (3—5). He has to risk being held up to ridicule as a poor sort of soldier, who could not put up with friendly horseplay but ran off telling tales and getting his comrades in trouble. Since he cannot very easily meet this kind of countercharge directly, he anticipates it by trying to show that the incident was something more extreme than an ordinary outburst of soldierly high spirits.

Always in an account of "life in the service" a speaker has to gamble on the kind of experience that the jurors may remember from their youth. Will they cherish memories of riotous evenings and take the side of the wayward private against the officer, or will they be more straitlaced and support the cause of authority?[33] Here the plaintiff has to take the risk of

32 It may well be that Ariston has exaggerated the savagery of the attack and the injuries and indignities that he suffered (and his mother's alarm when he was taken home, 54.20). H. J. Wolff, in a lecture delivered before an audience of lawyers, "Demosthenes als Advokat," Schriftenreihe der juristischen Gesellschaft e.V. 30 (1968), 16—17, suggests that he lacked witnesses to prove that it was the defendants who struck the first blow and that this is why he refused the *proklesis* of the defendants (27), who offered their slaves for interrogation (these slaves, even under severe *basanos*, would certainly support their masters' version). In fact, the narrative, by showing Ariston outnumbered from the start, invites the conclusion that he could not possibly have provoked a quarrel (7—8). He had to decide whether it was better tactics to refuse the challenge or face their evidence and try to discredit it. For the tactics of the speech see also M. Morford, "*Ethopoiia* and character-assassination in the *Conon* of Demosthenes," Mnemosyne 19 (1966), 231—48.

33 Apollodorus, in the speech "Against Polycles," appeals to members of the jury who have seen military service (50.3), and apparently expects (or hopes) that they will

expecting them to support authority. He cannot gloss over the incident, because that leaves the defendant too good an opportunity to represent him as a spoiled and self-important young man who needed to be taught a lesson, incapable of putting up with a little inconvenience and fond of magnifying his aches and pains.

In the speech *Against Meidias* Demosthenes represents himself as the victim of an outrageous personal assault, like Ariston in *Against Conon*. The scale of the *Meidias* is much larger and involves important political considerations, but there are some interesting similarities in the narrative portions of the two speeches. Ariston says he might have charged Conon with criminal *hybris*, but was content to bring a civil action, as his friends advised (54.1). Demosthenes, however, at the advice of his friends, has indicted Meidias by the process of *probole*, so as to obtain a vote of condemnation in the public assembly (21.2). He will have to show, therefore, that the assault at the Dionysiac festival is a serious enough offence to justify legal action by *probole*. He will also argue, like Ariston, that this final outrage is the end of a series of lawless acts, since Meidias first conceived a deadly hatred for him many years ago, when he tried, unsuccessfully, to interfere with his prosecution of his guardians (78–82).

The narrative begins with the incident in the theatre at the Dionysia, when Demosthenes was choregus and Meidias struck him in full view of the audience and tried to prevent his chorus from entering the competition (13–17). The secondary narrative of earlier events comes later (77–127), after a long and elaborate argumentative section in which the enormity of the offence is explained. Like the speaker in *Against Conon*, Demosthenes describes not what Meidias did but what he, the choregus of his tribe, suffered:[34] "I volunteered to undertake the training of a chorus and was lucky enough to be allotted first choice of flute-player. Public opinion was favourable to me; at least there was applause when I made my offer and when the luck of the lot turned out in my

approve of his generosity towards his men when he was trierarch, though official-dom would condemn it as bad for discipline (50.35). Tales of army and navy life are not common in classical Greek literature; it is only Xenophon who has much to tell us about the humorous side of camp life, e.g. Anab. 2.2.19–20; 4.1.14; 4.4.11–12; 7.3.29–33.

34 A few verbal similarities with "Against Conon" are worth mentioning: 21.13: τρίτον ἔτος τουτί, 54.3: ἔτος τουτὶ τρίτον. 21.78: οὐδ᾽ εἰ γέγον᾽ εἰδὼς οὐδὲ γιγνώσκων ὡς μηδὲ νῦν ὤφελον, 54.3: ἐσκήνωσαν ... ἐγγὺς ἡμῶν, ὡς οὐκ ἂν ἐβουλόμην. 21.78, 54.5: εἰσεπήδησαν. And for the progress from abusive language to acts of violence, 21.79, 54.5. In the first narrative section there is no act of Meidias mentioned which Demosthenes did not witness himself. In the second section he is careful to note when he is relying on hearsay: ὡς ἐγὼ τῶν παραγε-νομένων τινὸς ἐπυνθανόμην (21.85). Cf. 54.7: ταῦτα γὰρ ὕστερον ἐπυθόμεθα.

favour; but Meidias' behaviour was very different; he made trouble for me in every way" (13—15).

He "passes over" some incidents lightly, saying that, however unpleasant they may have been to him personally, "to you, who were not directly concerned, they might not seem to warrant legal action" (15). And in quick succession he describes how Meidias was partly successful in his attempt to ruin the costumes, bribed the chorus trainer (fortunately the flute-player took over his duties), and attempted to influence the archon, the other choregi, and the judges; he nailed up the doors giving entrance into the orchestra,[35] which was damage to public property, and finally assaulted Demosthenes—"an outrageous insult to me, and one of the main reasons which robbed the tribe of victory, when it was on its way to winning the prize" (19).

One might think that the incident would now be "amplified" with insistence on very detail, but Demosthenes drops the subject quite suddenly, and goes on to mention, but not to describe, some outrages of Meidias against other people: "And many of the victims, gentlemen of the jury, terrorized by his arrogance and by the companions who attended on him and his wealth and all his other advantages, took no action aginst him. Any who did try to bring suit found themselves unable to proceed, and some agreed to a settlement, thinking perhaps that they were lucky" (20).[36] He is shifting the attention of the jury from himself to the character of Meidias. Instead of magnifying the sufferings which he and others have endured, he has to think of the main object of the speech, which is to show that Meidias considers himself "more powerful than the laws" and that his *hybris* is a political as well as a personal outrage.

Demosthenes is following the same tactics as he had used in earlier speeches that he had written for political prosecutions. The object of the narrative is not merely to present the "facts," because the strictly relevant "facts" are not really in dispute. As in the actions against Androtion, Timocrates, Leptines, and Aristocrates between 355 and 350, which are prosecutions under *graphai paranomon*, the object of the legal action is to

---

35 τὰ παρασκήνια φράττων. Apparently this means blocking the door from the stage buildings and forcing the chorus to go outside and use the public entrance. Cf. A. W. Pickard-Cambridge, The Theatre of Dionysus in Athens, 23—24.

36 If Demosthenes never delivered this speech, but made a settlement with Meidias out of court, as is commonly believed (Dion. Hal. Ad Amm. 1.4; Aeschines 3.52; cf. Cloché, Démosthènes, 96—98), he is on rather dangerous ground here, as in 39 when he criticizes officials who were victims of assault and settled out of court and in 120, where he takes an even stronger line. H. Erbse, "Über die Midiana des Demosthenes," Hermes 84 (1956), 135—51, offers some good arguments in support of his belief that the speech *was* delivered substantially in the form as we have it.

make the breach of the law appear politically significant, so that the defendant will be shown as an undesirable person, unreliable and unfit for public responsibility. It is the same in the later duels between Demosthenes and Aeschines.

All these speeches are open to the criticism that Aristotle pronounces in the opening chapter of the *Rhetoric*: "The only task of the litigant is to show that a fact is or is not so, that an event happened or did not happen. Whether it is important or unimportant, in accordance with justice or not, in cases where the lawgiver has not made it clear, is for the juror to decide himself. It is not for the contending parties to instruct him" (1. 1354a). Aristotle disapproves of any attempt to play on the feelings of the jury and considers it outside the proper province of rhetoric to discuss methods of influencing their feelings: "Writers are discussing matters not strictly relevant to the art when they lay down rules about the proper content of an exordium or a narrative or any other part of an oration, because what they are concerned with here is simply to put the juror in a certain frame of mind" (1. 1354b).

Despite these strict views about the proper function and limits of forensic oratory Aristotle knows very well that speakers in court do not limit themselves to argument about the facts and the law. In "deliberative" speeches before a legislative assembly speakers do not always confine themselves to the question, Is this proposal expedient or inexpedient to the community? They often introduce the issue of "the just" and "the honourable" as well as "the expedient," and likewise in courts of law "the expedient" will often play a part as well as "the just."[37] When the issue of political expediency plays a part in a lawsuit, we call it a political trial. And if a pleader wants to convince the jury that the conviction of a defendant is politically expedient as well as legally justified, we shall not be surprised to find him using methods that Aristotle considers more appropriate to deliberative oratory.

One such method is the appeal to parallels or examples (*paradeigmata*) from history or literature, and this may involve the use of narrative. In conventional rhetorical theory this is only a secondary type of narrative, but the extensive use of narrative by Demosthenes in political trials can

37 After his introductory remarks about the three kinds of oratory, Aristotle continues: τέλος δὲ ἑκάστοις τούτων ἕτερόν ἐστι, καὶ τρίσιν οὖσιν τρία, τῷ μὲν συμβουλεύοντι τὸ συμφέρον καὶ βλαβερόν· ὁ μὲν γὰρ προτρέπων ὡς βέλτιον συμβουλεύει, ὁ δὲ ἀποτρέπων ὡς χεῖρον ἀποτρέπει, τὰ δ' ἄλλα πρὸς τοῦτο συμπαραλαμβάνει ἢ δίκαιον ἢ ἄδικον ἢ καλὸν ἢ αἰσχρόν· τοῖς δὲ δικαζομένοις τὸ δίκαιον καὶ τὸ ἄδικον, τὰ δ' ἄλλα καὶ οὗτοι συμπαραλαμβάνουσι πρὸς ταῦτα. τοῖς δ' ἐπαινοῦσιν καὶ ψέγουσιν τὸ καλὸν καὶ τὸ αἰσχρόν, τὰ δ' ἄλλα καὶ οὗτοι πρὸς ταῦτα ἐπαναφέρουσιν (Rhet. 1. 1358b).

hardly be described as secondary or digressional. His narratives are sometimes, but not always, blended with argument, and they are not confined
to the conventional place after the introductory section. And his object is
no longer, as in a simpler forensic speech, to describe what has happened,
but "to show the kind of thing that has happened and will happen again
unless certain measures are taken."

It is not until he composes the *First Philippic* and the *Olynthiacs* that
Demosthenes starts using narrative extensively in political speeches before
the Assembly. He seems to have profited from his experience in political
trials in the few years before 351, and to be adapting for use in the
Assembly the technique which he had used in these trials.[38] These
speeches, therefore, and especially their narrative sections deserve more
careful examination, if we are to understand his development as a political
orator.

The earliest of these speeches, *Against Androtion*, was written to be
delivered by Diodorus as second speaker for the prosecution. The technical charge was that Androtion had violated a constitutional rule by proposing that a crown be awarded to the Boule, though it had not provided
for the building of ships, as the law specified. Diodorus begins, in the
manner of the *Meidias*, by mentioning a series of "outrages" perpetrated
by Androtion against himself and the first speaker, Euctemon (22.1–3),
and then goes on to examine some of the legal arguments that the defence
may be expected to use (4–11). The law, no doubt, has often been
neglected in the past, but he refuses to recognize any appeal to that sort
of precedent (6–7). And while he thinks it appropriate to recall events
from the past which show how important it has been for Athens to have a
shipbuilding law and to maintain its supply of triremes, he warns the jury
not to listen to "irrelevant" narrative from the other side: "I understand
he will tell some story to the effect that the Boule was not to blame for its
failure to build ships, but that the treasurer of the ship-building fund
absconded with four and a half talents" (17). He is denying the defendant
the opportunity of telling a story that may arouse sympathy.

Androtion's "illegal" proposal is supposed to be doubly "illegal"; he
is supposed to be barred from public life by a notorious career as a "male
prostitute" and by his father's failure to pay a debt that he owed the
treasury (21–34). Will it be suggested that he deserves credit for his
diligence in collecting arrears of taxes from recalcitrant tax-payers? The
suggestion is rejected indignantly: "This will make people think that you
value money more than the law" (45). Thus while rejecting the narrative

38 Cf. Chapter IV, section ii, below.

of the other side the speaker prepares the way for his own narrative, which begins in section 47 and continues to the end of the speech—the story of this "worthy man's" political career.

Androtion's supposed misdeeds have to be amplified with some very obvious rhetorical δείνωσις if the story is to be an impressive one. His behaviour in collecting arrears of taxes is supposed to reveal a contempt for democratic principles and a disregard for human dignity—he takes advantage of critical times to have special emergency measures passed, he takes the Eleven with him to the houses of Athenian citizens and breaks into their privacy, a procedure which recalls the evil days of the Thirty (49—52):

"What are you to think of it, men of Athens, when a poor man, or maybe a rich man who has had many expenses and for some perfectly good reason happens to be short of money, had to climb over the roof of his neighbour's house or creep under the bed so as to avoid being seized and dragged off to prison, or had to submit to other indignities that befit a slave but not a free man, and in the sight of his own wife, whom he had married as a free citizen?" (53).

There is no evidence to support this lurid tale. Evidently the jurors were not convinced, since they acquitted Androtion of the charges against him, but in the speech *Against Timocrates*, which was written for Diodorus when he returned to the attack, we find Demosthenes still employing the same method. The defendant is Timocrates, but the attack on Androtion begins in section 7: "He accused me of killing my own father, when he prosecuted my uncle for impiety because he associated with me. But he received less than one fifth of the votes and had to pay a thousand drachmas, so that I escaped disaster, thanks to the gods and thanks to you—those of you who were on the jury." If the jury will believe this, they will believe almost anything that the speaker tells them about Androtion. After a reference to the tax-collecting scandal and some other supposedly dishonest methods by which he raised money,[39] and a quick breathless passage describing how Timocrates pushed through some legislation which saved him from prosecution, the speaker says he will tell the whole story "from the beginning" (8—10).

It is Euctemon, the co-prosecutor of Androtion, who holds the centre of the stage first. He had learned that the trireme carrying Androtion and Melanopus and Glaucetes as ambassadors to Mausolus had captured an enemy ship on the high seas, and they had not turned over the price of its cargo to the Athenian treasury. Following the proper

---

39 The speaker regrets his failure to secure a verdict against Androtion ("I wish I could have had my way and convinced you how much he deserved punishment," 8), not taking the trouble to point out that the formal ground of prosecution was something quite different.

procedure he reported the matter first to the Boule and then, after their authorization, to the Assembly. His correct behaviour, at every stage,[40] is contrasted with the irregular antics of Androtion and his fellow-ambassadors: "Euctemon's speech in the Assembly met with universal approval. Up leapt Androtion and Glaucetes and Melanopus (watch now, to see if I am being truthful), with shouts, complaints, and abusive language, exonerating the trierarchs, admitting that they had the money, saying that any application for it should be made to them. And after you heard what they said (when they finally came to an end of their shouting and screaming), Euctemon made the perfectly proper motion that the people should demand the money from the trierarchs, but they could shift the responsibility to the persons in possession of the money; that in case of dispute there should be a legal hearing,[41] and the person who was found to be at fault should be declared a debtor to the state. They prosecuted Euctemon's motion as being illegal; the matter came before your court; to make a long story short, the court decided that his motion was in order and he was acquitted of the charge. What was the next proper step then? The state should receive the money and the person who misappropriated it should be punished. There was no need at all of further legislation" (12—14).

Timocrates now enters the story and becomes its central figure. He offers his services, at a price, to Androtion and his companions (14), and proposes to introduce legislation which will save them from paying what they owe—and in fact, so we are told, they have not yet paid the treasury a single drachma. After the existing state of the law and the rules of legislation have been explained, the text of Timocrates' proposal is read out (39), and it is shown how it contravenes existing statutes and (very strangely) contravenes an earlier law proposed by Timocrates himself (41—64).

The speaker is leading up to the point when he can accuse Timocrates of disregarding constitutional principles, using democratic procedure to introduce oligarchic features into Athens (76—78), and trying to

---

40 The proper technical terms are used: ἐμήνυσεν Εὐκτήμων, προσῆλθε τῇ βουλῇ, προβούλευμ᾽ ἐγράφη, προὐχειροτόνησεν ὁ δῆμος, ἔθεσαν τὴν ἱκετηρίαν, ἀπεχειροτονήσαθ᾽ ὑμεῖς μὴ φιλὶ εἶναι. The jurors are presumed to be familiar with the technicalities of legal and constitutional procedure, though it is not taken for granted that they are equally competent to understand details of business and accounting. Cf. pp. 44 — 46, supra.

41 διαδικασία, a hearing to decide which of two or more individuals has the stronger claim to some advantage or the responsibility for a debt or some other liability. Cf. Lipsius, Att. Recht. 463—67. It is not considered appropriate to explain why Euctemon's motion might have been thought illegal—it is enough to show that it was in fact declared legal.

establish the kind of law that one might have expected from a member of the Thirty (90). As in *Against Androtion*, the narrative has prepared the way for these accusations. Then, once he has shown, as he maintains, that this illegal proposal was made purely in the interests of Androtion,[42] he returns to the scandalous tax-collecting episode. The story as told in the earlier speech is repeated, with a few necessary changes to show that Timocrates took part: "I have things to tell you which will be entirely unfamiliar to you, unless some of you were present when Euctemon brought his action" (159).[43]

The alarming tale may be neither fair nor truthful. But any appearance of anti-democratic behaviour will be damaging to Timocrates, since he had claimed to be proposing a "philanthropic" measure, which would protect the common man against summary imprisonment and give him until the ninth prytany to find the money that he owed the state before any punitive measures were taken against him.[44] Demosthenes has adapted the narrative very shrewdly with Timocrates in mind as the principal object of attack. The story of the unfortunate man who had to climb up on the roof or hide under his bed to avoid arrest[45] is left out (perhaps it had merely roused the jury to laughter). It is thought enough now to represent this man as "not only frightened to show himself in the Agora, but thinking himself unsafe even in his own house" (24.165). Other ways are found of bringing out the cruelty and avarice of Timocrates (just the kind of man who would sell his services to Androtion) and his disregard for the rights of Athenian citizens (though he was "sorry" for a thief like Androtion): "You went to their houses taking with you the Eleven and the Apodectae and your retinue of attendants, showing no pity for anyone, but tearing down doors, snatching up bedding, and taking a servant girl as pledge of payment, if there happened to be one" (197).

Like Androtion Timocrates is supposed to have behaved badly about his father, when he was imprisoned for failure to pay a debt to the treasury. Androtion was content to let his father escape from prison

---

42 The announcement that proof is complete is made in 108—09. The arguments that follow in 110—54 are badly organized and carelessly written and are commonly taken to be fragments of an unrevised early draft, not presumably shown to Diodorus or intended for inclusion in the finished version; the speech certainly is better without them. Cf., e.g., Orsini's introduction to the speech in the Budé edition, Plaidoyers politiques I 119—21.

43 Orsini suggests that this passage was included "à la demande expresse de son client" (Budé ed., p. 121), and if Diodorus had not been consulted he might have objected at being asked to repeat a narrative that had not achieved its purpose in the former trial.

44 Cf. 24.72—88.

45 22.53. Cf. above p. 65.

(22.56, 24.168), which was bad enough for a man who insisted that taxes must be paid to the last obol, but Timocrates, who could perfectly well have paid his father's debts, never lifted a finger to help him (24.101). Where the one was lax, the other was hard-hearted and mean (we need not worry whether there is any truth in these accusations). Androtion, a former male prostitute, was accused of taking prostitutes into custody, though they did not owe any money (22.56). His own experience gave him no sympathy for female members of the oldest profession (22.56). But Timocrates is accused of "selling" his sister to an enemy of Athens, a Corcyrean ambassador who lodged at his house, and then claiming to have made a good marriage for her (24.202−203).

There is perhaps more purely slanderous accusation in these speeches than in any that Demosthenes wrote. They illustrate very clearly the unscrupulous malice that prevailed in Athenian public life, though they offer remarkably interesting examples of the orator's skill in adapting narrative to his purpose.

The other two speeches written for *graphai paranomon* during these two years are of quite different character.

Against Leptines was delivered by Demosthenes himself.[46] Leptines had introduced a bill which would abolish grants of *ateleia*, believing that this would increase tax payments and enforce liturgies more extensively. Demosthenes objects that it will be a great mistake to abandon the traditional method of rewarding benefactors of Athens; and he offers examples to show how well some benefactors have earned their grants of *ateleia*, like Leucon of Bosporus (30−40) and Epicerdes of Cyrene (41−45). This is the orthodox rhetorical method of proof by *paradeigma*.[47] But he does not expand his *paradeigmata* into a narrative section, as orators sometimes did;[48] he does not take the opportunity to describe how the grain trade with the Crimea developed and how Leucon established friendly relations with Athens; he is content to explain why it has always been desirable to show appreciation for Leucon's co-operative attitude. There is, therefore, no proper narrative section in *Against Leptines*.

In the speech *Against Aristocrates*, on the other hand, there are long sections of narrative, since the jury cannot be expected to give a reasonable judgment unless they are put in possession of the "facts." Charidemus was a well-known soldier of fortune, who had been active in Thrace as a mercenary commander in the service of Thracian princes, and he had

---

46 The case against Leptines came on in between the suits against Androtion and Timocrates (in 354 B.C.), that against Aristocrates not until 352.
47 Cf. Aristot. Rhet. 1. 1356b.
48 Cf., e.g., Cic. De Inv. 1. 19.27; Ad. Herennium 1. 8.12.

been made an Athenian citizen because of his supposed services to Athens. Aristocrates now proposes a resolution that "anyone who kills Charidemus shall be subject to arrest anywhere in the territory of our allies" (23.16), and the speaker will maintain that this resolution is unconstitutional, wrong in principle, and contrary to Athenian interests. He will argue that Aristocrates has other things in mind besides the interests of Athens and that Charidemus is not a true friend of Athens at all, but her worst enemy (6), who may cause Athens to lose control of the Thracian Chersonese, if he is given a free hand.

The speaker's first task, therefore, is to explain the situation in Thrace, and this is done very simply. At the death of King Cotys (whose name will presumably be familiar to members of the jury) the Thracian kingdom was divided between three rulers, Amadocus, Berisades, and Cersobleptes; Berisades is now dead, and Cersobleptes is trying to obtain the whole kingdom for himself, and Charidemus is working for him. If Charidemus receives any special favour from Athens, the Greek military advisers with Amadocus and the sons of Berisades (of whom one is a native Athenian and two are honorary citizens of Athens) will take it as a warning that they had better not offer much resistance to Cersobleptes, unless they are prepared to risk the disfavour of Athens. The Athenian supporters of Charidemus evidently want it made clear to the world that Charidemus has official Athenian support in his efforts to help Cersobleptes. The speaker expects the jury to agree with him that a Thrace united under Cersobleptes is not in the best interests of Athens, but he lets them draw this conclusion for themselves. He does not tell them yet what final arrangement in Thrace would suit Athens best or what would assure Athenian control of the Chersonese.[49]

After this preliminary narrative the speaker goes on to show that the proposal of Aristocrates is illegal and dangerous, using *paradeigmata* from recent history to illustrate the folly of such measures.[50] Then comes his third task, which is "to examine the career of Charidemus and make clear to you the fantastic impertinence of the people who sing his praises"

---

49 He does not give them the answer until 102—03, when he explains that, just as a strong Sparta or a strong Thebes is contrary to Athenian interests, so it is undesirable that one man should control all Thrace; it is the rivalry between Thracian rulers that guarantees the safety of the Chersonese for Athens. Even there the proof is over-simplified, confined to the familiar *paradeigma* of the balance of power between Sparta and Thebes.

50 E.g., how Miltocythes was deterred from resisting Cotys by an Athenian resolution (104) and how untrustworthy Cotys was, though Iphicrates thought it more important to stand by him, than to show gratitude for the honours he received from Athens (128—32).

(144).[51] As in *Against Androtion* and *Against Timocrates* Demothenes has designed a narrative to illustrate a man's untrustworthy character, but in contrast to those speeches the story is told in a straightforward style without rhetorical amplification; indeed the speaker's restrained manner gives him the opportunity to complain about political orators "who make speeches and propose resolutions for pay" (146).[52]

The story of Charidemus begins with his early career as a soldier in the ranks fighting against Athens and then as captain of a pirate ship—a disreputable start, but it was his way of making a living and "I pass over these details" (148). More important is his first betrayal of trust when he hands back to the Amphipolitans the hostages he is supposed to surrender to the Athenians, thus preventing Athens from recovering Amphipolis. Timotheus engaged the services of his mercenary force, but he deserted to the Thracian prince Cotys, taking the Athenian triaconters with him (149). Then when the Athenians captured him at sea and brought him to Athens, instead of being punished for his treachery, he was taken into Athenian service, honoured with crowns, and made an Athenian citizen (150–151).[53]

As the war with Cotys went on, he undertook to recover the Chersonese for Athens, without any intention of doing so (the letter containing his offer is presented in evidence). And after leaving Timotheus' service, he showed himself just as treacherous in the service of the relatives of Artabazus, the rebellious satrap of the Hellespontine area (Artabazus himself had been captured by the satrap of Lydia, Autophradates).[54] He seized for himself the fortresses in the Troad, which he was supposed to pillage for his employers; then, finding himself in difficulty, without any supplies for his men, he sought the usual solution of men in

51 This makes it plain that the real object of the prosecution is to discredit Charidemus. The whole plan of attack is similar to that of Aeschines in prosecuting Ctesiphon more than twenty years later.

52 Though the Athenians regard political speakers as πονηρότατον τῶν ἐν τῇ πόλει πάντων ἐθνῶν, they nevertheless rely upon them for the judgments they pass on other individuals: οὖς γὰρ αὐτοὶ πονηροτάτους νομίζετε πάντων, τούτοις περὶ τοῦ ποῖόν τιν' ἕκαστον χρὴ νομίζειν πεπιστεύκατε (147). This passage reminds us how important it was for a political speaker to develop the art of characterization.

53 We are not told, of course, what services he had rendered to deserve these honours; it is for the defence to try and prove that such services outweigh his reputation for treachery.

54 ὡς ἀπόμισθος γίγνεται παρὰ τοῦ Τιμοθέου (154) does not necessarily mean that he was dismissed, but rather that Timotheus would not (or could not) continue to pay for his services (but if the jury choose to put the worst interpretation on what is said, the speaker will not object). It is not said who Artabazus and Autophradates are, nor with whom Athenian sympathies lay; there is no point in admitting that the Athenians were happy that he should support Artabazus (nor in suggesting that he "betrayed his trust" because he was not paid regularly).

trouble: "And what is that? Your kind-heartedness, men of Athens, or whatever name you choose to give it" (156). Once again he offered to recover the Chersonese for Athens, if they would send him ships, and Artabazus, his liberty now recovered, let him go, fearing a clash with Athens if he did not. But Charidemus, instead of keeping his word to the Athenians, "hired himself out again to Cotys, and laid siege to the towns that were still in your hands, Crithote and Elaious" (158).

There has been no suggestion so far that anyone might doubt the accuracy of this narrative, but in case anyone should think Charidemus seriously intended to help Athens in the Chersonese after leaving Artabazus' service, it is pointed out that he went straight from the Troad to Abydos, "a place that had always been hostile to you," which would never have received him after the letter he sent to Athens "unless they knew perfectly well that he was deceiving you and were themselves a party to the deception." And from Abydos he crossed the strait to Sestos, which was in Cotys' hands (158–160). The argument is supported by various letters, including a despatch from the Athenian commander in Crithote (161). It is left for the defence to explain why the Athenians should have trusted him. The story, as it is told, leaves the impression that Athenian behaviour was just as illogical as the behaviour of Charidemus was treacherous.

The narrative continues. Cotys is killed (his murderer does Athens a good turn!) and the new situation gives Charidemus his chance to recover the Chersonese for Athens and settle the kingdom of Thrace in the way that suits Athens. The new king, Cersobleptes, is only a young fellow, and the Athenians have sent out Cephisodotus as strategos with triremes, the very man whom Charidemus wanted to have with him, the man to whom he had written when he was in trouble. But instead of helping Athens Charidemus wages open war with their forces for seven whole months. Their ships anchor at Perinthos, expecting co-operation from him, and he makes a vicious attack on them, causing heavy loss of life; they attack the pirate base at Alopeconnesus, and he supports the pirates against them, a gratuitous act of hostility, since Alopeconnesus is in Athenian territory and his duty to Cersobleptes does not oblige him to defend the place. And his good friend Cephisodotus suffers; after being obliged to sign a most discreditable pact with Cersobleptes, he is relieved of his command, put on trial when he returns to Athens and fined five talents, narrowly escaping a death sentence (163–167). Even if the facts are all there waiting for Demosthenes to use them, he has arranged them in a perfect pattern of contrasts.[55] Charidemus' treachery to Athens is aggravated by

55 We may well wonder whether it was Charidemus' letter that induced the Athenians to send out Cephisodotus as general (cf. E. Schwartz, Demosthenes' erste Philippi-

treachery towards his friend; he took Athenian lives and nearly caused his friend's death. And his treachery is matched by Athenian lack of logic, honouring Charidemus as a benefactor and punishing his unfortunate victim, Cephisodotus: "What are we to make of this lack of logic, men of Athens?" (168).

The tale of treachery and murder is not finished yet. Cersobleptes' rival Miltocythes had been consistently loyal to Athens, though treated very shabbily by them, and now he is betrayed into Charidemus' hands. And Charidemus, "knowing that his life would be saved if he were taken to Cersobleptes, since it is against Thracian custom to kill members of their own people," makes sure of his death by handing him over to "your enemies the Cardians," who butcher his son before his eyes and then drown him in the sea (169). This shocking act angered all Thracians and gave new strength to Cersobleptes' other rivals. Indeed Athenodorus, the Athenian military commander serving with them, was able to make Cersobleptes sign the kind of treaty that Athens wanted. But following the pattern of the story the Athenians match the stupid savagery of Charidemus with another piece of stupidity. They give Athenodorus no support at all, and when they send out Chabrias to replace Cephisodotus they give him only a single ship. Cersobleptes therefore repudiates the treaty he has signed, and Charidemus forces Chabrias to sign an agreement even more discreditable than the one he had prepared for Cephisodotus. And the Athenians, as might be expected, showing no respect for the high reputation of Chabrias and refusing to listen to his defenders, remove him from his command and send out a ten-man commission to deal with Cersobleptes (170–172). But it is only in 357 that Cersobleptes is induced to sign a treaty that is "just and satisfactory" (173).[56] This was the year when the Athenians made a successful expedition, thanks to Chares and his mercenaries. Cersobleptes was ready to be a friend of Athens when Athens was strong enough to make enmity unwise.

Chares and Athenodorus, the men who have worked well for Athens, are mentioned only incidentally, and it is evidently no part of the orator's

ka, 24; L. Vorndran, Die Aristocratea des Demosthenes, 25–26), and doubt whether it is strictly accurate to describe Charidemus' treatment of him as "ungrateful." Vorndran, as a pupil of Drerup, is quick to seize upon any example of an "advocate" misrepresenting the facts. One of the difficulties in this speech is that Demosthenes gives so few chronological indications, and without being sure of dates it is often difficult to know how valid his interpretations are. Cf. P. Cloché, "Athènes et Kersebleptès de 357–6 à 453–2," Mélanges Glotz I 215–26 (Paris 1932).

56 The text of this treaty is partially preserved in an inscription, Tod, Gk. Hist. Inscr. II 151. Cf. P. Cloché, "Le traité athèno-thrace de 357," Rev. de Philologie 46 (1922), 5–13.

intention to give particular praise to the people who have neutralized the influence of Charidemus. There has been a tendency in modern times to regard this oration as a political speech directed against the party that stood behind Aristocrates' proposal,[57] that is against the party that supported Cersobleptes as the man most likely to check Philip's aggressive moves into Thrace. It is important to notice, however, that the names of the leaders of this party, whoever they are, are never mentioned. Aristocrates is treated very gently, the attack is concentrated upon Charidemus and Cersobleptes, and the number of dramatis personae is carefully restricted. The immediate object of the speech is clearly to prevent a resolution being passed which will show faith in Charidemus and Cersobleptes. There is no effort to discredit any leading politician in Athens, unless some members of the jury choose to think so. And Philip plays a much less prominent part in the speech than might be expected, if it represents a serious effort to influence Athenian policy towards Macedonia.

In this speech we see the orator making full use, for the first time, of the tendentious kind of narrative of public events which is characteristic of his later manner in *On the Embassy* and *On the Crown*. He was evidently pleased with this oration and used parts of it in subsequent addresses to the Assembly.[58] His experience in this case also seems to have taught him that narration and interpretation of narrative were effective methods of explaining matters of public policy, more effective sometimes than appeals to principles and examples from the past. Though he remains a notably paradeigmatic orator and the peroration of *Against Aristocrates* consists in great part of orthodox *paradeigmata*,[59] we can observe how he

57 Cf., e.g., the discussion in Jaeger, Demosthenes, Chap. V, 98—106. Jaeger believes that Demosthenes wrote this speech because of strong political convictions, because "he hoped that by his treatment of the affairs in northern Greece he would obtain a decision giving him solid ground to stand on in his further resistance to the official policies" (100). But Jaeger is surely mistaken in thinking that the speech is a plea to reject the policy of "a strong and united Thrace allied with Athens" (105). People who believed in that policy would not want to see Cersobleptes in control of Thrace if he was unreliable, and the object of the speech is to prove that he and Charidemus are totally unreliable.

58 It was no doubt a common practice of orators to contrast the luxury of contemporary living with the modest style that contented even the great men of older days, but in 3.25—29 Demosthenes repeats not only the sentiments but much of the phraseology of 23.106—09. Likewise 13.21—24 is modelled on 23.196—200, and such repetition is not an adequate reason for thinking Oration 13 spurious. Cf. Chapter IV, below, p. 122.

59 Examples of modest rewards given to men of olden times who did great services to Athens: Themistocles and Miltiades (196), Menon (199), Perdiccas (200), compared with the extravagant rewards to so-called benefactors of recent years, Ariobarzanes, Timotheus, and others (202). Examples of severe punishment for misdeeds, which would be passed over lightly now: Themistocles and Cimon (205).

74

learns to make a larger use of narrative in the *Philippics* than in his earlier political speeches. This aspect of his development, however, must be postponed until Chapter IV, after other qualities of his earlier forensic work have been examined in Chapter III. *On the Embassy* and *On the Crown* will be discussed separately in Chapter V.

In 191 it is anticipated that the defence will invoke the principle οὐ δεῖ μνησικακεῖν to justify the support of Cersobleptes and offer the parallel of Athenian treatment of Sparta; and it has to be shown that this *paradeigma* does not apply to the present situation.

Chapter III

The Interpretation of Narrative: Character and Motivation

A prosecutor's story should make it easy to believe that the defendant is a dishonest man of unwholesome character, motivated by greed or malice or cowardice; a defendant will want to represent himself as activated by prudence or caution or genuine altruism. A clever orator's story should lead inevitably to the desired conclusion. But the "bare facts," substantiated by evidence, very rarely contain "the whole truth" that he wants to establish; they will not be enough to make the jurors confident that they are giving the right verdict. Some necessary additional detail can be worked into the narrative in such a way that it appears to be substantiated by the evidence. But a speaker usually has to take further steps to make his interpretation appear preferable to the version presented by his adversary.

An Athenian speaker, equally in the Assembly or in the courts, may be looking ahead beyond the judgment that will be passed on that day. He will want to be able to say on subsequent occasions, with some show of accuracy, that the jury or "the people" found his adversary not only at fault or incompetent (as partner or trustee, ambassador or office-holder), but untruthful, untrustworthy, unpatriotic, of unsound character. If a litigant has to take further action before he gains his object, a favourable impression of his own character and a prejudice established against his adversary will be very helpful; and if a politician has to take legal action to follow up a challenge delivered in the Assembly or the Council, he can strike a useful blow in advance by attacking his opponent's reputation. The speeches of Thucydides offer some interesting evidence of this practice in politics.[1]

The fierce vindictiveness of Athenian politics explains some of the characteristics of Attic oratory. A speaker is not satisfied to show that a certain person did or did not do what he is said to have done. He will want

---

1 For example, Nicias accuses Alcibiades of purely selfish motives, of irresponsible ostentation, and of using improper methods to influence voters, and Alcibiades has to answer these charges (6.12–13, 16–17). Pericles' opponents attack him in the Assembly before they indict him and obtain a verdict against him in the courts (2.59–65). We may doubt whether the accusers of Pythodorus, Sophocles, and Eurymedon had much evidence that these men were bribed in Sicily (4.65), and some vigorous efforts to blacken their character (in their absence) must have preceded the trial.

76

also to make it plain that a man of this kind was bound to behave like this, using the argument from probability to strengthen his case. Demosthenes often begins with a strong complaint about the character of the opposing party, so that the jury will be prejudiced against him from the start. The narrative will then appear to illustrate his character and show him behaving as such a man might be expected to behave. The speaker may pretend that the story reveals the man's character, but he wants the jury to listen to it with their conclusions about his character already formed.

Many novelists offer a character sketch before starting a story which supplements, complicates, or qualifies the initial description. This is a way of arousing the reader's powers of analysis; it presents him with a problem of character. Demosthenes' purpose is a simpler one. He wants to show the jury that there is no problem of character at all, that the man is behaving just as one might have expected (unreasonably, shamelessly, with almost incredible cruelty), if one had known what manner of man he was; unfortunately the victim had not known, and had made the mistake of trusting him.

As was shown in Chapter II, the short narrative with which Demosthenes often begins his speeches resembles in certain ways the narrative of a tragic prologue. But a dramatist does not develop a tragic plot in the same way as an orator presents his case in court. The audience in a theatre waits to see the leading characters involved in actions and situations in order to learn what kind of people they are; it would not take much interest in a play which announced in advance what sort of people these characters were and then showed them acting as might be expected.[2]

2 Nevertheless the leading characters in a tragedy are not complete strangers to an audience that is familiar with mythology. Many of them are already established as brave or cowardly, loyal or disloyal, cruel or gentle. If such characteristics are pointed out early in the play, the purpose is not necessarily to remind us of what we already know, but to tell us that other characters in the play share this knowledge. Thus the serving-woman says of Alcestis:

πῶς δ᾿ οὐκ ἀρίστη; τίς δ᾿ ἐναντιώσεται;
τί χρὴ γενέσθαι τὴν ὑπερβεβλημένην
γυναῖκα; πῶς δ᾿ ἂν μᾶλλον ἐνδείξαιτό τις
πόσιν προτιμῶσ᾿ ἢ θέλουσ᾿ ὑπερθανεῖν;
καί ταῦτα μὲν δὴ πᾶσ᾿ ἐπίσταται πόλις   (Eur. Alc. 152—56).

This tells us that Alcestis is beloved and admired by everyone, and makes us wonder what they think of Admetus. And when Chrysothemis tells Electra:

καίτοι τὸ μὲν δίκαιον οὐχ ᾗ γὼ λέγω,
ἀλλ᾿ ᾗ σὺ κρίνεις   (Soph. Electra, 338—40),

or Ismene tells Antigone:

τοῦτο δ᾿ ἴσθ᾿ ὅτι
ἄνους μὲν ἔρχει τοῖς φίλοις δ᾿ ὀρθῶς φίλη   (Soph. Ant. 98—99),

the object is more to help us understand how the situation strikes a person of less

Aristotle in the *Poetics* (1450a) insists that characters in a play are not shown doing certain things in order to illustrate their *ethos*, but that the action, the plot, is itself the *telos*, the most important thing in tragedy. He says elsewhere, in the *Ethics* (2.1103b), that we acquire moral qualities by doing certain actions, and this was normal Greek thinking; only by "doing worthy deeds" did one "become a good man." It is not surprising, therefore, that he should say the same thing in the *Poetics*: οὔκουν ὅπως τὰ ἤθη μιμήσωνται πράττουσιν, ἀλλὰ τὰ ἤθη συμπεριλαμβάνουσι διὰ τὰς πράξεις, "the characters in a play do not perform certain actions in order to illustrate their character, but their actions involve certain elements of character." This Greek sentence has been understood differently by different interpreters of Aristotle, but this translation seems to be what is demanded by the language as well as by the line of argument; by certain actions persons "include" or "imply" certain characteristics.[3]

Aristotle makes it quite clear that *ethos* is not a fundamental element in presenting tragic actions, since many of his contemporaries wrote tragedies without *ethos*.[4] Evidently he did not think a narrative was necessarily dull or unskilful because it paid little attention to characterization,[5] but his point here is to establish the logical priority of action over character in tragedy; he thinks a dramatist should show character as consequence

heroic mould than the protagonist, than to tell us anything we do not know about the protagonist.

3 Editors and critics of Aristotle have been disposed to believe that the subject of συμπεριλαμβάνουσι is the "playwrights," and that the meaning is simply "include." For more detailed discussion of the passage, with reasons for rejecting this interpretation and also for rejecting the alternate reading συμπαραλαμβάνουσι, which some editors of the "Poetics" prefer, see L. Pearson, "Characterization in Drama and Oratory — Poetics 1450a 20," CQ 17 (1968), 76—83.

4 Poetics 1450a 25: αἱ γὰρ τῶν νέων τῶν πλείστων ἀήθεις τραγῳδίαι εἰσίν, καὶ ὅλως ποιηταὶ πολλοὶ τοιοῦτοι.

5 Critics seem more willing now than they were fifty years ago to agree with Aristotle that characterization is a relatively unimportant aspect of Greek tragedy. For recent discussion see A. M. Dale, "Ethos and Dianoia, 'Character' and 'Thought' in Aristotle's Poetics," AUMLA 11 (1959), 3—16, reprinted in A. M. Dale, Collected Papers (Cambridge 1969), 139—55; G. H. Gellie, "Character in Greek Tragedy," AUMLA 20 (1963), 241—55; C. Garton, "Characterization in Greek Tragedy," JHS 77 (1957), 247—54; and the more detailed analysis in F. Zürcher, "Die Darstellung des Menschen im Drama des Euripides" (Basle 1947). The influence of the law-courts on the Attic drama is generally recognized, but it is necessary to remember that the experience (and the responsibility) of the juror differed greatly from the experience (and the artistic pleasure) that a dramatist hoped to give members of his audience. In the courts a juryman hoped to understand what sort of people were presenting their cases to him, so that he could distribute praise and blame fairly. His task was easier if the persons involved and their problems could be related to his own experience. Some Athenians (if we can trust Aristophanes) thought Euripides was at fault in making his characters resemble ordinary persons; but if an orator failed to do this, how could the jury be expected to pass a reasonable and just verdict?

of action, not action as consequence of character. In forensic oratory Demosthenes achieves his purpose most commonly by the opposite method, by first establishing character and showing the action as its logical consequence. After setting forth the facts, he can then return to the character of the principal agent and offer this to the jury as the final and most important factor in determining their verdict, reminding them that a man of such a character is likely to repeat what he has done. In tragedy character is not established until the action has been set forth, and it is the action, the result, to which the attention of the audience returns. This is the note on which Greek tragedies end: τοιόνδ' ἀπέβη τόδε πρᾶγμα.

Aristotle may be drawing a contrast between tragedy and oratory. An orator may introduce details for no reason except to illustrate some aspect of his own or his opponent's character. It might be argued, therefore, that if the *telos* of tragedy is πράξεις, the real *telos* of a forensic speaker is ποιότης[6] —that his object is to show what kind of man his adversary is and what kind of punishment such a man deserves. He explains his misfortune first, but his *telos* is to convince the jury that the man who caused it deserves to be punished or at least must give adequate compensation.

Forensic oratory can never dispense with characterization. Unless a speaker can show that his adversary is a man of bad character, acting from discreditable motives, or that he himself is of good character and well-motivated, he has no case to present to the court. A speech-writer faces a problem of characterization, and often offers a study in contrast between plaintiff and defendant. A man who prepares his own speech faces, perhaps for the first time in his life, the difficulty of describing and establishing a man's character, whether his own or someone else's.[7] But it is a task that he cannot avoid.

Aristotle thinks that the good character of the speaker is one of the strongest points in his favour: "There are three kinds of argument," he says, "which speech can produce, those that depend on the speaker's *ethos*, those that depend on putting the listener in a certain frame of mind, and those that depend on demonstrations or apparent demonstra-

6 Plutarch applies this lesson to the writing of biography, saying it is not always the most spectacular actions that reveal *arete* or the lack of it, but sometimes a trifling detail—καὶ ῥῆμα καὶ παιδία τις ἔμφασιν ἤθους ἐποίησε μᾶλλον ἢ μάχαι μυριόνεκροι (Alex. 1). He remarks that painters look for the features οἷς ἐμφαίνεται τὸ ἦθος, and he will use a word like ἔμφασις or μίμησις to describe accurate representation, while Aristotle avoids both words in his discussion of rhetoric, not wanting the art of rhetoric to be confused with the less responsible "poetic" arts.

7 When one thinks how skilfully Plato reveals the character of Socrates, it seems a little ungracious of him that he should be so scornful of the art of rhetoric.

tions in the course of the actual speech." When he says "the speaker's
ethos," he makes it clear that he does not mean his already established
character, but the *ethos* that he establishes in his speech, by speaking in
such a way that he commands respect and is thought worthy of belief.[8]
He disagrees sharply with writers of rhetorical textbooks who give no
weight to the speaker's character. He insists that character "really counts
for almost more than anything else," σχέδον ὡς εἰπεῖν κυριωτάτην ἔχει
πίστιν τὸ ἦθος.[9]

This does not necessarily mean that an orator should make a deliberate effort to reveal his own character. Cicero's rather heavy-handed
attempts to represent himself as a modest man can never have deceived
anyone, and Demosthenes shows a surer touch in *On the Crown* when he
says he knows it will irritate an audience to hear a speaker praising himself, but he cannot refute the charges against him without speaking of his
own achievements and "I will try to do this as modestly as I can."[10] The
impression of himself that an orator conveys will depend not only on
what he says but on his bearing and manner of speech. Contrast, either
explicit or implicit, with the deplorable character of his opponent is also
an effective method, and Demosthenes employs it with great skill. When
he ridicules Aeschines for his pride in his "beautiful voice,"[11] he contrives
to give the impression that he is more modest about himself and has no
great opinion of his own oratorical talent[12].

Cicero, in the *Verrines*, tries to achieve the same effect by a more
explicit comparison. Young Caecilius is trying to get himself accepted as

8 τῶν δὲ διὰ τοῦ λόγου ποριζομένων πίστεων τρία εἴδη ἐστίν. αἱ μὲν γάρ εἰσιν ἐν τῷ
  ἤθει τοῦ λέγοντος, αἱ δὲ ἐν τῷ τὸν ἀκροατὴν διαθεῖναί πως, αἱ δὲ ἐν αὐτῷ τῷ
  λόγῳ, διὰ τοῦ δεικνύναι ἢ φαίνεσθαι δεικνύναι. διὰ μὲν οὖν τοῦ ἤθους ὅταν οὕτω
  λεχθῇ ὁ λόγος ὥστε ἀξιόπιστον ποιῆσαι τὸν λέγοντα. τοῖς γὰρ ἐπιεικέσι πιστεύομεν
  μᾶλλον καὶ θᾶττον, περὶ πάντων μὲν ἁπλῶς, ἐν οἷς δὲ τὸ ἀκριβὲς μή ἐστιν ἀλλὰ τὸ
  ἀμφιδοξεῖν, καὶ παντελῶς. δεῖ δὲ καὶ τοῦτο συμβαίνειν διὰ τοῦ λόγου, ἀλλὰ μὴ διὰ
  τὸ προδεδοξάσθαι ποιόν τινα εἶναι τὸν λέγοντα (Rhet. 1.1356a).
9 Fortunately the context leaves us in no doubt concerning the meaning of *ethos* in
  this passage—it means a person's moral character, whether he is worthy of respect
  or not. Later rhetoricians use the term *ethos* differently, as when they talk of
  ἠθοποιία (for which Lysias was often praised) and the "ethical quality" of a
  speech. Thus in [Dion. Hal.] De Arte Rhet. 11.1 it is formally announced that
  there are four standards by which a speech must be judged: ἦθος, γνώμη, τέχνη,
  λέξις. And ἦθος is twofold, κοινόν τε καὶ ἴδιον, the general moral tone of the
  speech and the particular manner in which it is appropriate to the speaker (2), in
  terms of his nationality, origin, age, natural tendencies, fortune in life, and occupation (3). These are qualities in a speech which Aristotle is inclined to take for
  granted, and he is talking a quite different language.
10 18.4.
11 Cf. especially 19.337, and also 19.199,206; 18.280,291.
12 Aeschines tried to make him look ridiculous by recalling the occasion when he was
  seized with a fit of nervousness in Philip's presence and found himself tongue-

Verres' prosecutor instead of Cicero, and Cicero represents him as totally unprepared for the task, an uneducated man but so absurdly conceited that he seems not to be frightened by the prospect of opposing the wily and experienced Hortensius—"I devote all my spare time to study, but I shake with terror when my turn comes to speak."[13] This kind of direct comparison is difficult for a man like Cicero, who is not naturally modest, and in the *Philippics*, at the close of his career, he is generally content with implied comparison between himself and Antony.

When an orator is describing the kind of man his opponent is, exactness or completeness may be neither necessary nor desirable; it is more important to pick out characteristics that the audience will understand and that will arouse the reaction that the speaker wants. Good examples of this kind of description can be found in Theophrastus' *Characters*,[14] and both Demosthenes and Isaeus offer further material for sketches in this style.

The sketch or caricature of Aeschines that Demosthenes tries to present in *On the Embassy* and *On the Crown* includes the characteristic of ἀπειροκαλία, "lack of good taste." Aeschines, he says, cannot distinguish pedantry from true understanding of literature or history, though he makes pompous appeals to cultural tradition with long quotations from familiar authors. And Demosthenes himself has to defend himself from the charge that he is "fond of abusive language"; he explains, therefore, that virulent invective is contrary to his usual practice and that he resorts to it reluctantly, in retaliation for "the numerous lies that Aeschines has told," and has no alternative but to explain what kind of man this is—here is a "collector of trash and gossip, a trickster from the Agora, a neglected piece of rubbish," using absurdly high and mighty language: "There he was, like an actor on the stage, yelling out 'O earth and sun and true worth,' and the rest of it, and invoking 'Intelligence and Culture that help us distinguish good from evil'" (18.126-27).

The sketch of ἀπειροκαλία is merciless—an uneducated man talking pompously about "true worth" (*Arete*) and "culture" (*Paideia*): "No really cultivated person would ever speak like this about himself, he would blush with embarrassment if he heard anyone else doing so. But people

tied—after th°y had all been expecting a masterly speech from him! (2.34—35). Demosthenes says nothing of the incident.

13 Div. in Caec. 13.41.

14 It has never been quite clear what the purpose of Theophrastus was in writing these sketches. For the most recent discussion, with references to earlier literature, see R. G. Ussher, "The Characters of Theophrastus" (London 1960), Intro. 3—12. L. Radermacher, "Anfänge der Charakterkunde bei den Griechen," Symbolae Osloenses 27 (1949) 19—24, points out that the origins of "Typenschilderung" must be sought in rhetoric.

who lack culture, as you do, and are stupid enough to think they have it, all they can do is offend their listeners whenever they open their mouths; they cannot succeed in appearing like cultivated people" (18.128).

Aeschines' parents are represented as uneducated and unlikely to have set their son very high ideals, his father working in a school as a slave and his mother officiating, with her son's assistance, in religious rites of very doubtful reputation. The jury will not despise a man because his origins are humble, but the grotesque details of Aeschines' youth are evidently thought necessary in the portrait that Demosthenes wants to present—the picture of a dignified and slightly pompous speaker with occasional theatrical mannerisms, whom one might take for a conservative gentleman of the older school unless one was warned that the manner was deliberately cultivated to give that impression, the solemn language and manner learned on the stage, part of the stock in trade of a man who lived by his wits, motivated solely by the desire for wealth and power; a man who had fought his way to the top by disreputable methods and was constantly acting a part which he did not really know how to play.

This is the portrait of Aeschines which Demosthenes wants the jury to have before them as his career is set out for them, this is the character which the narrative of events is meant to illustrate. Details in the narrative that are not substantiated by evidence may be more readily believed if they fit into the pattern of behaviour suggested by the character sketch. The character is there for the sake of the narrative. In long speeches, like *On the Embassy* and *On the Crown*, it becomes necessary to recapitulate and re-elaborate the portrait at intervals; the tactics of argument can be seen more plainly in earlier and simpler speeches.

In Isaeus' speeches the difference in character and behaviour between the opposing parties is frequently emphasized. In particular he likes to show how different they have been in their attitude towards a testator, his client modest and generous, his adversaries shameless and greedy, ready to do anything to obtain the money and deprive the rightful heir of his inheritance. The contrast can be drawn either by a detailed narrative, which consistently illustrates their differences in character, or by a strictly curtailed narrative coupled with a warning to the jury that the details supplied by speakers on the other side cannot be accepted as true, because they do not fit the known character of the persons involved. Isaeus' speeches offer good examples of both methods.

In his first oration, *On the Estate of Cleonymus*,[15] the speaker begins with a series of contrasts. In the past, like properly brought up boys, he

15 This speech, as well as Orations 2, 3 and 8, was examined in Chapter I, supra, pp. 15—17, to illustrate the skill of Isaeus in adapting his narrative to the needs of the

and his brother never entered a law court even out of curiosity, but now they are threatened with poverty unless they put up a fight in court for their uncle's estate. It hurts them deeply to quarrel with a member of the family,[16] but their opponents (who have no family feeling) are determined to empoverish them. Everyone knows, he says, how fond of them their uncle was, and though he left a will which made no mention of them, he tried to change it before his death, but was prevented by these men.

Devoted as they are to their uncle Cleonymus, they are careful not to charge him with negligence in waiting so long before changing a will that cut them off without a legacy. They say that this unfortunate will had its origin in Cleonymus' quarrel with their other uncle, Deinias—a quarrel which they are unwilling to discuss, fearing that it might harm his reputation if they revealed details (8—11). Their reticence is all part of their effort to make people think that they are "very decent young fellows".[17]

The speaker in this case has to rely almost entirely on the argument from character. Cleonymus' will was perfectly legal, and whatever his intentions may have been, he did not in fact change it. They hope to convince the jury that he wanted to make some last-minute changes when he thought he was dying, and was prevented by their adversaries. But they have no positive evidence of his intention, since neither of them was with him when he died, and their only hope is to discredit whatever story their opponents tell by insisting on their lack of scruple; the jury will be asked to interpret the narrative and complete the gaps in it on the assumption that "these men are totally lacking in shame." The speaker and his brother may have a weak case in law, but they hope to prove that they have a strong moral right to the inheritance.

The same kind of argument is employed in the eighth oration, *On the Estate of Ciron*, which begins with a severe attack on the character of the opposing party: "It is enough to make one angry, gentlemen of the jury, when, in addition to claiming property to which they have no right, people think they can destroy the just provisions of the law by their arguments.[18] This is what these people are now trying to do. Our grand-

---

case. The discussion that follows is intended to bring out other aspects of his skill and technique, and repetition will be avoided as far as possible.

16 1.1,6. Instead of insisting on their own scruples, the speaker quickly calls the jury's attention to the insensitive attitude of their opponents, their ἀναισχυντία and αἰσχροκέρδεια (7—8)—a perfect example of establishing one's own character by implied contrast with the adversary.

17 Cf. Wyse, The Speeches of Isaeus, p 178, who remarks that the nephews have a very weak case, but the exordium is "designed to give the speaker an engaging air of youth and innocence."

18 This would of course be an appropriate reply to the first oration, which is a request to annul a legal will.

father Ciron did not die without issue. We are children of his legitimate daughter, but they lay claim to the estate as nearest of kin, and they offer us a grave insult (ὑβρίζουσιν) by refusing to recognize us as his daughter's children; in fact they say he never had a daughter at all. The explanation for this behaviour of theirs is their avarice (πλεονεξία) and the size of the estate which Ciron left, which they have forcibly appropriated (βιασάμε-νοι) and taken into their possession. And they have the effrontery (τολμῶσι) to say that he left no property, while at the same time they put in a claim to his estate" (1–2). Contempt for the law, *hybris*, violence, and avarice make up a formidable list of accusations, in addition to their lies and their shameless pretence that the estate is not worth worrying about, when their only concern is to gratify their avarice.

Against such utterly unscrupulous people,[19] who have witnesses prepared to give false testimony, the only answer is a full narrative of the "facts." Unfortunately there is little evidence to support their detailed narrative. The only witnesses who would have immediate knowledge of Ciron's first marriage and the birth of his daughter are his old family servants, and they are in the hands of "these dishonest schemers," who refuse to hand them over for interrogation. They are fully entitled to refuse this challenge to surrender their slaves, but it is hoped that the jury will think they are afraid to let their servants talk.[20]

After his narrative the speaker reminds the jury of the tactics he has used: "If you knew the shamelessness of Diocles and the kind of man he has shown himself in other matters, you would not doubt a word of what I have told you" (40). He recalls some further examples of high-handed and semi-criminal behaviour (43) and notes, as a crowning touch, that he was caught in adultery and suitably punished (μοιχὸς ληφθεὶς καὶ παθὼν ὅτι προσήκει), calling witnesses to support his allegation (44–46).

The same method of argument, less artistically employed, can be observed in some of the spurious speeches in the Demosthenic corpus, the work of unknown authors. In Oration 44, *Against Leochares*, the speaker begins with a contrast between the contending parties. Leochares, he says, is making many false statements in order to claim an inheritance to which he has no legal right, and has therefore forced him and his father to bring suit: "And I beg you, gentlemen of the jury, to help my father and me, if we are speaking the truth, and not to let poor and powerless men be outmanceuvred by dishonest tactics. We have come to court putting our trust in the truth, and we shall be content if we are permitted to have

19 The speaker says it is the most "shameless" attempt to obtain property belonging to others that has ever been made in the Athenian courts (4). Cf. the similar statement made by Demosthenes about his guardians (27.7).
20 See chapter I above, p. 15 and note 23.

what the law allows us. But these men have always relied on careful planning and the outlay of money—understandably, since it is no great matter for them to spend money that is not their own; and so they have provided themselves with plenty of people to speak on their behalf and give false testimony for them. Now my father, whom you see here, I must explain, has unmistakeable evidence to prove his poverty and his lack of experience. This is something you all know, since he works regularly as a crier in the Piraeus; such an occupation indicates not only that he is without money, but also that he has no time for other matters, since he has to spend the whole day in the Agora. If you bear these things in mind, you must recognize that we would never have come into court if we were not putting our trust in the justice of our cause" (44.3—4).

Here the speaker is insisting that "we are just ordinary honest hard-working people," before he offers any detail that explains his accusations and before embarking on his narrative. He also tries to make it clear that his claims are very modest. His adversary, Leostratus, is claiming the estate of Archiades for his son Leochares, and has made a formal statement, in a *diamartyria,*[21] that he is the legally adopted son of Archiades and also that he and his son are the nearest surviving relatives. The speaker claims, convincingly, that he and his father are nearer relatives,[22] but he is quite prepared to recognize the adoption, if it can be established as legally valid, and makes a great show of being "reasonable": "Even if their claim is not strictly legal, but their case is shown to be a fair and equitable one, on this basis too we will yield to them" (44.7—8).

The narrative soon shows how important it is for the speaker to emphasize the contrast in character between himself and his father, on the one hand, and Leochares, his father Leostratus, and his grandfather, Leocrates, on the other. The property of Archiades, who died many years previously, has passed through the hands of various members of the family; the story is quite complicated, and the attempt of Leostratus to claim the property for his son is based on a manoeuvre of doubtful legality.[23] The speaker encourages the jury to believe that Leostratus is

21 A *diamartyria* was a formal statement before witnesses, affirming or denying the legality of an action or claim, and was frequently a prelude to litigation. Cf. Lipsius, Att. Recht III 854—55.
22 The speaker's father, Aristodemus, is a grandson of Archiades' brother. The father of Leochares is great-grandson of Archiades' daughter. The male line has preference.
23 Leocrates, after taking over the estate of Archiades as his adopted son, subsequently inherited his own father's estate, and was permitted by Athenian law to substitute his son Leostratus as the "adopted son" of Archiades, so that he took over the property (cf. Lipsius, Att. Recht III 518); he in his turn (at his father's death) went back to the family house, leaving a son to take his place; and when that son

deliberately cheating simple honest people, by recalling the long history of shameless and violent behaviour in his family—beginning with his father, Leocrates, who obtained possession of Archiades' estate by taking advantage of the good nature of the dead man's brother, Meidylides, the speaker's great-grandfather. Meidylides and his descendants have been content with less than their full legal rights, while Leocrates and his son and grandson have forced their way into an inheritance to which they have no right at all[24]. It is appropriate, therefore, to ask the jury, as a matter of principle, "to help people who are not grasping, but will be content if they can have what the law allows" (28).

Not all litigants can say that they are young and inexperienced, and *Against Dionysodorus* is written for an experienced man of business (a cleverly written speech, but not by Demosthenes, since it is clearly later in date than 323).[25] The speaker, who has lent Dionysodorus money to finance a trading venture, proclaims his full confidence in the courts and says only fools would provide cash in exchange for a mere scrap of paper unless they had confidence in the force of Athenian law. His difficulty (he says) is that Dionysodorus has no shame and no fear of the courts (56.1—2), and since he has not left Athens seems to have no fear of losing his case. He had tried to make the speaker break the law by signing a contract that authorized his shipper to take grain from Egypt to Rhodes, instead of bringing it direct to Athens as the law required (5—6). And though the speaker insisted on altering the contract and obeying the law, the shipper took his Egyptian grain to Rhodes and sold it there just the same, since the price was higher there than in Athens; and now he will maintain that the speaker has connived at this breach of the contract and

died, without issue, he attempted first to reinstate himself as the heir to Archiades' property and (as an alternative) to substitute another son, Leochares—both manoeuvres of very doubtful legality.

24 Before telling this part of the story the speaker says he had better explain the details, to show "what desperately violent people these men are" (16) and how Leocrates εἰσποιεῖ αὐτὸν υἱὸν τῷ Ἀρχιάδῃ καὶ ἐνεβάτευσεν οὕτως εἰς τὴν οὐσίαν (19). Meidylides, who might have objected, gave way (being good-natured and not in need of money) and "we" (his family) "kept quiet and made no move," ἡσυχίαν εἴχομεν (20), ὑπεμένομεν πάντα (24). The contrast of βία and ἡσυχία is normal, and prepares the way for a protest against the present claim. Demosthenes himself prefers not to drive the point home so hard. In 36.15 he describes how Phormio is persuaded by members of the family to let Apollodorus keep certain sums of money, rather than make an enemy of him by insisting on his rights; he makes no comment and lets the incident speak for itself.

Leostratus, in his turn, is shown to be guilty of "shamelessness and greed" (ἡ ἀναίδεια καὶ ἡ πλεονεξία τοιαύτη ἐστὶν αὐτοῦ), as well as παρανομία and βία. Final proof that his present claim is dishonest is his "shamelessness" in trying to obtain the *theoricon* to which he has no right (38).

25 Cf. Gernet, Budé ed., Plaidoyers civils, III 134.

is expecting to gain by it, despite his show of respect for the law. He has no chance of winning his case or recovering his money from Dionysodorus unless he convinces the jury that he is an honest man who respects the law, unlike his adversary. But he cannot simply proclaim his honesty and he does not; it is the manner and style, the *ethos* of the speech, which must show his character, in contrast with the shamelessness of his adversary.[26]

A man who has lent money and is trying to recover it may have to face the popular prejudice that bankers and moneylenders are merciless people, determined on obtaining their pound of flesh at all costs. In Oration 49, *Against Timotheus*,[27] Apollodorus is trying to recover money that his father, the banker Pasion, had lent to the distinguished but impoverished general, Timotheus. It would not have been easy to represent a man like Timotheus as an ordinary "shameless scoundrel," but Apollodorus says Pasion lent the money out of pure kindness, "thinking it more important to help Timotheus in his need than to retain a large balance in his reserve,"[28] and is then able to tax Timotheus with ingratitude towards a benefactor, always a damaging accusation.

Apollodorus uses cruder methods in the first speech *Against Stephanus*. This speech was composed by an experienced and competent speech-writer, if not by Demosthenes himself,[29] and it can be argued that Apollodorus was in such a desperate situation that only drastic tactics could save him. His earlier attempt to discredit Phormio had failed completely. The speech *For Phormio*, written by Demosthenes and delivered by a friend of Phormio, had made such a powerful impression on the jury that they would not listen to Apollodorus' reply. Now he accuses Stephanus of giving false testimony on Phormio's behalf and charges Phormio with

26 Blass, in looking for signs that the speech is not by Demosthenes, says that it lacks *ethos* ("Ethos freilich ist ebensowenig vorhanden," Att. Bered. III 587). He seems not to recognize the means by which the speaker commends his character to the jury, by being careful not to give himself any very positive personality.

27 This speech is perhaps the work of Apollodorus himself; like other speeches by the same author (Apollodorus or his speech-writer) it shows some shrewdness, though it is not a well-written speech. Cf. L. Pearson, "Apollodorus, the Eleventh Attic Orator," in The Classical Tradition, Studies in Honor of Harry Caplan (Cornell Univ. Press 1966), 347–59.

28 Now Pasion is dead, and Timotheus is deceitfully trying to persuade the jury that he does not owe ὃ μετὰ χάριτος ἔλαβε (49.3–4).

29 Though admirers of Demosthenes would be happy if the speech could be proved spurious, nothing inappropriate has been found in its language and style, and it is commonly regarded as genuine. Cf. Blass, Att. Bered. III 467–73; Sandys & Paley, Select Private Orations of Demosthenes (3rd ed., Cambridge 1896), II 39–47; G. Hüttner, Demosthenis oratio in Stephanum prior num vera sit inquiritur (Ansbach 1895). For some additional remarks see L. Pearson, "Demosthenes (or Pseudo Demosthenes) 45," Antichthon 3 (1969), 18–26.

using dishonest methods to obtain the verdict. He hopes to convince the jury that Phormio is a thoroughly disreputable character, who cheated his employer, the banker Pasion, from the beginning, seduced his wife and forged a will which enabled him to marry her after her husband's death, waiting until Apollodorus, her elder son, was absent on trierarchic duty before actually making her his wife.

This is the story that Apollodorus unfolds. Abusive remarks are scattered throughout the speech, but there is no valid evidence to support his accusations and Phormio is not provided at the start with the kind of character that can carry such a story. It is not until the closing section of the speech that a consistent portrait is attempted.

Apollodorus argues that the story told by the other side at the previous trial is absurd and inconsistent, that a "will" of Pasion which authorized Phormio to marry his widow is incredible, "because he could not have trusted a rogue like Phormio." Phormio, however, enjoyed a good reputation among business people in Athens, and Apollodorus could hardly expect the jury to accept his version of the story unless he convinced them from the start that this reputation was undeserved. At the end of the speech he says Phormio had the habit of ingratiating himself with successful people and abandoning them when they ran into difficulties (63–65), and of putting a surly expression on his face, so as to make sure that no one would ask him inconvenient favours (68–69). Even if they are believed, these accusations are not substantial enough to upset the story told by the other side; they would be useful only as corroborative details after a convincing narrative had revealed an unpleasant and untrustworthy character.

Unfortunately for Apollodorus his slanderous remarks are likely to damage him more than they will damage Phormio. The jury may find it hard to forgive him for his disloyalty to his mother's memory, when he says that Phormio seduced her and that perhaps Phormio and not Pasion is the father of his younger brother Pasicles.[30] Unless his accusations are believed, his own character will suffer severely, and the jury may think they understand why Pasion had no confidence in him and preferred to trust his servant Phormio.

On the other hand the speech *For Phormio* (36), which Demosthenes wrote for the earlier trial, was delivered with great success by a friend of Phormio and it is considered to be perhaps the very best of his private

---

30 Apollodorus first merely hints at this, saying "he married my mother when I was away on service as trierarch," ὃν τρόπον δέ, οὐκ ἴσως καλὸν υἱεῖ περὶ μητρὸς ἀκριβῶς εἰπεῖν (3), but is quite blunt about it later in 84: ἐγὼ γὰρ ὁμομήτριον μὲν ἀδελφὸν ἐμαυτοῦ Πασικλέα νομίζω, ὁμοπάτριον δ᾽ οὐκ οἶδα, δέδοικα μέντοι μὴ τῶν Φορμίωνος ἀδικημάτων εἰς ἡμᾶς ἀρχὴ Πασικλέης ᾖ.

orations. It contains a character sketch of Phormio, which is the most ambitious tribute of this kind that he ever attempted.

Phormio's friend, who delivers the speech, begins immediately by insisting on the contrast between Phormio and Apollodorus. He explains that they have entered a special plea, a *paragraphe*, to prevent Apollodorus bringing suit (since his suit is clearly inadmissible), in order to free Phormio from the harassing attentions of Apollodorus which have been continued for many years. Phormio is without experience in the courts, and the speaker himself is not a professional orator who will try to mislead the jury, but Apollodorus is represented from the start as a *sycophantes*, a man who thrives on litigation. Phormio has done everything possible to reach a settlement, fulfilled all his obligations and done Apollodorus many favours, but the harassment has continued just the same (1—3). This is a way of telling the jury that Apollodorus is not only a troublesome person who is trying to deceive the court, but guilty of gross ingratitude as well. Phormio's own character begins already to take on some form by contrast with his opponent.

This is the same technique of contrast that Isaeus had used in Orations 1 and 8 and that Demosthenes himself had used in the first speech *Against Aphobus.* That was his first appearance in court, and his youth spoke for itself, but he wanted to show how Aphobus was taking advantage of his inexperience by forcing him to bring suit, instead of letting members of the family resolve their differences (27.1). The next step was to contrast the greed and heartlessness of Aphobus and his fellow guardians with the kindly forethought of his own father in making provision for his children's future. He "thought about" his children as death approached, choosing two close relatives and an old friend as trustees and treating them generously in the expectation that this would make them more conscientious (4—5). But they had no thought except to enrich themselves, as they helped themselves to their legacies (6,13) and divided the rest of the property between them, not even trying to conceal what they were doing. Their shamelessness is emphasized immediately and repeatedly (7,16,18), though nothing is said about heartlessness until later (ὠμότατ' ἀνθρώπων, 26). To show that he is not himself greedy for money as they are, Demosthenes points out that he is using a lower rate of interest than the law actually specifies in calculating what is due to him (17,23) and giving them a generous allowance for expenses (34,36). In protesting about their shamelessness and meanness[31] he notes how one of them refused to back up another, if he could do so without damage to

31 ταῦτ' οὐ μεγάλη καὶ περιφανὴς ἀναισχυντία; ταῦτ' οὐχ ὑπερβολὴ δεινῆς αἰσχροκερδίας; This is the same vocabulary that Isaeus uses, cf. supra, p. 82, and n. 16.

himself (42,43), and Aphobus never paid young Demosthenes' teachers (46)—evidently "a man who could not even keep his hands away from little things," μηδὲ τῶν μικρῶν ἀπεσχημένον (47).

In similar style in *For Phormio* the contrast between Phormio and Apollodorus continues to be emphasized as the story unfolds. When Apollodorus first began to make trouble, after his mother's death, Phormio was persuaded by the committee of arbitration to let him have the three thousand drachmae that he claimed, and "he preferred to keep on friendly terms rather than make an enemy out of him on this issue" (15). But Apollodorus has shown no such conciliatory spirit, but has invented new grounds for complaint, even though he previously granted him a release from all claims. It is a sign of his shamelessness that he behaves "as though previous events are not likely to be known," "as though the men who could testify to them were all dead" (16—17). The story shows Apollodorus guilty of ingratitude, greed, and shameless *sycophantia*. The only familiar accusation missing from the list is "contempt for the law,"[32] and this is soon added when he is charged with disregarding the law which prohibits further complaints once a release from all claims has been granted or after a statutory limit of five years: "The law, gentlemen of the jury, lays down the time limit quite clearly; more than twenty years have passed, but Apollodorus is asking you to regard his *sycophantia* as more important than the laws according to which you have sworn to judge the case" (26).

Before warning the jury that Apollodorus will try to defend his character by pointing to his trierarchies and his generosity in the service of Athens, the speaker tells him he will have to admit that Phormio resembles his father, Pasion, more closely than he does; and when he sneers at Phormio, he is really sneering at his own father and is guilty of disloyalty to his own family (a charge which the speaker in Isaeus' first oration makes against his adversaries).[33] He is therefore told that his objections to accepting Phormio as a stepfather are ludicrous (28—31) and his complaint that his father's will was forged is "utterly shameless" (33). Unlike his industrious father he has been guilty of gross extravagance—this accusation follows almost inevitably and makes it hard for him to rouse much sympathy when he protests that he spent the money in the service of the city (39).[34]

---

32 The term παρανομία, used in the speech "Against Leochares," does not occur here or in the speeches against his guardians, and is in fact not common in the genuine speeches (it occurs only once in Isaeus, 6.48).
33 Cf. supra pp. 81–82.
34 In Oration 38 ("Against Nausimachus and Xenopeithes?") the defendants are charged with disregarding the law by bringing an inadmissible case (after granting a release

The way is now ready for the tirade against Apollodorus' character which follows (43—48). His ostentatious manner of life and his expensive clothes and his extravagant ways with *hetairai*, married man though he is (45), are bad enough, but he is dishonouring the memory of his father when he sneers at Phormio, the successful former slave, since his own father had been a slave and had made his way in the world by honest industry. His attitude is ridiculous and contemptible, and the jury may conclude that he is extremely thick-skinned (εἰς τοῦθ᾽ ἥκεις ἀγνωμοσύνης, 46) or not quite sane (εἰς τοῦθ ἥκεις μανίας, 48). They will certainly understand why his father had so little respect for him and preferred to entrust his business to Phormio. Demosthenes does not turn him into a monster and a caricature, as he does with Meidias,[35] and he has some serious things to say about the worthy character of Phormio.

This speech is unique among the private speeches of Demosthenes because of its final appeal, asking the jury to respect and uphold integrity of character and "goodness of heart" (τρόπου ἐπιείκεια) such as Phormio possesses (58—59). One must suppose that the speaker had a genuine regard and affection for the man whom he was representing and was able to deliver this tribute convincingly. After re-emphasizing the ingratitude and extravagance and litigiousness of Apollodorus, he tells the jury that Phormio saved Pasion's bank from collapse at a critical time when many bankers were totally ruined (49—53). Witnesses are called to testify to discreditable incidents in the career of Apollodorus, and evidence is then offered in favour of Phormio's good character including his public services. Phormio, instead of suing people, like Apollodorus, has helped many people in need; his thrift and skilful management, unlike Apollodorus' extravagance, saved the bank from ruin and made possible his generous contributions to the city.

The contrast is now fully developed:

"In all these ways, men of Athens, Phormio has been of service to the city and to many of your number. He has never done any injustice to anyone, neither in affairs of the city nor privately, nor has he done Apollodorus any wrong. He asks you, he entreats you, he begs you to save him, and we his good friends join with him in this entreaty to you. There is another point that should be made. Evidence has been read to you showing that he had command of money far beyond anything that Apollodorus or any individual has in his possession. This is because Phormio's credit, where it is known, is worth all this

and after the time limit has passed) and with gross extravagance, which they say has been in the cause of the city. The charges have not been preceded by the kind of characterization that is so important in "For Phormio," and the speaker draws attention to his restraint in not attacking the character of his opponents—μή με φῶσ᾽ κακῶς αὐτοὺς λέγειν (26).

35 Cf. below pp.105—11. For an appreciative description of the characterization in Oration 36 see Bruna Veneroni, "Démosthène logographe," REG 79 (1966), 640—54.

money and much more; this is why he can do so much, whether in his own interest or in your service.

"Do not surrender all these advantages, do not let this abominable man overthrow what Phormio has built up, do not set up a shocking example to suggest that the property of hard-working and modestly living men can be taken from them in your court by scoundrels and professional litigants. This wealth is far more useful to you if it rests in his hands. You have seen the witnesses, heard from them how he behaves to people who are in need. And these services he has done not for the sake of any gain or profit, but out of pure kindness and goodness of heart. It is not right, men of Athens, to betray a man like this and let Apollodorus have control" (57—59).

The way has been carefully prepared for this final appeal. The narrative has been consistent and well-documented, the individual accusations refuted,[36] and explanations have been given of details which Apollodorus maintained were incriminating or suspicious. It is not considered necessary to tell the jury much about the financial situation of the bank or the methods by which Phormio saved it from disaster; it is enough to let his success illustrate his ability and integrity, just as his good character explains his success.

It was necessary to establish the good character of Phormio and to discredit Apollodorus in order to make further legal action on his part difficult if not impossible—and the speeches *Against Stephanus* show how weak the position of Apollodorus was when he tried to renew the attack. In some suits it may be possible to prove a technical case by establishing the "facts," but it will not be easy to prove malicious intention or semi-criminal motive without making it clear what manner of people are concerned. When Demosthenes sues his guardians it is not enough to establish the fact that his father's estate has dwindled and that he has failed to obtain what his father intended. If the jury think that Aphobus and his fellow-trustees were unlucky or perhaps a little less competent and prudent than they might have been, the probability is that they will treat them leniently. If Demosthenes is to obtain a satisfactory judgment—a sum of money large enough, so that he can be content if he succeeds in exacting about half of it—he must prove that they were, at best, shame-

---

36 The charge that Phormio kept for himself a personal investment (ἀφορμή) left in the bank by Pasion is refuted by a convincing story of Pasion's procedure, showing what a man of his financial shrewdness would do (4—6). And when Apollodorus chooses the shield-factory instead of the bank as his share of the inheritance, he is said to be admitting that no such "private investment" existed, since it would make the bank much the more valuable property (12). And even if Phormio had been dishonest, why should he treat young Pasicles with strict fairness (as shown by his making no complaint) and try to cheat the wily Apollodorus (22)? These are all arguments from probability, which would have much less force if it could not be taken for granted that the speaker's judgment about the character of the various persons was correct.

fully negligent, probably not only dishonest, but shameless, greedy, and contemptuous of the law as well.

The narrative in the first speech *Against Aphobus* is arranged so as to illustrate these characteristics, with the additional touch of meanness (αἰσχροκέρδεια). But some instances of "utter shamelessness" are reserved for the latter part of the speech, just as they are in *For Phormio*. It is not until he is near the end that he mentions "the most monstrous lie of all"−a statement by Aphobus before the arbitrator that the elder Demosthenes left a "cache" of four talents buried in the house, a statement which he expected to be believed on the strength of his "bare word," without any evidence to support it (53−54). It is one more sign of "shamelessness" that Aphobus should expect such a fantastic story to be believed.

The protest about lack of shame is repeated several times in the paragraphs that follow, and the final detail that completes the portrait of these despicable guardians is left to the end−they left no provision at all for Demosthenes' young sister, despite the dowry that her father had set aside for her, so that young Demosthenes, in addition to all his other troubles, must somehow find a dowry for her (65−66). This final touch of inhumanity is very effective, and the speech ends, as it began, with the contrast between totally unscrupulous men and a helpless young fellow in the depths of misery (ὁ πάντων ταλαιπωρότατος, 66).

In the second speech *Against Aphobus* Demosthenes adds a few new touches to the portrait. He describes how his father, when near to death, called the three men in and let them hold the children in their arms, as a formal indication that he was leaving them in their care−and now Aphobus asks for pity! (15−16). Then he tells of the trick that Aphobus played on the young Demosthenes to force him to undertake a trierarchy (17)[37]. Comment is unnecessary, because the story shows his complete lack of pity for the young and helpless. It serves as an admirable introduction to the final appeal, in which Demosthenes asks the jury to pity him and once again contrasts his father's concern for his wife and children with the selfish cruelty of Aphobus (τῷ σχετλιωτάτῳ πάντων ἀνθρώπων, 19).

Judgment is given against Aphobus and he replies by prosecuting one of Demosthenes' witnesses on the charge of giving false testimony. An attempt to evade justice is one more example of his contempt for the law, as well as his meanness and avarice, and Demosthenes takes advantage of the opportunity to point this out in the third speech *Against Aphobus*.[38]

37 The incident is described with more detail in the "Meidias" (21.78−80), where it is used to illustrate the *aselgeia* of Meidias.
38 This speech, however, presents a number of problems, and it is very doubtful if

In the speeches *Against Onetor*, Demosthenes says he faces an opponent tougher and even more unpleasant than Aphobus—ηὕρηκα πολὺ
τοῦτον ἐκείνου δυσκολώτερον (30.1). The jury had ordered Aphobus to
pay ten talents, and as part of his attempt to collect what was due to him,
Demosthenes tried to take possession of a farm. He was forcibly ejected
by Onetor, who said that the property was his, that his sister was divorced
from her husband, Aphobus, who should have returned the dowry and
had pledged this property to cover the amount that was due. Demosthenes
says nothing about documents in his speeches, and Onetor may have
papers to show that the property was legally pledged to him before the
case against Aphobus came into court. Even if this is so, Demosthenes
hopes to represent Onetor as an accomplice of Aphobus in his design to
defeat justice. If he tells a coherent and convincing story, which fits in
with the case presented in the previous trial, he may discredit Onetor to
such a degree that the jury will overlook the legal technicality and give
judgment against Onetor on the basis of his bad character.

The complaint against Onetor is for illegal ejectment, a δίκη ἐξούλης,
but Demosthenes intends to prove that he has a legal right to take over the
property and that Onetor is guilty of a carefully meditated fraud to prevent him from obtaining what Aphobus owes him. The narrative is very
brief, but the motives of all parties are made quite clear. Onetor's sister,
whose name we are not told, was previously married to Timocrates; this
marriage was dissolved and Timocrates, instead of returning the dowry,
agreed to pay interest on it, at 10 % per annum. The reason for this
arrangement, Demosthenes argues, was plain enough. Onetor was eager
that his sister should marry Aphobus (a man of considerable property,
with Demosthenes' estate added to the estate he had inherited from his
father!), but since he and Timocrates expected that Demosthenes would
obtain judgment against his guardians when he came of age, he did not
want to let Aphobus have the dowry, in case it should be considered part
of the guardians' property and be liable to seizure in part payment of their
debt to Demosthenes.[39]

Demosthenes delivered it in the form in which it is preserved. Cf. Gernet, Budé ed.,
Plaidoyers civils I 63–70.

39 Such a fear may not have been justified; no law is cited which would inform the
jury whether or not the dowry was protected against demands from the husband's
creditors. But for the purpose of the argument it does not matter what the law is;
Onetor's fears can be real, even if he does not understand the law: δῆλον δὲ καὶ ἐκ
τῶν εἰκότων ὅτι τούτων ἕνεχ᾽ ὧν εἴρηκα ὀφείλειν εἵλοντο μᾶλλον ἢ καταμεῖξαι
τὴν προῖκ᾽ εἰς τὴν οὐσίαν τὴν Ἀφόβου τὴν οὕτω κινδυνευθήσεσθαι μέλλουσαν
(30.10). This sentence is not evidence of any law, only of what these men
thought—"they chose" is the equivalent of "they said to themselves that."

The dowry, therefore, remained in the hands of Timocrates. And when judgment was given against Aphobus, it was pretended that this marriage also had broken up, that Aphobus had not returned the dowry (which he never received!) but had pledged the farm to Onetor in lieu of the amount: "He had the impertinence to give this as the reason for ejecting me from the property" (30. 6–8).

Nothing is said yet about the date of this supposed divorce. And was the property transferred before Aphobus came to trial—and how long before? Argument about dates will come later. The immediate concern of Demosthenes is to explain the motives of the various parties. Timocrates, he says, was not short of money and could easily have raised the amount of the dowry (10–11); the only reason for not letting it out of his hands must be the fear that Demosthenes might claim it. This explanation will seem much more plausible if Onetor can be presented from the start as a dishonest man familiar with the ways of the law and fully capable of devising a clever fraud.

The way is accordingly prepared for this narrative by remarks about Onetor's character in the opening sections of the speech. Like Aphobus, he refused to consider any settlement or discussion, but "threw me off the property in a quite outrageous manner" ($\dot{\upsilon}\beta\rho\iota\sigma\tau\iota\kappa\tilde{\omega}\varsigma$ $\pi\dot{\alpha}\nu\upsilon$, 2). A display of *hybris* is a sign of bad character, and Demosthenes concludes that he is "facing contrived arguments and lying witnesses" in the case (3). A history of past misdeeds would be useful, but it is equally easy to suppose that Onetor is clever enough to keep them concealed; any members of the jury who have regarded Onetor as an honest man will learn now how wrong they were: "Yes, I shall show you not only that he never handed over the dowry (he says that the piece of land was pledged to him in lieu of the dowry which should have been returned), but that he devised a plot against my property from the beginning. Also I shall show that this woman, in whose interest he expelled me from the farm, has not parted company from her husband" (4).

A witness will testify that he saw Aphobus in the house with her when she was ill, after the suit was already filed (34), and there are three servant women who "knew perfectly well that she was still living with her husband," but Onetor has refused to let them be examined under torture (35–36). Perhaps a sketch of the woman's character will be a substitute for evidence. She is, it is suggested, a young woman who cannot do without a husband. She moved from Timocrates to Aphobus without a day's interval between them. Is it credible that, if she really left Aphobus three years ago, she has not yet found another husband, young as she is and with a wealthy brother who is able to provide a good dowry (33–34)? Aphobus and Onetor may pretend to be "simple, honest people" (30.24;

31.11), but the whole course of events is intelligible only when one realizes that they are devious and clever.

Demosthenes reconstructs events on the basis of presumed intentions and motives and character, and before long he is treating as established "fact" what began by being merely "probable." When his opponents tell a story which does not conform with his ingenious reconstruction, he can say it is inconsistent with the "facts." Onetor maintained that the dowry was indeed paid to Aphobus, not all at once, but it had been paid in full within two years, before the divorce took place. An incredible story, says Demosthenes: "A man who, from the start preferred to owe the amount of the dowry and pay interest on the amount owed, so that the dowry would not be in danger like the rest of the property, how is it conceivable that such a man paid it in full after I had already brought suit against Aphobus? Even a man who had been confident at the start of that period would have tried to get the dowry back when I brought suit. It won't do, gentlemen of the jury" (16). They cannot produce witnesses to the payment of the dowry—here they are pretending to be "simple people," when everyone knows their procedure was carefully planned.[40]

A jury might have some sympathy with Onetor, if he were guilty of nothing more shocking than using a little force to prevent Demosthenes setting foot on a disputed farm-property. But if he is a cunning scoundrel, engaged in a plot to cheat an unfortunate young man out of his inheritance, the whole thing takes on a different aspect. It is the same in the first speech *Against Boeotus*, where the speaker must do more than prove a technical breach of the law. This speech (Oration 39) is with good reason recognized as a genuine Demosthenic speech; but the speaker, Mantitheus, was unsuccessful in his action, and like Apollodorus in his prosecution of Stephanus, when he made a second attempt, he was content with a cruder and less sophisticated effort—his own work, perhaps, or the work of a less expensive speech-writer than Demosthenes. The complaint against Boeotus is that he is using the plaintiff's name, Mantitheus.[41] This might strike a jury as a trifling matter, and Mantitheus has to begin by explaining that it is not a trifling matter at all: "Because he says he is the son of my own father" (39.2).

---

40 τοιαύταις τέχναις καὶ πανουργίαις ὡς ἁπλοῖ τινες εἶναι δόξοντες ἡγοῦνται ῥᾳδίως ὑμᾶς ἐξαπατήσειν, ἁπλῶς οὐδ᾽ ἂν μικρὸν ὑπὲρ τῶν διαφερόντων, ἀλλ᾽ ὡς οἶόν τε ἀκριβέστατα πράξαντες (24).

41 It is difficult to be sure exactly what kind of lawsuit Mantitheus is bringing. Legal scholars, though not without misgivings, are inclined to think it must be a δίκη βλάβης, because the speaker says he will describe "how much harm the defendant is doing (ὅσα βλάπτει) to the city as well as to me" (39.5). Cf. Gernet, Plaidoyers civils II 13–14, and the works listed on p. 59, n. 29, above.

He goes on to describe how the man sued his father, with the help of some notorious professional litigants, an ἐργαστήριον συκοφαντῶν⁴² (well known to the jury), complaining that he was being deprived of his rights as an Athenian citizen:

"Now I must be frank with you, gentlemen of the jury. My father did not want to go into court; he was afraid, like any other man active in politics, that he might meet someone there to whom he had done an injury on some other occasion; he had also been deceived by this man's mother, who had sworn to him that, if he offered her the chance to make a sworn statement on this question, she would decline the offer, and once that was done it would be an end of the matter, and there would be no more trouble. Accordingly he saw to it that she received some money, and offered her the oath to swear. But instead of declining the offer, she accepted it and declared under oath that not only the man here in court but his brother also were my father's sons. When this happened, my father had no choice but to introduce the boys to the phratry—there was no point in arguing about it. He introduced them, formally adopted them as his sons, and (I will not give all the details) registered them in the phratry at the feast of the Apaturia, this man under the name of Boeotus, the other under the name Pamphilus (I had already been registered as Mantitheus). My father, as it happened, died before he could have them registered in the deme; and this man goes along to the members of the deme, and registers himself, not as Boeotus, but as Mantitheus. It will be my task to show you how much damage he does, first to me, then to you, the citizens of Athens, by behaving as he has done" (39.3—5).

It is more important for the speaker to convince the jury that the defendant and his associates are undesirable characters, acting from discreditable motives, than to reveal what he may think are the true facts of the case. The result is that modern readers of the speech are uncertain whether his father was or was not married to Plangon, the daughter of Pamphilus. The speaker is also careful to avoid any remark about the legality of his father's behaviour if he registered as Athenian citizens two young men who may not have been his legitimate sons.⁴³ He never criticizes his father, and is careful not to show disloyalty to him—unlike the defendant who took advantage of his supposed father's vulnerability as a politician and is now hoping to get the better of his supposed brother by a shameless act of fraud. It has to be shown that this fraud is serious; and

---

42 Among its members he mentions Mnesicles and Menecles, "who got sentence passed on Ninus" (τὸν τὴν Νῖνον ἑλόντα). The same phrase occurs in 40.9. In 19.281 Demosthenes mentions a certain Glaucothea, who organized religious rites "on account of which another priestess was put to death," and according to a scholion on the passage (Oratores Attici, ed. Baiter-Sauppe, Zürich 1845—54, II 94) this priestess was Ninus, a reputed witch or sorceress. No more is recorded, but evidently the scandal was well known.
A notorious "underworld gang" (ἐργαστήριον μοχθηρῶν ἀνθρώπων) is mentioned in 32.10 (Chapter II, above, p. 53).

43 Cf. Chapter II above, pp. 58—59, with notes 28 and 29.

the jury may be persuaded to take a serious view of it if they are convinced that the man with whom Mantitheus is being forced to share his
name is a scoundrel, with no scruples and no respect for the law.

This seems to be the opinion that Demosthenes and his client
reached, and the speech is written on this basis. The speaker insists that he
is not greedy for money: "Over the matter of my father's estate I have
given in to them; although by rights it all belonged to me, when my father
adopted them I was willing to be content with taking only a third part of
it" (6). Boeotus, on the other hand, is represented as a greedy, shameless
sycophantes, and the portrait is developed in greater detail by comparing
him with his supposed father, Mantias. He obtained his share of the inheritance when his mother took advantage of Mantias' "simplicity" in
order to provide him with a father, and "he has brought two or three
actions against me in order to obtain money" (25). Mantias, as the jury
will remember, managed his financial affairs badly, and could hardly have
afforded to maintain two wives.[44] The jury might be disposed to think
that a malicious *sycophantes*, with his mind constantly on money, was
hardly likely to be the son of such a father.

The point is not argued, but the man's shamelessness needs further
demonstration. He rejected the name Boeotus, which he had obliged his
"father" to give him when he was registered in the phratry—"a strange
thing to say that Mantias was his father, and then take the bold step of
undoing what he did" (21). But his statement before the arbitrator was
"quite monstrous" ($\pi\rho\tilde{\alpha}\gamma\mu$' $\dot{\alpha}\nu\alpha\iota\delta\acute{\epsilon}\sigma\tau\alpha\tau\text{o}\nu$) — that his father celebrated his
"tenth day" after his birth and gave him the name Mantitheus at that
time; and the witnesses that he offered were "people in whose company
he had never been seen before" (22). It was sheer impertinence on his part
to think that his worthless witnesses would be believed, when reliable and
well-informed persons will testify that his mother subsequently introduced him into her tribe, not the tribe of Mantias—a thing she would
never have done if his "father" had celebrated his "tenth day" as he
asserted (24). Further lies (27) and further unpleasant characteristics are
attributed to him, leading to the conclusion that he is an "impossible
person" ($\tilde{\omega}$ $\chi\alpha\lambda\epsilon\pi\acute{\omega}\tau\alpha\tau\epsilon$ $\text{B}\text{o}\iota\omega\tau\acute{\epsilon}$, 34).

---

44 39.25–26. This passage cannot be used as evidence to support the belief that
bigamy was in some circumstances legal in Athens, as implied by Diog. Laert. 2.26
(cf. W. K. Lacey, The Family in Classical Greece, London 1968, 113, 142–45).
Demosthenes is merely saying that bigamy is "a rich man's hobby," not that it is
legal.

Another good contrast between plaintiff and defendant, in regular Demosthenic style, can be found at the beginning of the speech *Against Spudias* (41):[45]

"If I had not made every effort and tried my hardest to reach a settlement, leaving the decision in the hands of friends, I would have to blame myself for choosing the troublesome alternative of coming to court instead of agreeing to accept a small loss. But what has happened is that my efforts to be courteous and friendly in my approach to him only made him the more contemptuous of me. And our whole attitude towards coming to court seems to be quite different. He thinks nothing of it, since he has been accustomed to it by many appearances here; but what frightens me is that my lack of experience will make it impossible to explain things to you (41.1–2).

The brief narrative tells a strange story. Polyeuctus, who had two daughters but no son, adopted his wife's brother Leocrates, and gave him his younger daughter in marriage; his elder daughter was married to the speaker. Then Polyeuctus quarrelled with his adopted son: "I don't know why I should describe the quarrel, but he removes his daughter from Leocrates and gives her to Spudias. Leocrates was angry at this, and brought suit against Polyeuctus and Spudias; they had to come to a general settlement, and the final conclusion was that Leocrates should retain whatever property he had brought into the family and cherish no grudge against Polyeuctus; and that both parties should consider that all claims had been satisfied" (4).

No other instance is known of an adoptive father disinheriting his adopted son in this manner, taking away his wife,[46] and giving her to a new husband, and the speaker might have made the story easier to understand if he had told us something about the character of Polyeuctus or Leocrates or the reason for their quarrel. But he is interested only in explaining the character of Spudias, whom he accuses of robbing him of money that is due to him. Polyeuctus is now dead[47]; he had not been able to give the speaker the full amount of the dowry that was promised to him when he married the elder daughter; but before he died he had arranged for a house to be pledged to him as security for the ten minas that were still due, and so long as Polyeuctus was alive and Leocrates was

---

45 For the language and idiom of the speech see R. Ruehling, "Der junge Demosthenes als Verfasser der Rede gegen Spudias," Hermes 71 (1936), 441–51.

46 Instead of taking these words literally, we may believe that a divorce took place, on the wife's initiative, with her father's approval, as suggested by Burkhardt, De causa orationis adversus Spudiam Demosthenicae (Leipzig 1908), cf. Lipsius, Att. Recht, 518, n. 71. But we are not told that this is what happened, and Gernet is sceptical: "Nous ne sommes pas assurés que l'ἀπόλειψις fût permise à l'épouse d'un fils adoptif" (Plaidoyers civils II 52–54).

47 The *hypothesis* states dogmatically that Polyeuctus died ταῖς θυγατράσι καταλιπὼν τὸν κλῆρον ἐξ ἴσου, but gives no further explanation.

still in the picture,[48] there was no question or difficulty about it: "But Spudias will not allow me to receive the rent which it brings in" (5).[49]

But Spudias is not only mean and dishonest in refusing to part with the money, in contrast with the honourable attitude of Polyeuctus and Leocrates; it is revealed that he made no effort to pay debts which he owed to Polyeuctus and Polyeuctus' wife, and the conclusion is drawn that "he has no regard for the laws or the provisions of Polyeuctus' will or the documents or persons that bear witness to his obligations" (6). He is also represented as an ungrateful son-in-law, since he complained of the arrangements made by Polyeuctus (12), and worst of all he is "shameless." Just as Demosthenes, in prosecuting Aphobus, described the scene when his father was dying and entrusted his children to the care of their guardians (28.15), so here the speaker describes how Polyeuctus made his last will in the presence of Spudias and his wife. Spudias made no complaint at the time about its provisions, and his shamelessness in trying to evade them will be clear to the jury: "He knows the true facts just as well as I do, even better . . . but he is not ashamed to talk in a way that is in sharp contradiction with his behaviour" (24).

The speaker goes on to say: "Often, when you have recognized that one act of fraud was perpetrated, you have taken this as a sign that other complaints against the defendant are well founded. But in this case the defendant has convicted himself on every point" (24). He appears to be saying that in this case an appeal to the argument from probability (based on the defendant's past behaviour or his presumed character) is hardly necessary, but that in other cases the jury has considered argument from character as a substitute for direct evidence. It is a statement that should be borne in mind when reading *On the Embassy* and *On the Crown*.

In *Against Pantaenetus* the speaker is far from certain about all the facts, and it is particularly important for him to persuade the jury that Pantaenetus is a thoroughly unpleasant character, so that they will reconstruct the course of events in a way discreditable to him. The speaker and Evergus lent Pantaenetus money on the security of a mining operation at Maroneia in Attica. Evergus then became involved in a dispute with Pantaenetus which took them into court, and judgment was given in favour of Pantaenetus. Now when the speaker returns to Athens, after an absence of several years, he finds Pantaenetus ready to bring suit against

---

48 Before he "had withdrawn" (ἐξεκεχωρήκει), and ceased to be a member of the family.
49 According to the *hypothesis* Spudias insisted that the house must be regarded as common property to the two families. In that case, one might ask, why did he not allow the speaker one half of the rent? We are not told who is in possession of the house.

him, charging, among other things, that he gave instructions to a slave to damage his property.

The speaker counters with a *paragraphe*, maintaining that there is no basis for the suit, that the charges are ridiculous in view of his prolonged absence from Attica (23—24), and that "this is the most shameless example of *sycophantia* that has ever occurred in the Athenian courts" (3). He talks of meeting with Mnesicles[50] and other creditors of Pantaenetus and his inability to sort out the whole story of their experience ("everything was lies and confusion").[51] His main task is to show what an unpleasant person Pantaenetus is: "I recognized him for a person of bad character (κακοήθη, 16). I noted how from the start he abused Mnesicles in speaking to me. He had been on the most friendly terms with Evergus, and then quarrelled with him. And when I first landed in Athens, he professed to be delighted to see me, but dropped his friendly manner when he was faced with having to pay what he owed. In fact, he was anyone's friend until he got the advantage of them and obtained what he wanted, after which he turned against them and quarrelled with them" (15).[52]

The time has now come to reveal the true intentions of Pantaenetus. He is trying to ruin the speaker, Nicobulus, by grossly malicious charges. He has asserted that Nicobulus sent a slave to rob one of his slaves who was taking money to Athens in part payment of a mining concession, so that when the money failed to arrive he (Pantaenetus) was entered as owing the treasury twice the amount. Nicobulus pulls this accusation to pieces, insisting that its lies are stupid (24) as well as "shameless" (27), but does not take time to answer other accusations (Pantaenetus has accused him of fraudulent dishonesty towards members of his own family, as well as *hybris* and violence).[53] He prefers to emphasize the difference

---

50 It was Mnesicles who had induced the speaker to take over the mining property that Pantaenetus had pledged to him as security for a debt. He is said to have "sold us" the property (11), because in this kind of transaction giving security takes the form of a sale—πρᾶσις ἐπὶ λύσει, cf. Lipsius, Att. Recht, 692—93; Gernet, Plaidoyers civils I 225—26. The property formally changes hands, with the understanding that the repayment of the debt will redeem it. Thus the speaker talks of the *ergasterion* and the slaves ἃ ἡμεῖς ἐπριάμεθα παρὰ Μνησικλέους (12).

51 It appears that Pantaenetus borrowed further sums on the security of this property which was already pledged to the speaker and Evergus.

52 In "Against Aristocrates," in his account of the soldier of fortune's career, Demosthenes develops this characteristic at some length, to show that Charidemus is no true friend of Athens. Cf. Chapter II, above, pp. 68—73.

53 ἐνταυθὶ πόλλ' ἄττα καὶ δεινά μοι ἅμ' ἐγκαλεῖ καὶ γὰρ ἀείκειαν καὶ ὕβριν καὶ βιαίων καὶ πρὸς ἐπικλήρους ἀδικήματα (33). The charge of defrauding *epikleroi* (heiresses holding property in trust for their sons) is a charge of αἰσχροκέρδεια.

between himself and Pantaenetus, pointing out how scrupulously he has met his legal responsibilities.

In order to illustrate the gross *aselgeia* of his adversary (42), the same kind of violent contempt for the law that is attributed to Meidias, he tells the jury about "the gang of assistants" (τὸ ἐργαστήριον τῶν συνεστώτων) that Pantaenetus uses. With this gang as a kind of bodyguard, "he comes up to me and does a shocking thing. He reads out to me the text of a long challenge, asking that a certain slave, who (he says) has full knowledge of these matters be handed over to him for interrogation". The terms of the challenge were grossly unfair, but "wishing to have the full weight of justice on my side, I consented" (39–41). But instead of having the papers sealed and copies held by all parties, he produces a new text of the challenge and, without waiting for the official interrogator, starts handling the slave roughly himself.

An indignant outburst follows about the false front that Pantaenetus has tried to present to the world throughout his life, in contrast with the speaker's "simple and natural" behaviour.[54] Now that he has told the jury what kind of man Pantaenetus is, he can take for granted that all his successes in court have been won dishonestly, and he warns them: "When he deceived those jurors, do you suppose he would hesitate to deceive you?" (47). And he tells them more about the "gang" that is helping with false testimony: "This big fellow, Procles, a filthy, loathsome man, and Stratocles, the biggest and most plausible rogue. As for himself, he will have no scruples about bursting into tears and bewailing his lot" (48).

Nicobulus is a money lender, and Pantaenetus has taken advantage of the prejudice against money lenders: "Nicobulus, he says, is generally disliked; he walks fast and speaks in a loud voice, and carries a stick" (52). The speaker in *Against Dionysodorus* had defended the money lender's trade in a semi-humorous manner, preferring this indirect manner of self-defence.[55] Nicobulus treats the accusations more seriously, calls witnesses to speak in defence of his character, and justifies his way of doing business in an interesting attempt at self-portraiture:

"Now while I have full faith in the honesty of money lenders, I suppose that some of them are understandably disliked in Athens, when they make a business of lending money with complete disregard of human feeling or anything else so long as they make a profit. I have had personal experience of such people, because I have often borrowed money, besides lending it to Pantaenetus, and I don't like them, but that does not mean that I cheat them or harass them with dishonest lawsuits. A man

---

54 καὶ ἔγωγ᾽ ἐνεθυμήθην, ὦ ἄνδρες δικασταί, ἡλίκον ἐστὶ πλεονέκτημα τὸ κατα-πεπλάσθαι τὸν βίον· ἐγὼ γὰρ ἐμαυτῷ ταῦτα πάσχειν ἐδόκουν καταφρονούμενος τῷ ἁπλῶς καὶ ὡς πέφυκα ζῆν (43).
55 Cf. above, pp. 85–86.

like me, who has worked hard sailing the seas and risking his life, who has made a little money and invested it in a loan, since he wants to help someone else and at the same time not let the money go to waste, why should anyone class such a man among those people? Or do you insist that anyone who lends you money should be regarded as a public enemy?

I will ask the clerk to read out statements from witnesses, as evidence of my behaviour towards persons who have signed agreements with me and people who have sought my help" (53—54).

It is by contrast with his adversary that Nicobulus hopes to establish his own good character, and he turns to his own account this charge of "walking fast" and "speaking loud": "This is the kind of man I am (the man who walks fast), and this is the kind of man you are (the one who walks quietly). Now about my walk and my speech, gentlemen of the jury, I will be quite frank with you. I cannot deceive myself, I am well aware that in these respects I am not one of those men who have been blessed by nature, who can turn what nature gave them to their own advantage" (55). Apollodorus uses very similar language in the first speech *Against Stephanus* (45.77), comparing his own "natural" manner with the "pose" adopted by his adversary; if he "walks close to walls, with a surly expression on his face" (45.68), this is not a sign of modesty but an indication that he dislikes his fellow-men.[56] Nicobulus has complained constantly that Pantaenetus' accusations are irrelevant, and it may make a good impression at the end of his speech when he pleads guilty to some characteristic that is no fault of his own.

This small show of generosity and his portrait of himself as a modest and tolerant person prepares the way admirably for the final plea to the jury, which is based on a sound legal point. Pantaenetus had granted him a release from further claims and declared himself satisfied, and in such circumstances the law does not permit legal action to be renewed, even if a severe offence has been committed (58—60). The same plea, in a similar form of words, is used in *Against Nausimachus and Xenopeithes* (38.21—22), but is far less effective, because it lacks the preparation that leads up to it here.

In the speeches of the Demosthenic corpus which for one reason or another must be regarded as not genuine, no speaker is ever found who

---

56 οὐ τοίνυν οὐδ᾽ ἃ πέπλασται οὗτος καὶ βαδίζει παρὰ τοὺς τοίχους ἐσκυθρωπακώς, σωφροσύνης ἄν τις ἡγήσαιτ᾽ εἰκότως εἶναι σημεῖα, ἀλλὰ μισανθρωπίας, and this pretence of modesty is contrasted with the manner of people who walk ἁπλῶς ὡς πεφύκασιν (45.68). In similar manner the "false show" that Pantaenetus puts on is contrasted with the speaker's "natural" manner (37.43, see note 54 above). The similarity between these two passages has been taken as an indication that Demosthenes wrote Apollodorus' speech (cf. p. 86, note 29 above), but it is equally likely that this contrast of speech and gait is a *topos*.

uses this kind of vigorous character-painting as a substitute for detailed narrative. It is also only fair to notice that Demosthenes often uses it when his client has a weak case and seems to have little chance of winning it. If on the other hand a garrulous client provided a speech-writer with plentiful information, however irrelevant by modern forensic standards, the speech-writer's art consisted in arranging it into the kind of narrative that presented appropriate portraits.

In the speech *Against Conon*, which is written in a style reminiscent of Lysias, as ancient critics point out,[57] the narrative is presented in such a way that specific remarks about character are unnecessary. It is also full of relevant detail and free from irrelevancies. The story of the speaker's experience is easily intelligible without any need to remind listeners that this or that point deserves special attention, and it leads of itself to the conclusion that the speaker is a person of very different character from Conon. But undue emphasis on the contrast is perhaps tactically unwise, since the speaker might lose the sympathy of the jurors if he presented himself directly and deliberately as too "proper" a young man. His task is to tell his story modestly without any vigorous effort at self-justification, and this seems to be what the ancient critics mean by clever *ethopoiia*.

If a speaker is not sufficiently modest in talking about himself and his achievements, there is always the danger that he will irritate the jury and that his opponent will make him look ridiculous. Demosthenes feels it necessary to apologize for self-praise at the opening of *On the Crown* (18.3—4), and when he wants to show the good qualities of a client he usually does it by tacit comparison with the unpleasant characteristics of his adversary. Apollodorus, on the other hand, is a speaker who has no compunction about revealing what he thinks are good points in his own character, and there are no more egotistical speeches in the entire collection of Attic oratory. In the speech *Against Polycles* (50), when he wants to contrast his public spirit and generosity as a trierarch with the reluctance of his adversary to take over the trierarchy from him, his speech is full of what he did himself, in order to make the other man appear mean and irresponsible.[58] In fact he makes himself appear over-indulgent and lavish, and it becomes only too clear why Polycles was unwilling to take over a crew which had been pampered by an indulgent captain.

---

57 Cf. Chapter II, above, pp. 59—60.
58 What he does is to tell "the whole story from the beginning," explaining how much money he spent beyond the line of duty, so as to have a good crew and a splendidly equipped ship (50.7—9), how he had to borrow money to raise cash (13, 17) and so on; and he explains that his object in telling all this story is to show how generously he gave his services (21).

His contrast between himself and his adversaries is more effective in *Against Nicostratus*. He has taken the unpopular step of "informing against" Nicostratus, making an official report that certain slaves are not his legal property, but the property of Arethusius, and subject to seizure by the state, since Arethusius is in debt to the treasury. No litigant wants to be a thought a trouble-maker or a *sycophantes*, and the author of the *hypothesis* comments: "Since this procedure is disagreeable and likely to arouse antagonism, there is a narrative of the injuries he has received from Arethusius, to make it clear that his legal action is taken not because he is malicious, but because he has good reason to take vengeance."[59] Apollodorus is quite frank about his desire for revenge and says he "has not half time enough" to describe all the villainous things that Nicostratus and Arethusius have done (3). He makes much of the ingratitude of Nicostratus, his former neighbour in the country, with whom at one time he had been on the best of terms: "There was nothing I would not do for him, and he was helpful to me, looking after my property when I was away" (4). But now, after he has rescued Nicostratus from captivity, when he was captured by an enemy ship and held prisoner in Aegina, threatened with a life-time of slavery and suffering terrible hardships (he had to borrow money to find the ransom to buy the poor man's freedom!)—he finds Arethusius and Nicostratus conspiring to play a whole series of dishonest tricks on him; Arethusius once actually attacked him on the road from the Piraeus and tried to throw him into a quarry (17).

The details are piled up, to illustrate the ingratitude and "shamelessness" of his opponents, their greed for money and disregard for the law —the usual picture—while the speaker represents himself as loyal and generous to his friends, scrupulous and public-spirited in recognizing his civic obligations. Apollodorus confirms what Demosthenes seems to be telling us about the average man's sense of personal values in Athens;[60] the "good citizen" emerges as a standard type just as simply conceived as the shameless semi-criminal type.

---

59 ἵνα δοκῇ μὴ φύσει πονηρὸς ὢν ταῦτα πράττειν, ἀλλ᾽ ἀμυνόμενος τὸν ἀδικοῦντα (53, Arg.). As the language of the *hypothesis* shows, it was still recognized in later antiquity that legal procedure "in the public interest" was regarded more sympathetically if the plaintiff had a personal grievance against the defendant.

60 There are numerous indications in Thucydides and the dramatists that Athenians in the fifth century applied these standards of conduct, and it is perhaps hardly surprising that the orators of the fourth century should write as though Socrates had never questioned their validity as ethical criteria. Cf. L. Pearson, Popular Ethics in Ancient Greece (Stanford 1962), esp. chaps. 5—7 and, as an introduction to a study of the fourth-century attitude, "Popular Ethics in Fourth Century Greece," Arts, Journal of the Sydney University Arts Association 5 (1968), 16—29.

Aeschines and Meidias are the two men whom Demosthenes is determined to portray in the blackest possible colours, to show that they are unfit for the responsibility of public office. And he devotes special care to their portraiture. Aeschines deserves special treatment, and the final chapter of this book will be devoted to *On the Embassy* and *On the Crown*. But the present chapter may suitably finish with some consideration of the portrait of Meidias. He is given the usual semi-criminal qualities of *hybris, aselgeia,* and *anaideia,* and he tries to be more powerful than the laws (66); there is something about him that suggests the slightly superhuman or sub-human tyrant rather than a mere opportunistic politician. From the very start of the speech *Against Meidias* he is made to appear more like a monster than a man, and everything that he does is on a gigantic scale.[61]

Demosthenes begins by telling the jury: "I imagine you all know the *aselgeia* and the *hybris* with which he treats everyone" (1). He also takes for granted that they approve of his procedure in indicting Meidias by *probole,*[62] "because I was not only assaulted by him at the Dionysia, but suffered many other brutalities from him throughout the time that I was choregus" (1). Everyone has urged him not to relent in prosecuting such a "fearless, loathsome, and totally intolerable person," and he takes the chance to indicate, by comparison, what he is like himself. He has no need to explain his strong feelings, since he is not merely avenging a personal grievance but helping the entire Athenian public to exact just punishment from a man who "has committed an assault not only on me, but on you and the laws and the entire population" (7). He cannot be ready to forgive or compromise, like so many speakers in private actions: "I have kept faith with you, men of Athens. I am here, as you see, to prosecute the case. I might have been content to take the large sums that were offered to me if I would drop the matter, but I refused them; I had to face many requests, many tempting offers, yes, and threats as well" (3).

Demosthenes, then, is obliged by his responsibility to the public to be firm and unyielding, but the gentleness and forbearance of the general

61 Cicero follows a similar method in the "Verrines," and it is by no means impossible that the figure of Verres owes something to Demosthenes' Meidias. Cf. L. Pearson, "Cicero's Debt to Demosthenes: the Verrines," Pacific Coast Philology 3 (1967), 49–54.

62 The procedure of προβολή was the correct method of raising a complaint about an offence against the festival. The first step was to hand in the complaint to the prytany of the Council (this was προβάλλεσθαι), after which the matter would be put before a meeting of the Assembly and a formal preliminary vote passed (in this case it "condemned" Meidias); this preliminary vote had only formal value, but was expected to have a great influence in determining how the jury voted when the case came to trial. For details see Lipsius, Att. Recht, 211–19; Bonner & Smith, The Admin. of Justice, II 24–25.

public can be contrasted with the violence of Meidias. The special rules of the Dionysiac festival, as laid down by law, are read out, and the comment is made: "And so, men of Athens, you, the people, have gone so far in gentleness and piety as to suspend for the duration of these days the right of exacting satisfaction for misdeeds previously committed; but Meidias will be shown to have done, on these very days, things that deserve the extreme penalty" (14). It is an ingenious device to compare Meidias with his public victim. It enables Demosthenes to be sparing with remarks of self-pity or self-praise, and he makes his grievance seem less personal by associating himself with the public which has suffered as much as he has.

This comparison leads into the narrative,[63] and the tale is told economically without any insistence that Meidias reveals his character by his constant disregard for the sacred character of the festival. But it is noted that many people in the past, whom Meidias had mistreated in one way or another, decided that legal action against him would be too dangerous—because of his arrogance, his wealth, and the friends he had attending on him (19—20). Unlike these people, who apparently "thought it was in their interest to make a private settlement", Demosthenes is concerned not with suiting his convenience or with collecting damages, but with maintaining the law and protecting the rights of the public (40).[64] It is still the Athenian people that represents forbearance, in contrast with the arrogance of Meidias. Even the law about *hybris*, which protects the slave as well as the free man, is upheld as an example of Athenian *philanthropia* (48).

Meidias, like the defendants in the case *Against Conon*,[65] is expected to complain that far too much fuss is being made about a minor matter and that he is the victim of absurd legalistic intolerance, and since Demosthenes cannot play the part of gentle forbearance, he insists constantly that the law, which demands a severe penalty, is fundamentally "philanthropic" in character. He says remarkably little about his own character in the early part of the speech. Even when the opportunity offers to show his public spirit, in volunteering to undertake the *choregia* (13), he passes it by, and he says nothing about the money he spent in giving his chorus magnificent costumes (as one might have expected Apollodorus to do, if he had written the speech).

In fact, instead of developing the contrast between himself and Meidias, it is the contrast between the *hybris* of Meidias and the *philan-*

---

63 Cf. Chapter II, above, pp. 61—63.
64 πᾶν γὰρ τοὐναντίον ἐκείνοις αὐτὸς μὲν οὔτε λαβὼν οὐδὲν οὔτ' ἐπιχειρήσας λαβεῖν φανήσομαι, τὴν δ' ὑπὲρ τῶν νόμων καὶ τὴν ὑπὲρ τοῦ θεοῦ καὶ τὴν ὑπὲρ ὑμῶν τιμωρίαν δικαίως φυλάξας καὶ νῦν ἀποδεδωκὼς ὑμῖν (40).
65 Cf. Chapter II, above, pp. 60—61.

thropia of Athenian law which is developed further. The law forbids certain persons to take an active part in festival performances, for example, persons who have lost their civic rights because of some misfortune which brought on the legal penalty of disenfranchisement. But such is the *philanthropia* of the law and its concern for the peace and order of the festival, that a choregus who wishes to challenge the civic status of one of his rival's performers must pay a fine for violating the truce of the festival. Instances are known of skilled performers who have been engaged illegally; and an example is recalled of an occasion when no choregus dared to interfere, because he could not stop the man from performing unless he came out and took him by the arm and led him away: "And from this personal assault everyone shrank. Is it not strange, is it not shocking? Those choregi thought they might have won the competition, if it had not been for this man performing; they had perhaps spent all that they possessed on their contribution to the festival; yet not one of them dared lay hands on a man, though the law permitted it. So strict, so pious, so proper was their attitude, that despite the money they had spent and the strain of the competition they had endured, they had a higher regard for the wishes of the people and the solemnity of the festival. But Meidias, a private individual, who has spent no money, just because he has quarrelled with a man and is at odds with him, assaults him, a choregus with full civic rights who is spending money on the festival—assaults him and strikes him, with no thought for the festival or the laws or for what the people will say or for the god!" (60–61).

The rhetorical *amplificatio* of the passage[66] would catch the attention of every experienced listener; it is not only the enormity of Meidias' offence that is heightened, but his unpleasant character. He has no excuse like drunkenness or erotic passion, that might earn him sympathy, not even the fear of losing or wasting money, since he is a rich man. "Shamelessness" is the only word for his behaviour (εἰς τοῦτ᾽ ἀναιδείας, 62). Further *amplificatio* follows and comparison with other examples of assault in a public place. Finally Demosthenes brings himself back into the argument, remarking how lucky it was that he did not attempt to defend himself or hit back (74). The opportunity to compare his self-restraint

---

66 In orthodox rhetorical form, the *amplificatio* would be worked out as follows: "If it was reprehensible for a choregus, who had spent money in the hope of winning a prize, to take someone by the arm who had no right to be there, even though the law would have permitted him to take such action, how much worse that Meidias, a man with no official position, with nothing to gain by intruding, should come forward without any just *prophasis*, and not just take by the arm, but strike and προπηλακίζειν a choregus, who had every right to be there and who was spending his money in the service of the city." Cf. Blass, Att. Bered. III 333–34.

with the brutality of Meidias is plain to see, but even now he hesitates to call himself *sophron* and prefers to think it was lucky that he restrained himself,[67] because the only way to deal with *hybris* and *aselgeia* is through the courts (76).

He has returned to these key words with which the speech opened, and now he goes back to earlier years to describe how the quarrel between them started (through no fault of his), and this enables him to show that Meidias was an equally unpleasant person many years ago. When Demosthenes was involved in the struggle with his guardians, Meidias appeared suddenly with his brother and challenged him to undertake a trierarchy or accept an exchange of property (*antidosis*). If Demosthenes had accepted the *antidosis*, he would apparently have surrendered control of the case against Aphobus along with his property, and so he decided to take the trierarchy and put up the money which would cover its cost, in order to be able to press his charges against his guardians.[68] But Meidias and his brother showed their character by their offensive behaviour. They pushed their way unceremoniously into the house,[69] tore down the doors, as though the property had already been transferred, and used obscene language in the presence of Demosthenes' young sister, "the sort of language that you might expect from such men" (79). Meidias' career of *hybris* and *aselgeia* had already started, and Demosthenes was learning the ways of the law (78–81). He hopes some of the jurors will remember how this "plot" was contrived.[70]

67 καὶ ἐμαυτὸν μέν γε, ὦ ἄνδρες Ἀθηναῖοι, σωφρόνως, μᾶλλον δ' εὐτυχῶς οἶμαι βεβουλεῦσθαι, ἀνασχόμενον τότε καὶ οὐδὲν ἀνήκεστον ἐξαχθέντα πρᾶξαι (74).

68 The purpose of the legal manoeuvre is explained more clearly in 28.17: ἵν' εἰ μὲν ἀντιδοίην, μὴ ἐξείη μοι πρὸς αὐτοὺς ἀντιδικεῖν, ὡς καὶ τῶν δικῶν τούτων τοῦ ἀντιδιδόντος γιγνομένων, εἰ δὲ μηδὲν τούτων ποιοίην, ἵν' ἐκ βραχείας οὐσίας λειτουργῶν παντάπασιν ἀναιρεθείην. There is no mention here of Meidias or his brother; Demosthenes tries to obtain a hearing, but making no progress and not having time to spare, raises money on the security of the house to pay for the trierarchy. The legal details about *antidosis* are not as clear as one might like them to be. Cf. Lipsius, Att. Recht, 590–99; W. A. Goligher, "Studies in Attic Law, II," Hermathena 14 (1907), 481–515; and Gernet, Introduction to Oration 43, Budé ed., Plaidoyers civils II 71–75.

69 εἰσεπήδησαν ἀδελφὸς ὁ τούτου καὶ οὗτος εἰς τὴν οἰκίαν, ἀντιδιδόντες τριηραρχίαν (78). The challenge and the offer of exchange is in the name of Thrasylochus (cf. 28.17), but "it was Meidias who arranged everything."

70 καὶ ταῦτ' ἐστὶ μὲν παλαιά, ὅμως δέ τινας ὑμῶν μνημονεύειν οἴομαι· ὅλη γὰρ ἡ πόλις τὴν ἀντίδοσιν καὶ τὴν ἐπιβουλὴν τότε ταύτην καὶ τὴν ἀσέλγειαν ᾔσθετο (80). "Plotting" is a serious accusation. Cf. the emphasis on ἡ ὅλη ἐπιβουλή in "Against Zenothemis" (32.2) and the "plot" that Nicobulus is supposed to have devised against Pantaenetus (37.23). Meidias' plan to destroy the chorus' costume is also described as a "plot" (ἐπεβούλευσεν, 16). Demosthenes makes sure that the jury will not forget the *hybris* and *aselgeia* of Meidias "not only against me and my family," ἀλλὰ καὶ εἰς τοὺς φυλέτας δι' ἐμέ (81). Cf. 88, 92, 97, 98, 99, 100.

Next comes the story of the unfortunate arbitrator Straton, a worthy and absolutely honest man, but neither wealthy nor ambitious for public prominence (πένης μέν τις καὶ ἀπράγμων, 83). He was trying to settle the difference between Demosthenes and Meidias, and Meidias, despite threats and an offer of money (fifty drachmas!) could not make him alter the verdict he had given against him. On the very last day of the arbitrators' term of duty, Straton (like many others) did not put in an appearance, and Meidias contrived, by dubious means, to get a sentence passed against him *in absentia* which deprived him of civic rights (87). Here was a shocking example not only of his *aselgeia* and his contempt for the law but also of his extreme cruelty; and, as later in the theatre, it was not any large sum of money that he stood to lose—a mere thousand drachmas, which he never paid anyhow (88–91). Poor Straton, a pathetic, speechless figure, who can just stand up on his feet, is introduced into court, to show what happens to an honest, poor man who tries to stand up to this rich bully. If he had been less scrupulous, he might have accepted Meidias' fifty drachmas and been left in peace.

Demosthenes takes full advantage of the ethical relevance of the contrast between these two. Men must expect life to reward them according to the contribution that they make to it: "For example, I am modest and merciful in my relations to other men, I give help to many; it is appropriate that everyone should repay such a man in kind if the occasion occurs,"[71] but Meidias is "a violent person, without pity for anyone, who does not even regard his fellow man as a human being" (101), he expects people "to lick his boots when he insults them" (προσκυνεῖν τοὺς ὑβρίζον-τας, ὥσπερ ἐν τοῖς βαρβάροις, 106). What right has he to expect mercy when he shows none? The quality of cruelty has now been added to his *hybris* and his shamelessness and his expectation that money can accomplish anything that he wants (109).[72] He is also a *sycophantes*, who exploits the resources of the law without regard for justice or truth, as shown not only by his treatment of Straton, but by his attempts to accuse Demosthenes of dodging military service and even of murder (103–105).

---

71 ἐγὼ οἶμαι πάντας ἀνθρώπους φέρειν ἀξιοῦν παρ᾽ ἑαυτῶν εἰς τὸν βίον αὐτοῖς ἔρανον παρὰ πάνθ᾽ ὅσα πράττουσιν. οἷον ἐγώ τις οὑτοσὶ μέτριος πρὸς ἅπαντάς εἰμ᾽, ἐλεήμων, εὖ ποιῶν πολλούς. ἅπασι προσήκει τῷ τοιούτῳ ταῦτ᾽ εἰσφέρειν, ἐάν του καιρὸς ἢ χρεία παραστῇ (101). An *eranos* can mean a loan without interest, given as an act of friendship; but the passage seems to suggest something like contributions to a "benevolent fund," which give the contributor the right to assistance when he needs it. Cf. Gernet's note in the Budé ed. The sentiment is repeated in 184–85.
72 τί γὰρ ὡς ἀληθῶς πέρας ἂν φήσειέ τις εἶναι κακίας καὶ τῶ᾽ ὑπερβολὴν ἀναιδείας καὶ ὠμότητος καὶ ὕβρεως; (109).

The next step is to show that he has no regard for religion, that he is impious (ἀσεβής). His attempt to transfer the charge of killing Nicodemus from Aristarchus to Demosthenes is called "an act of impiety" (104),[73] but it is not until later that we see exactly what is meant. It is "impious" to accuse a man of murder and nevertheless permit him to do things that could not possibly be tolerated if the man really had the stain of blood on his hands. Though he accused Demosthenes of murder, he did nothing to stop him from officiating at religious ceremonies and offering sacrifice on behalf of the city (114–115). But since there was not a shadow of truth in the accusation, this was less serious impiety than his treatment of Aristarchus. One day he enjoyed his hospitality, next day he called him a murderer in the Council, next day he went back again to his house, took him by the hand, and perjured himself swearing that he had said nothing to hurt him. This is real "impiety", to call a man a murderer and then deny having made the charge, and to risk the infection of blood-guilt by entering the house of a man whom one has charged with murder (120).

Demosthenes offers to answer any questions the jury may want to ask about these incidents or other episodes in the life of Meidias, since he has copious notes and is willing to read from them "for as long as you wish to listen" (130). But the monstrous side of Meidias' character is complete, and it only remains to add the finishing touch that will make the portrait credible. Meidias has some lesser faults which make him at the same time human and ridiculous. For example, he is a persistent fault-finder. He complained that the cavalry regiment with which he served on an expedition to Euboea was "a disgrace to the city" (132). But he was hardly in a position to complain after doing his best to avoid serving with them and making an absurd exhibition of himself on the campaign; he never put on his breastplate, rode on a silver saddle, and carried around a collection of expensive clothes and cups and casks of wine, which the customs officers confiscated. At least that is the story that circulated; true or not, people were ready to believe it of a man like Meidias (133–134).

What makes Meidias ridiculous is that he is boastful, ostentatious, and a coward. In his speeches in the Assembly he likes to talk proudly of his generous public services—which, on closer examination, turn out to be more imaginary than real (154–155). He built an enormous house at Eleusis, and his wife drives to the mysteries in a carriage drawn by a team

---

73 ὃ καὶ δεινόν, ὦ ἄνδρες Ἀθηναῖοι, καὶ σχέτλιον καὶ κοινὸν ἐμοὶ γ' ἀσέβημα, οὐκ ἀδίκημα μόνον, τούτῳ πεπρᾶχθαι δοκεῖ, τοῦτ' ἐρῶ ... καὶ οὔτε θεοὺς οὔθ' ὁσίαν οὔτ' ἀλλ' οὐδὲν ἐποιήσατ' ἐμποδὼν τοιούτῳ λόγῳ, οὐδ' ὤκνησεν (104). Demosthenes never mentions Nicodemus, but Aeschines says he was responsible for the charge of evading military service and that Demosthenes employed Aristarchus to get rid of him (2.148).

of white horses; and he has the habit of making a pompous progress through the Agora, with three or four attendants, making loud remarks about his valuable possessions (158). But any claim to gallantry as a cavalry officer is totally absurd[74]. He could not sit a horse well enough to ride through the Agora in a procession (171) and he never owned a horse of his own, for all his display of wealth (174). It is true that he did make a gift of a trireme to the navy, and he boasts about it constantly (160); but it was a long time before he produced it, and it was only to avoid service with the cavalry on an expedition that might have been dangerous; he never sailed on board his own ship until his cavalry regiment was called out for active service, and then "this miserable coward deserted his post and went on board his ship" (164). The opportunity of comparing him with some braver and less fortunate Athenians is not passed by (165).

Many elements in this portrait of Meidias will be repeated in the portrait of Aeschines—pomposity, boastfulness, love of his own voice, constant public speaking but never to any good purpose, fault-finding (the word βασκανία is used constantly in the later speeches, but not in *Against Meidias*), and a painful, though absurd, unwillingness to face danger and responsibility. The final result, in both cases, is more like a caricature than a portrait, and the resemblances should warn us not to take it very seriously.

The picture is built up with quite alarming skill, so that every detail serves its purpose, but we are forced to conclude that Demosthenes is not even trying to present a realistic portrait in these speeches or in any of the speeches where he vilifies an opponent. There is something highly conventionalized about the various character sketches in this rogues' gallery, but taken individually it is easy to believe that each one of them had a devastating effect.

---

74 *Hybris* is the only word to describe what he did—a man like Meidias denouncing the regiment publicly in a speech to the Assembly (132, 135). His *hybris* and *aselgeia* continue to be emphasized (137, 138, 140, 143), and other words to describe his behaviour are φρόνημα (131), λοιδορία (132), θρασύτης (132), φιλοπραγμοσύνη (137), ὑπερηφανία (137), ἀηδία, ἀναισθησία (153).

Chapter IV

Argument and Advice: Addresses to the Assembly

i. First Group

On the Symmories, For the Megalopolitans, On the Freedom of the Rhodians

Demosthenes' reputation as a speech-writer was solidly established before he made his first speech in the Assembly in 354, but there is no indication that he had spoken very often in the courts himself. Apart from his early litigation with his guardians, he is reported to have delivered the oration *Against Leptines* himself, and he may have spoken *On the Trierarchic Crown*, though the evidence is not conclusive.[1] It is not known that he delivered any other forensic speech during these years; the speech *Against Meidias*, if it was in fact delivered, belongs to the year 347. But experience in the courts was a different thing from addressing the Assembly. We need not believe that a better delivery and a changed manner on the platform are the only reasons for his subsequent success after an initial failure. Whatever the difference in the manner of delivery, the *First Philippic* and the *Olynthiacs* are strikingly different in style from the earlier speeches.[2] The written text by itself reveals the increased confidence he feels and his command of the task that he faces. We should try to discover, if we can, the stages by which he learned the best way of adapting his forensic method to a "deliberative" political speech.

A new speaker in the Assembly has to introduce himself like a speaker in the courts, and in *On the Symmories* Demosthenes distinguishes himself from speakers who praise the Athenians of former times and try to "win a reputation for skill in oratory" (14.1). This manner of introduction, which recalls passages in Thucydides and Isocrates,[3] is comparable to the introduction that he often uses in private speeches, as a way of telling the jury that the speaker is not a professional orator and will present the facts of the case without any flights of rhetoric. But here

---

1 Cf. Blass, Att. Bered. III 243, 264—66, Pickard-Cambridge, Demosthenes, 40, 117, Jaeger, Demosthenes, 65.
2 Cf. Chapter I above, pp. 23—24, and also L. Pearson, "The Development of Demosthenes as a Political Orator," Phoenix 18 (1964), 95—109.
3 Cf. Chapter I above, pp. 24—27.

he does not explain the real point of the comparison with other speakers. Does he mean that those who praise the men of old are urging the Athenians to behave "in a manner worthy of their ancestors" by making a bold attack on the Persian king?[4] Instead of making his point clear, he thrusts it aside: "In my case I shall try to tell you of the manner in which, as it seems to me, you should make military preparation" (2). Once this is understood, he says, "all our immediate alarm will disappear," but he must first make "a few preliminary remarks about our relations with the King."

A speaker in the courts normally begins by explaining the situation; he has to tell the jury how he has been wronged before he asks them to restore his rightful property or avenge the outrage he has suffered. His order of topics is: "My adversary, injustice, restoration or punishment by a just verdict." But here Demosthenes starts talking about the solution before he has explained what the trouble is. He does not begin by saying "As you are aware, relations with the King have become strained," in the manner of a litigant who begins, "My adversary has treated me abominably." If he was following the usual pattern of a forensic speaker, his order of topics would be: "The King, a dangerous situation, a policy that will restore confidence." But instead of the order βασιλεύς, φόβος, παρασκευή, we have παρασκευή, φόβος, βασιλεύς.

In contrast with a forensic speech the lack of descriptive detail is quite remarkable. We are not told what the King has done, why Athenians are alarmed, what exact purpose will be served by a policy of rearmament.[5] There is no equivalent to the narrative that is generally necessary in a forensic speech, and Demosthenes makes haste to set forth his own opinions:

"I think it is expedient to wait and make sure that when you start war the step is an honourable one and a just one. But you must make all necessary preparations; that is the basis on which everything else rests" (3).

These are very proper sentiments, and he goes on to say that if the King makes a clear aggressive move he will unite all Greeks against him, but if Athens provokes him by taking the initiative, he will be able to make friends among the Greeks (if he spends money in the right quarter). Athens should not tolerate Persian imperialist designs, but if proper preparation is made and nothing foolish done in haste, a defeat in war

4 Cf. e.g. Pickard-Cambridge, Demosthenes, 119–20, and Croiset's note in the Budé edition.
5 Cf. Chapter I above, pp. 29–31.

need not be feared (4–9). What he has not told us is why certain persons are asking for a declaration of war, and why war is not only foolish but cannot be justified.

He is equally uncommunicative about his political affiliations. His language does not indicate whether he is a supporter or an opponent of Eubulus or a man who has not yet thrown in his lot with either party.[6] He may wish to show his independence from party ties, but there is nothing in his introduction to make the audience think that his judgment in matters of armament and finance is worthy of respect. A litigant has to establish his personal integrity, not his experience in public affairs or his political judgment, and his use of the first person singular need not give an impression of egotism. But in a political speech an unknown speaker cannot take for granted that people will be ready to listen to his personal opinions. Here the statements of personal opinion—"I think that"—come one after the other. The word ἐγώ occurs with remarkable frequency in the opening paragraphs; as time goes on, Demosthenes will learn to use it more sparingly.[7]

Once the preliminary question of "relations with the King" has been settled in this dogmatic manner, the plan for rearmament is presented more modestly and the first person singular is no longer so prominent.[8] Demosthenes insists that every man must meet his responsibility, that the right attitude is all-important,[9] and then offers his proposals for the organization of symmories and the building and manning of triremes and other details, after which he finishes with further arguments to prove that the Persian menace is not really serious (29–40).

The recommendations, with appropriate argument in support of each item, are made without any significant rhetorical embellishment, but the speech as a whole is dominated by a *logos-ergon* contrast in the Thucydi-

6 Cf. Chapter I above, p. 22. Cloché, Démosthènes, 44–45, thinks that the request for money to be spent on armament would be impossible for a member of the so-called "Eubulus party," but Jaeger, Demosthenes, 73–78, believes Demosthenes is still a faithful supporter of Eubulus and that the proposal to spend money on armament is not meant seriously—that the request for money was part of a design to damp down martial enthusiasm. It is not easy to believe that Demosthenes was so devious in his methods at this stage of his career.

7 There are about twice as many examples of it in sections 1–14 of "On the Symmories" as in the corresponding sections of Orations 15 and 16, but in the "First Philippic" the emphasis on self has almost disappeared, and Demosthenes now prefers to say that things "seem to him" rather than "I think."

8 There is a return to the "I think" style after section 31. Cf. 31, 32, 34, 35.

9 ἐστὶ τοίνυν πρῶτον μὲν τῆς παρασκευῆς, ὦ ἄνδρες Ἀθηναῖοι, καὶ μέγιστον οὕτω διακεῖσθαι τὰς γνώμας ὑμᾶς ὡς ἕκαστον ἑκόντα προθύμως ὅ τι ἂν δέῃ ποιήσοντα (14). The theme will recur in the "Olynthiacs."

dean manner.[10] It appears first in the opening sentence, which adapts the thought of Pericles in the Funeral Oration; most speakers who praise the dead cannot match the deeds of men of old with their words;[11] Demosthenes will therefore reject such *logoi* in favour of the more practical theme of *paraskeue*; he will do Athens a real service by offering a concrete proposal for military preparation.

He goes on to say that it is in the interest of Athens to wait until she can take up arms against Persia in the cause of justice, but she should nevertheless make "all necessary preparations" (3). There is no conflict here between justice and expediency, but he reminds them that there is a conflict between the private interests of individuals and "the common interest of all." The series of contrasts is elaborate, between word and deed, general and particular, intention and result, appearance and reality, the individual and the community. He is trying to show, as so often in his later speeches, that he has the true interests of Athens at heart and that his advice is valuable. But this sententious introduction is a poor substitute for a more straightforward attempt to catch attention and win the respect of his audience.

A distinctive quality about this speech, which all critics have noticed, is its Thucydidean "brevity" or concentration of expression. Not only are words used economically, sometimes at the expense of clarity, but the *cola* are shorter; each group of five or six words introduces enough new thought to justify a brief pause.[12] This means that, even though the speech is harder to follow, it puts less strain on the speaker, who has the opportunity to pause for breath quite frequently; and the pace of the speech is slower; it could be delivered in the manner that suits Thucydidean speeches. The *First Philippic*, by contrast, makes higher demands on the orator's technique, and perhaps reflects the intensive training to which Demosthenes is supposed to have submitted himself. The private orations, written as a rule for speakers with no particular experience or training, are not only easier to follow but easier to deliver; they are technically much less demanding. On the other hand their pace is not slow, because they are

10 It is strange that neither ancient nor modern critics of the speech have drawn attention to this.

11 οἱ μὲν ἐπαινοῦντες, ὦ ἄνδρες Ἀθηναῖοι, τοὺς προγόνους ὑμῶν λόγον εἰπεῖν μοι δοκοῦσι προαιρεῖσθαι κεχαρισμένον, οὐ μὴν συμφέροντά γ᾽ ἐκείνοις οὓς ἐγκωμιάζουσι ποιεῖν. περὶ γὰρ πραγμάτων ἐγχειροῦντες λέγειν ὧν οὐδ᾽ ἂν εἰς ἀξίως ἐφικέσθαι τῷ λόγῳ δύναιτο κτλ.

12 Hermogenes (Περὶ Εὑρέσεως IV 3, Spengel, Rhetores Graeci, II 241) says that a *colon* may vary in length from seven syllables to something longer than a dactylic hexameter. As an example of a long (and highly demanding) μονόκωλος περίοδος he quotes 1.24: εἶτ᾽ οὐκ αἰσχύνεσθε εἰ μηδ᾽ ἃ πάθοιτ᾽ ἂν εἰ δύναιτ᾽ ἐκεῖνος, ταῦτα ποιῆσαι καιρὸν ἔχοντες, οὐ τολμήσετε;
Nothing like this will be found in "On the Symmories." In fact, if one compares,

meant for delivery before a fairly small audience inside a building. When Demosthenes first started to speak in the open air before the Assembly, he would quite naturally think a slower pace would be necessary; and we might expect his pace to increase, as his technique improved and his self-confidence increased.

The structure of *On the Symmories* is simple enough, though he obscures the design by jumping to conclusions in the opening section. Blass calls its arrangement symmetrical,[13] since the central portion, which is concerned with means of rearmament, is preceded and followed by a discussion, in more general terms, of "relations with the King." The method and manner of argument is quite similar in the speech *For the Megalopolitans*. Demosthenes first compares himself with other speakers, but without any complex Thucydidean antithesis, and then goes on, in the same style as in the earlier oration:

"There are other matters which I want to explain to you later, if you are willing; but first of all I want to tell you what I think is best in the light of certain things which everyone will admit to be true" (3).

Just as everyone should admit that "the King is the common enemy of all," so here everyone should agree that neither Thebes nor Sparta must be weakened to such an extent that it will no longer be strong enough to act as a check on the other.[14] If Megalopolis is destroyed and Arcadia brought under Spartan control, that will make Sparta too strong.

In *On the Symmories* he had to be careful not to appear pro-Persian, and here he is careful to avoid giving the impression that he is pro-Theban; he is also careful to insist that, if they do intervene, their cause, their ἀρχὴ τοῦ πολέμου, must be a just cause; in contrast to the earlier speech, he maintains that if they intervene now, instead of waiting until Messene also is threatened, their concern for the Arcadians and for the preservation of peace will be recognized and respected.[15]

He also wants to tell the Athenians that they must not be deterred from the right course of action by their fear of losing the chance to recover Oropus, if they antagonize Sparta. He hopes to convince them that the recovery of Oropus is less important than maintaining the political organizations of Arcadia and Messenia. And he prepares the way for this conclusion very skilfully, saying that if Athens supports the Arcadians

for example, 14.8 with 1.8, it will be seen that the *cola* in the "First Olynthiac" cannot be broken up into *commata* so easily as in the earlier speech and will not allow the orator to take breath so frequently.

13 Att. Bered. III 278.

14 Demosthenes offers it as "something that no one would deny" that "it is not expedient for Athens that both Sparta and Thebes should be weak" (3–4).

15 16.9, cf. 14.3.

and helps them preserve their independence against Spartan attack, she will be following her traditional policy of helping victims of oppression (15). Using the same technique as in the law courts, he reinforces his point by blackening the character of Sparta. When Sparta has helped others to "recover what belongs to them," her motive has been purely selfish, not regard for justice but pure πλεονεξία (15). It would be a long time before Spartans ever showed any regard for the feelings of others (ὀψὲ γὰρ ἂν φιλάνθρωποι γεγονότες εἶεν, 16).

The advice which Demosthenes gave in *For the Megalopolitans* was not taken, partly because prejudice against Thebes had grown strong in the past fifteen years, and the anti-Spartan group in the Peloponnese turned to Philip for support, giving him the excuse that he needed for intervening south of the Isthmus. Critics of the speech have not been able to suggest better ways of presenting the case for intervention.[16] Those who complain that it lacks emotional impact should ask themselves whether a more emotional appeal would have been appropriate to the occasion.[17] Demosthenes states his case firmly and clearly and hence with more authority, as Maurice Croiset points out,[18] than was apparent in *On the Symmories*. Later in his career he might have analyzed the situation in greater detail, and it is interesting to compare his description in *On the Crown* of the "confusion and disunion" in the Peloponnese, as he saw it with subsequent events to guide him.[19]

The speech seems less theoretical and abstract than *On the Symmories*, because it explains the situation and the likely consequences more clearly. Its structure is very similar. The central portion (which is taken up with answering objections) is followed by a repetition of the arguments that made up the first part of the speech.

In *On the Freedom of the Rhodians* Demosthenes begins by complaining that it is easier to make a good proposal to the Athenians than to have it carried out. But instead of comparing his failure with the success of other speakers, he tells them that this time he has an attractive proposal to offer, that will give them the opportunity to refute accusations made against them and re-establish their good name. And in the manner of an angry litigant he attacks Mausolus, who said that he was a friend of the Rhodians and then went on to rob them of their freedom. The Rhodians cannot expect any help from Chios or Byzantium, and Athens will win all

---

16 Cf. e.g. Pickard-Cambridge, Demosthenes, 133.
17 Blass, who thinks that it is perhaps less well-written than "On the Symmories," complains that it lacks "ein höherer Aufschwung" without asking whether flights of emotional rhetoric would be appropriate here (Att. Bered. III 291).
18 Budé ed., Harangues, I 21.
19 18.18–19. Cf. p. 181 below.

the credit for saving them: "What greater blessing could you ask for? Good will without a taint of suspicion anywhere!" (3—4).

This is an introduction more in his later manner.[20] But instead of reinforcing his position with further description of their magnificent opportunity and further denunciation of Mausolus, he reminds the Athenians what good advice he gave them in the past and how they followed it. Later in his career he is always ready to ridicule Aeschines for taking pride in his speeches and claiming credit that does not belong to him, and he might be taken to task here for doing the same thing himself.[21] Only when he has finished patting himself on the back does he remind them that Athens will be following traditional policy and practice if she helps Rhodes to recover her freedom, and that preserving freedom in the islands is a prudent and feasible policy, as well as honourable and "just" (8—10). He is confident that their intervention will meet with very little resistance now that Mausolus is dead; an additional reason for intervention is that Artemisia, who has succeeded Mausolus as dynast of Caria, might not be able to keep the island out of the King's hands. It is their duty to save these people and "not cherish a grudge against them" (16).

Many people in Athens must have had bitter feelings towards the Rhodians, who had recently fought against them, and Demosthenes counters anti-Rhodian prejudice with anti-oligarchic prejudice. Artemisia had established an oligarchic régime in power, and he is on safe ground when he says: "It is just, men of Athens, that you who live under a democracy should show that you have the same regard for a democracy in trouble that you would like others to have towards you, if (perish the thought!) some disaster of this kind were to happen here" (21).

By a route neither rhetorically orthodox nor strictly logical he has found his way back to the theme with which the speech began, the opportunity offered to Athens to enhance her reputation, to save victims of oppression and rescue a democratic people from oligarchic rule in accordance with her traditional policy. He insists that it is "just" to intervene, but in case there are some people who cannot believe that aggressive intervention is ever "just," he tells the Athenians there are times when it is shameful to give "justice" as an excuse for inaction (29). This is an argument familiar from Thucydides and the dramatists, and it clears the way for an attack on politicians who want Athens to abandon her traditional policy.

---

20 The introductory remarks in "Olynthiacs" i and ii are in a similar vein.
21 Was the advice that he gave in "On the Symmories" actually followed? It is extremely doubtful. Cf. Chapter I, above, p. 35, note 61.

Like the plea for the Megalopolitans, this plea for intervention had small chance of succeeding, since Athenians would think that the dangers of involvement were greater than any advantages they might gain by it, and inaction would appear the safer course. It is perhaps arguable that greater coherence in argument would improve the speech, if a greater effort had been made to show definite advantages resulting to Athens if she helped to liberate the Rhodians. But it is doubtful if a less scrupulous speaker could have presented the prospect in such a way as to gain his point. Demosthenes is now trying harder to explain the problem and the challenge in terms of actual example from the past and observable detail from the present. His oratory will acquire more speed and movement when he offers more information and gives coherence to his argument by combining it with narrative.

Chapter IV

The Speeches in the Assembly Before 346

ii. Second Group:

First Philippic, On Financial Organization, First, Second, and Third Olynthiacs

All these speeches urge vigorous resistance to Philip. Demosthenes is equally insistent in all of them that Athenians must change their attitude towards using public money, their method of raising armaments, and their military strategy; he maintains that no specific measure will have any value, unless these fundamental changes are made. Once they are made, he expects individual proposals to emerge of themselves. Proposals which could take the form of a psephism are found only in the *First Philippic* and the *First Olynthiac*. He does not dare make a formal motion that the Theoric Fund be diverted to military purposes, since that would expose him to prosecution under a *graphe paranomon*.[1]

The *Olynthiacs* come before the *First Philippic* in all surviving manuscripts, and it is presumed that Callimachus put them in this order when he drew up his list of eleven "Philippic" orations.[2] But the *First Philippic* is clearly the first speech of the series, since it precedes Philip's attack on Olynthus in 349, which is announced in the opening sentence of the *First Olynthiac*. It probably belongs to 351.[3]

---

1 None the less he makes it plain in 1.19 that he thinks they should use the Theorica (though he does not actually mention its name) and in 3.10—11 he asks them to set up a legislative committee which will be able to repeal the law protecting this fund. In both these passages he is formally within the law; his words are evidently not grounds for action. Cf. below pp. 128 and 133.

2 For this list of Callimachus and his other *pinakes* see R. Pfeiffer, Callimachus, I pp. 344—49, esp. Frag. 443—46. The "Philippica" as listed by him evidently included the seventh oration ("On Halonnesus") and the eleventh ("Reply to Philip's Letter"), neither of which can be a genuine work of Demosthenes; and the "Letter to Philip", though certainly not a genuine document, was added as the twelfth item.

3 Spring 351 is the orthodox date, as Dionysius of Halicarnassus (ad Amm. 4) dates it in 352—51 (his belief that the second part of the speech, from 30 on, is a separate composition, has found no support in modern times). The only possible reference to any event later than 351 is in 17, where Demosthenes says that the triremes and horse-transport ships are needed ἐπὶ τὰς ἐξαίφνης ταύτας ἀπὸ τῆς οἰκείας χώρας αὐτοῦ στρατείας εἰς Πύλας καὶ Χερρόνησον καὶ Ὄλυνθον καὶ ὅποι βούλεται. Since we have no specific evidence for Philip's military interference at Olynthus until the

The *First Philippic* was delivered when some people still doubted Philip's hostility and had no suspicion that he was going to attack Olynthus. The situation in 349, when the *Olynthiacs* were delivered, is different, but it is not possible to distinguish the different situation at the time of each succeeding oration. Are the *Second* and *Third Olynthiacs* later than the *First* by days, weeks, or months, and can we be quite sure even that the *Second* is earlier than the *Third*?

The historian Philochorus, writing in the third century, recorded three separate efforts by the Athenians to save Olynthus, all unsuccessful (the last expedition arrived after the city had surrendered), and early commentators found it convenient to believe that each of these efforts was the result of one of the speeches.[4] It is a convenient solution, but there is no reference in any of the speeches to any military operation actually undertaken by the Athenians and no mention in any other speech of Demosthenes (or by Aeschines) of these speeches or the situations they were designed to meet. It has even been suggested that they were never delivered at all, but were circulated in pamphlet form, like the orations of Isocrates.[5] It is perhaps wiser to be content with thinking that the three speeches were delivered with quite short intervals between them.

attack in 349, a number of critics, following the lead of E. Schwartz, "Demosthenes' erste Philippika," in Festschrift f. Th. Mommsen (Marburg 1893), take this as a reference to his attack and date the speech in 349. Such a casual allusion to Olynthus, however, seems out of place at so late a date, and it is not difficult to believe that Philip made some demonstration there before 349. Jaeger is hardly accurate (Demosthenes, 116) in saying that it is now "customary" to prefer a later date than 351; an earlier date is regarded as certain not only by Blass (Att. Bered. III 300), but by Pickard-Cambridge (Demosthenes, 184, Autumn 351), Cloché (Dem. 73, Spring 351), and M. Croiset (Budé ed., Harangues I 32). For the most recent discussion see R. Sealey, "Dionysius of Halicarnassus and some Demosthenic dates," REG 68 (1955), 77–120, G. L. Cawkwell, "The Defence of Olynthus," CQ N.S. 12 (1962), 122–40, and J. R. Ellis, "The Date of Demosthenes' First Philippic," REG 79 (1966), 636–39 (he argues for January 350).

4 Dion Hal. ad Amm. 9–10 Philochorus, F. Gr. Hist. III A 328, F. 49–51. It is the scholiast (on the "Second Olynthiac") who represents each expedition as the result of one of the speeches: ἰστέον δὲ ὅτι φησὶ Φιλόχορος ὅτι τρεῖς βοήθειαι ἐπέμφθησαν, καθ' ἕκαστον λόγον μιᾶς πεμπομένης, ὡς τῆς πρώτης μὴ ἐξαρκούσης (Oratores Attici, ed. Baiter-Sauppe, II 55).

5 The "Flugschrift" theory was first developed in detail by E. Schwartz (see note 3 above), and taken up by various other German scholars. Cf. H. Bengtson, Gr. Geschichte (Munich 1950), 281. A very strong reply was made by C. D. Adams, "Are the speeches of Demosthenes to be regarded as political pamphlets?" TAPA 43 (1912), 5–22. For more recent discussion see H. Erbse, "Zu den olynthischen Reden des Demosthenes," Rh. Mus. 99 (1956), 364–80, who is inclined to think all three "Olynthiacs" were delivered in the course of a single meeting of the Assembly. M. Croiset, "Date de la troisième olynthienne," Mélanges Perrot (Paris 1903), 65–72, argued that the intervals between them cannot have been more than a few days. Cf. his note on Harangues I 90–91, and A. Momigliano, "Filippo il Mace-

The thirteenth oration contains no attack on Philip and was not included in the collection of *Philippics*, though it appears to belong between the *First Philippic* and the *First Olynthiac*. It contains a remark that the Athenians have voted to take action against the Megarians trespassing on the area of sacred land known as the Orgas (13.32), and in the *Third Olynthiac* it is mentioned that a military force has been sent out against the Megarians (3.20). Philochorus dated the Orgas incident in 350–49, and Didymus, like other ancient commentators, found no difficulty in accepting the speech as genuine.[6] It contains passages, however, which are almost identical with passages in the *Olynthiacs* and the speech *Against Aristocrates*, and its genuineness has been doubted in modern times by critics who are not prepared to believe that Demosthenes would repeat himself.[7] On the other hand it is a well written speech, its language reminiscent of the *First Philippic*, and it cannot be described as a patchwork of borrowed material. The present fashion, therefore, is to accept it as a genuine work of Demosthenes, while doubting if he actually delivered it. It shows no signs of being incomplete or unrevised, like the *Fourth Philippic*. It is useless to talk of "publication," since there is no evidence that Demosthenes ever "published" any of these political speeches.[8]

The purpose of the present discussion is to show how much these five speeches have in common, in sentiment, literary style, and vocabulary. It was in the course of preparing these speeches that Demosthenes developed into an influential and successful orator and found ways to adapt the methods he had used in forensic speeches. We should notice how he manipulates his arguments, how he meets opposition, and how he

done" (Florence 1934), 112–13, n.1. J. R. Ellis, "The Order of the Olynthiacs," Historia 16 (1967), 108–11, finds reasons (which are hardly convincing) for believing that the second speech preceded the first, but he does not decide by how long an interval.

There is no way of knowing how far and in what respects the revised written version may differ from the original spoken version. Some good suggestions are made by P. Wendland, "Beiträge zu Athenischer Politik und Publicistik, II, Isokrates u. Demosthenes," GGN, ph. hist. Kl. 1910, 289–91.

6 Didymus, In Dem. Comm. col.13, F. Gr. Hist. III A 328 F.158.

7 E. g. P. Foucart, BCH 13 (1889), 433–67. Cf. Blass, Att. Bered. III 401: "Daß nun die Rede so, wie sie ist, nicht von Demosthenes herrühren kann, ist fast allgemein zugestanden und in der That unzweifelhaft."

8 For discussion see M. Croiset, Budé ed., Harangues, I 70–73, who notes that Weil, in his stylistic analysis of the speech found nothing un-Demosthenic, and Jaeger, Demosthenes, 241–42 (n.24), who lists further bibliography. The Oxford text marks the speech as "spurious," like the "Fourth Philippic," but it is not clear what exactly is meant by this classification, that it was not written by Demosthenes, not delivered by him, or not intended for the eyes of the public.

presents an unpalatable conclusion in such a way that it can be neither ignored nor evaded.

Although the *First Philippic*, his first experiment with his new style, met with no great success, he must have soon made up his mind nevertheless that the change was for the better. The difference is immediately apparent in the introduction of the *First Philippic*, which is more modest and in the manner of a plaintiff who thinks it necessary to explain why he is bringing suit[9] —saying he would not have come forward if certain persons had been more reasonable, as in *Against Aphobus*:

"If Aphobus had been willing, gentlemen of the jury, to meet his obligations or to let members of the family settle our differences, there would be no need of litigation . . . But since he refused . . . I have no alternative but to try to obtain what is due to me in this court" (27.1).

Similarly in the first speech *Against Boeotus*:

"If this man claimed someone else as his father, and not *my* father, it might be thought that it was no business of mine by what name he chose to call himself, but as it is . . ." (39.2).[10]

This is the kind of conditional sentence with which he starts the *First Philippic*:

"If the subject proposed for discussion were a new one, men of Athens, I would have waited until most of the usual speakers had expressed their opinions; if I had been satisfied by some proposal of theirs, I would not have risen to speak; if I had not been satisfied, my turn to say what I thought would come after them. But since we are now discussing matters about which these men have often spoken in the past, I think I may be excused for being the first to come forward" (4.1).

The first task Demosthenes sets himself in the *First Philippic* is to change the attitude of the Assembly towards Philip (not their attitude towards himself, as a litigant might try to do, if he thought the jury felt some ill-will towards him). He tells the Athenians that they must recover their confidence, despite past mistakes and present difficulties (4.2), and that Athens has good precedent for recovering from such situations. He chooses his *paradeigmata* with care, recalling how splendidly they recovered from their defeat in the Peloponnesian War, how boldly they asserted themselves against a Spartan domination which weaker spirits might have thought invincible; and he invites them to compare the strength of Sparta in those days with "the present *hybris* of Philip" (4.3). Philip himself

9 The model, however, appears to be the opening of Isocrates, "Archidamus."

10 Cf. also the opening of "On the Trierarchic Crown" (51.1). Isaeus also likes his clients to present themselves as reasonable, patient men, who are willing to allow full credit and full freedom to others, but find themselves caught in a disagreeable situation. Cf. 2.1 and 10.1.

supplies another *paradeigma*; he had the courage and determination to overcome the troubles that he inherited at his accession (5–6).[11]

Demosthenes does not disguise the difficulty of the task or the austere prospect that the Athenians face, but he disarms opposition by describing it in terms which they cannot refuse to accept:

"If you are willing to become your own masters, and if each individual stops thinking he need never do anything himself but can expect his neighbour to do it" (7).

The speech reaches a quick conclusion by using a method of argument which allows no answer. Anyone who wants to recommend nonintervention or opposition by diplomatic means will have to ignore what Demosthenes has said and argue on totally different lines. He tells them that Philip is vulnerable, his subjects only too willing to rise against him if assured of some support, and that he is an arrogant threatening bully, like Meidias, whose reign of terror will collapse if it meets with determined opposition.[12] It is no use hoping that Philip will fall ill or die, because even if he does, unless they change their attitude, they will "make another Philip" (11). Demosthenes assumes that he has convinced his audience, and gives them no time to think:

"You recognize the facts, you are convinced that you must show yourselves willing and eager to take the right course. I shall not press the point. Now about the method of our military preparations . . ." (13).

The design for opposing Philip, as he explains it, is simple enough. Fifty triremes, with citizens prepared to man them, and triremes ready to transport cavalry; a hoplite force of two thousand, including five hundred citizens, and fast ships ready to ensure safe passage for them. *Paradeigmata* are offered to show that all will be well if there are citizens serving side by side with mercenaries, though a purely mercenary force will be inadequate (24). Citizens must be prepared to serve without pay, beyond what it costs to feed them, and on this basis it will cost ninety talents to maintain the armament. The speech as delivered included a written statement explaining how this sum was to be raised (πόρου ἀπόδειξις, 29),

---

11 The Athenians are particularly expected to notice the *paradeigma* of Philip's confident attitude (4.6).

12 His subjects are cowering in terror (κατέπτηχε, 4.8), because Athens will not move to help them; and Philip has reached such a point of *aselgeia* that he does not give Athenians the choice of remaining at peace, if they prefer it; and he sets traps for them (καὶ κύκλῳ πανταχῇ μέλλοντας ἡμᾶς καὶ καθημένους περιστοιχίζεται, 4.9) as if they were wild animals. Does this mean that Philip hardly thinks of his opponents as human beings, and that if they stop behaving like dumb animals, they can defeat him?

which has unfortunately not been preserved in our text.[13] The Athenians are told that everything will be easy "once you vote the change in attitude" (ἐπειδὰν ἐπιχειροτονῆτε τὰς γνώμας, 30).

Philip must be stopped, the chances of success are good, and they have been shown the kind of armament they need and how it can be maintained if they are willing to serve without pay. The next stage is to explain how much they can accomplish, if they put things into effect and keep a force always ready for action, within striking distance of Macedonia, based on Lemnos or Thasos or some other northern island. They will put a stop to those "sudden expeditions of his, to Thermopylae, to the Chersonese, to Olynthus and wherever he wants" (17); there will be no more incidents like "his invasions of Lemnos and Imbros, when he took Athenian citizens prisoner, his seizure of ships off Geraestus, which brought him a fantastic sum of money, and his landing at Marathon, when he took the sacred trireme away with him" (34). Systematic arrangements are needed to stop these raids of Philip. If military operations can be controlled by a law, they should run as smoothly as the ceremonies at the great festivals, and opportunities will not be missed, as they have been in the past (33–37).

Demosthenes interrupts his contrast between the errors of the past and the possibilities of the future by returning to the present, to remind them that Philip is really dangerous: "His *hybris* has reached such a point that he sends the Euboeans a letter like this" (37). The Athenians are warned against the politicians who try to mislead the people by concealing the disagreeable truth from them (38). They must not let themselves be deceived, they must anticipate events instead of being led by them, they must not let Philip keep the initiative, "fighting with him in the way that barbarians try to box," letting their hands fly to the places where they are hit, instead of putting up a guard (40–41).

He has been careful to tell them how their troubles can be cured before trying to shame them into action by this insulting comparison. Now he returns to the mood of optimistic fervour which marked the earlier part of the speech. They must recognize Philip's *hybris* not as a disaster but as an opportunity: "I think that some god, filled with shame at what was happening to Athens, put these aggressive designs into his head" (42). He reminds them of the decisions they have reached with him, warns them that Philip's ultimate aim is to attack Athens itself, and finishes by saying something about himself and the risk he is taking by speaking so freely:

13 A. Puech, "Les Philippiques de Démosthène" (Paris 1952), 65–66, supposes it was considered too technical in character to be worthy of publication, "et parce qu'il n'avait plus pour les lecteurs son intérêt d'actualité."

"I have said exactly what I think, concealing nothing. I know it is to your advantage to receive the best advice. I wish I were sure that it is to the advantage of the speaker who gives it. I should be much happier if I knew that. As things are, it is quite uncertain what will happen to me, but I have made my decision to tell you these things, because I know that it will be to your advantage to carry through this policy. May the future bring what is best for all of us!" (51).

Demosthenes likes to finish his earlier speeches with a word about himself, but he never says anything quite like this elsewhere.

The *First Philippic* is different from any of the earlier speeches because it is an emotional appeal,[14] an appeal to the Athenians' confidence in themselves and their pride as free men—"I think that the strongest force that can drive free men is their shame at what has happened" (10). Only one fifth of the speech (13—22) is taken up with setting forth the plan for military preparation, and the explanation that begins in section 23 is part of his appeal to their pride; they are offered snatches of dialogue to show how they have been deceiving themselves.[15] If the members of the Assembly have come as far as this with Demosthenes without protest, their pride will not let them ask for a higher rate of pay in the field than what he offers them; they must take their chance to show that they are neither mercenaries nor politicians, that they are fighting Philip "not just with resolutions and diplomatic correspondence, but with action" (30).

---

14 Cf. Pickard-Cambridge, Demosthenes, 188: "In order to rouse his countrymen to the pitch of enthusiasm which could induce them to take the steps which he urged upon them, Demosthenes appealed to every motive that could influence them—pride in the past, shame at the present, trust in the help given by Heaven to those who help themselves, alarm for the future if the danger were not averted by vigorous action. Beside the eloquence of this speech the earlier orations—with the exception of parts of the speech "Against Aristocrates"—seem cold."

M.Delaunois, "Du plan logique au plan psychologique chez Démosthène," Les études classiques 19 (1951), 177—89, writes as though this peculiarity of the "First Philippic" and the "Olynthiacs" had not been recognized by earlier critics. But his effort to explain the art of the speeches as though it consisted only in repetition of "themes" with variations (in the manner of Schubert rather than Beethoven) does less than justice to Demosthenes.

When the orator is anxious to produce a change in feeling rather than a precise concrete decision, there is less need for adhering to the conventional rules of rhetoric. In many speeches of Demosthenes, from now on until the end of his career, he is concerned to produce the change of γνώμη before he is ready for stricter argument.

15 "Are you at peace, Athenians?" "Good Heavens no, we are at war with Philip" (25). And a description follows of the manner in which this so-called war is being conducted. "Is Philip dead?" "No, but he is in poor health" (11). This is to show how they can be misled by false and irrelevant information.

He also appeals to their faith in Athenian democratic institutions; their machinery of government is perfectly adequate, and it is their responsibility to see that it is used efficiently, whatever mistakes have been made in the past (35—37). If less honest politicians have refused to tell them the unpleasant truth, they must take it as an insult (38). As he goes on, hoping that he has won their confidence, his language becomes stronger and the truth that he tells them becomes much less pleasant: "Your enemies laugh at you and your allies die with fright when you send out an expedition," "Things have reached such a low point that each one of your generals finds himself on trial for his life on two or more occasions, but you won't find him risking his skin fighting the enemy" (45—47). Instead of believing absurd rumours (48), they must face the facts; if they refuse to fight Philip in his country, they may have to fight him in Attica (50).

The *First Philippic* does not present a series of logical arguments or conform to any regular rhetorical pattern. Its primary argument lies in its appeal to the feelings of the Athenians.[16] When they fail to take decisive action as a result of his speech, Demosthenes may conclude that practical considerations weighed heavier with them than respect for their pride and tradition. It is possible that more firmly established politicians warned the Assembly against being carried away by this forceful newcomer, who seemed not to have reflected on what he was saying. That might explain why he begins the *First Olynthiac* with a special plea for a fair hearing: "You must listen eagerly to all who advise you; it is not only a speaker who comes with a useful idea carefully thought out who may give you the right answer; I think it is part of your special good fortune that many right answers come from men to whom they occur quite suddenly" (1.1).

When he delivers the *Olynthiacs* in 349, he has had time for reflection since the *First Philippic*, but despite his initial failure he has evidently made up his mind that his method is the right one. He tells them at the very beginning of the *First Olynthiac* that immediate military action is needed: "The crisis is such that it almost breaks into speech, telling you to intervene directly up there, if you are concerned about your own survival"

---

16 Cf. the excellent analysis of J. Sampaix, "Quelques notes pour l'étude littéraire de la 1ère Philippique de Démosthène," Nova et Vetera (Revue d'enseignement et de pédagogique belge) 19 (1937), 23—30.
G. O. Rowe, "Demosthenes' First Philippic: The Satiric Mode," TAPA (1968), 361—74, shows how Demosthenes exploited the element of absurdity in Athenian military operations and speaks of his using a "satiric mode" of persuasion. The term does not seem to me a very happy one, because (unlike any satirist) Demosthenes is using ridicule in order to rouse the positive emotions of pride and determination. He is leading to the right answer by showing what shamefully wrong answers some Athenians have given.

(1.2).[17] As in the earlier speech, he tells them first about the gravity of the situation and the opportunity that it presents, and devotes the central part of his speech to the form that their intervention should take. They must follow the same principles as before. They must come to the help of Olynthus, the object of Philip's present attack, and at the same time raid Macedonia with a second naval and military force, because intervention in one place alone will be useless (17–18). He adds some remarks about finance, and the allusion to the Theoric Fund, though indirect, is clear: "You have funds for military purposes, more than anyone else has; only you take them for yourselves, suiting your own convenience. If you will transfer these funds to the men who will serve on these campaigns, there will be no shortage of money" (19). He makes no formal motion (" 'Are you proposing that these funds be made into a military chest?' 'Certainly not' "). But he tells them bluntly that a general payment of *eisphora* will be necessary.

The earlier part of the speech contains many familiar arguments and some of the familiar phrases from the *First Philippic*. They must "pay taxes readily, go out on service themselves, and never give in" (6); and they must learn to be present on the scene of action, as Philip always is,[18] instead of arriving too late and losing their allies, after Philip has explained their absence in such a way as to make their allies lose faith in Athens.[19] Demosthenes expects them to understand that a new attitude is needed; he tells them how ruthless and unscrupulous Philip is, but finds a serious weakness in him, his autocratic power, which may be an advantage in war but will make Greek cities cautious and suspicious in dealing with him, because "constitutional governments always distrust a tyranny" (5). From the very beginning of the speech he insists that Philip's attack on Olynthus offers them an opportunity which they must not miss,[20] and as before[21] he reminds them of the opportunities that they have missed, at Amphipolis, Pydna, Potidaea, Methone, and Pagasae (8–9). They should give thanks to the gods[22] that they have this chance to recover their good

17 ἔστι δὴ τά γ᾽ ἐμοὶ δοκοῦντα ψηφίσασθαι μὲν ἤδη τὴν βοήθειαν καὶ παρασκευάσασθαι τὴν ταχίστην ὅπως ἐνθένδε βοηθήσετε (1.2), there must be παρασκευή as well as βοήθεια (cf. 4.32).
18 The verb παρεῖναι is used with emphasis in the "First Philippic," e.g. 4.5, 24, 47.
19 Philip knows how to exploit our shortcomings, δεινὸς ἄνθρωπος πράγμασι χρῆσθαι (1.3). But Athenians seem unable to take advantage of an opportunity, γέλως ἔσθ᾽ ὡς χρώμεθα τοῖς πράγμασιν (4.25).
20 οὐ δεῖ δὴ τοιοῦτον, ὦ ἄνδρες Ἀθηναῖοι, παραπεπτωκότα καιρὸν ἀφεῖναι οὐδὲ παθεῖν ταὐτὸν ὅπερ ἤδη πολλάκις πρότερον πεπόνθατε (8). For the language, cf. Isoc. Paneg. 160 and the frequent allusions to καιροί in the "First Philippic," 4.12, 18, 33, 35, 37.
21 Cf. 4.4, 35.
22 Cf. 4.42: δοκεῖ δέ μοι θεῶν τις, ὦ ἄνδρες Ἀθηναῖοι, τοῖς γιγνομένοις ὑπὲρ τῆς

name and put an end to Philip's career of aggression. The long list of cities and areas where Philip has taken over control illustrates his φιλοπραγμο-σύνη (14). He will attack Athens unless they intervene.

This grim warning did not come until the peroration in the *First Philippic*, and here too Demosthenes follows it by telling them that he is well aware what risks he is taking when he speaks so freely:

"I know quite well, men of Athens, that you often vent your wrath, when something goes wrong, not on the persons whose fault it is, but on the persons who are the last to speak on the question. But that does not mean that I should stop myself, out of regard for my own safety, from telling you what I think you should be told" (16).

The situation in the North is described in greater detail in the latter part of the speech in order to show Philip's difficulties and the real weakness of his position. He is hated and distrusted in Thessaly, and if he is not allowed to raise money there by port-taxes and market fees, he will find it difficult to pay his mercenaries (22). His personal character is also making difficulties for him, particularly among the Paeonians and Illyrians, who are accustomed to independence and strongly antagonized by his autocratic hybristic ways.[23] But though the Thessalians may hate him, they cannot stop him advancing through their country; nor can the Phocians and Thebans be trusted to put up much resistance. It is up to the Athenians to help free men recover their rights in the areas that he has overrun.

The attack on Philip's character gives additional force to this concluding section, and it has always been difficult to counter it. Historians in modern times have argued that it would have been useful to cultivate Philip's friendship as an ally against the Persian king,[24] and they have complained (with good reason) that the portrait which Demosthenes paints is a gross caricature. But they cannot say what reasons the Athenians might have had to trust him; if they believed (even before Demosthenes told them so) that he was treacherous and incapable of keeping his word, tyrannical and high-handed in his methods, how could any politician seriously recommend them to adopt him as their partner? Demosthenes jeers at Philip's admirers from time to time, and it cannot be

---

πόλεως αἰσχυνόμενος, τὴν φιλοπραγμοσύνην ταύτην ἐμβαλεῖν Φιλίππῳ. Philip's restlessness and refusal to be content with his successes is the weakness which offers the Athenians their opportunity.

23 1.23. In 4.8 it is pointed out that he is hated and feared even by people who appear outwardly to be on excellent terms with him, and his *aselgeia* is mentioned in 4.9.

24 Cf. e.g., J. von Ooteghem, "La politique de Démosthène," Revue belge de philologie et d'histoire 7 (1928), 915—55.

said that Isocrates answers the accusations very effectively or that his letters (if they are genuine) justify faith in Philip's pan-hellenic ideals. The argument from character is secondary, not primary, in these speeches, but it is used with the skill of an experienced speech-writer, who knows how to convince a jury.

Demosthenes uses some notable epigrammatic language in describing the situation at Olynthus. It has happened of itself (γέγονεν αὐτόματον, 7), and "practically cries out aloud" (2) calling upon the Athenians to intervene. A "true accountant" (δίκαιος λογιστής, 10) of the favours shown to Athens by the gods should be thankful to them for the gift of this wonderful opportunity.[25] To postpone the day of intervention is to behave like people who borrow rashly at high rates of interest so as to gain a short relief, and end by losing everything that they possess (15). Equally striking is the language used to describe the unexpected elements in Philip's progress. One moment he is making concessions, the next he is making threats (3). He was weak at the start of his reign, became powerful by a remarkable succession of attacks on Greek cities, and then went into Thrace: "There, after he had thrown out some kings and established others in power, he fell sick; he recovered, but instead of taking a rest he immediately attacked Olynthus" (13). This is described as his φιλοπραγμοσύνη, the way of life he "lives with" (ᾗ χρῆται καὶ συζῇ, 14). It makes difficulties for him, and the Athenians must regard his difficulty as their opportunity (τὴν ἀκαιρίαν τὴν ἐκείνου καιρὸν ἡμέτερον νομίσαντας, 24).

The special interest of the *Olynthiacs* is that the same arguments are used in all three speeches, but they are manipulated differently and with variation in emphasis. The Athenians have to be convinced that Philip is strong and dangerous, but not so strong that he cannot be stopped; that he is in a precarious situation and his power rests on an unsound foundation, but he cannot be left to fall through his own folly; that Athens has made serious mistakes, but it is not too late to correct them; that they must be proud of their great traditions, but not be content with thinking about their past greatness. The danger is that in putting too much emphasis on one argument he may weaken the force of another.

In the *Second Olynthiac* Demosthenes is more particularly concerned to expose the weakness of Philip. He disclaims any wish to describe his strength (3), because that would work in his favour. He says that Philip owes much of his supposed strength to traitors in Athens, but refuses to

25 *Kairos* and *Tyche* play a great part in the language of Demosthenes, but I cannot agree with Jaeger's view that he has a specially "active, alert faith" and regards opportunity as the moment "when divinity stretches out its hand to man." Cf. Demosthenes, 128—35, and Paideia, III 361—65.

enlarge on that subject. A fuller narrative might convince some people that Philip was invincible, even though the object of the speaker was to show how dishonest and untrustworthy he was. So, in the manner of a prosecutor, while he says he will tell the whole story (5), he gives examples that reveal the character of his adversary, how he took advantage of other people's simplicity:

"He said he would put Amphipolis in your hands, and contrived that notorious secret agreement—[26] that was how he led you on; then he won the friendship of the Olynthians by capturing Potidaea, which was an Athenian city, and handing it over to them—an affront to you, his former allies; and finally now he has won over the Thessalians by promising to give them Magnesia and to fight the Phocian war for them. Everyone who has had anything to do with him has been cheated by him; on every occasion he takes advantage of the lack of wisdom shown by people who don't know what he is like; this is the basis of his power" (6—7).

In a simple but perfectly apposite simile he tells them how unsound a basis this is: "Just as in a house and a ship and all such structures the foundations must be the strongest part, so in political activity the basis on which everything rests must be sound and honest" (10). Enough has been said to indicate that the time is ripe for intervention, and he calls for immediate action by Athens, making the same demands as before, but in fewer words (11—13). Then he returns quickly to the theme of Philip's weakness, the helplessness of Macedonia without support from Greek allies and the lack of any common interest between Philip and his present allies, who do all the work but receive none of the rewards or the glory.

Demosthenes has an anonymous witness, "a man who has been to the country" (17) and can reveal the true story about Macedonia—how the Macedonian troops are not by any means such splendid fellows as they are supposed to be and Philip does not want anyone of real ability or good character about him, but prefers men who will keep him company in his drunken orgies, where they dance "such dances as I cannot bring myself to mention to you," and shows his taste by welcoming mountebanks and writers of obscene verse who have been thrown out of Athens (19). The full battery of a ruthless prosecutor is turned on Philip, who is shown as an inhuman and cruel man and at the same time a devotee of riotous living and doomed to disaster, with the signs of *kakodaimonia* plain to see (20). Demosthenes lends dignity to this abusive attack with his famous passage about the "body politic:"

26 For discussion of this supposed agreement see now G. E. M. de Ste Croix, "The alleged secret pact between Athens and Philip," CQ 13 (1963), 110—19.

"It is the same as in the human body; a man may be unaware of any trouble so long as he is in good health, but the slightest indisposition can throw everything into disorder and reveal any latent weakness, a fracture or sprain or whatever it may be; likewise with cities and autocrats, so long as the fighting is outside their own territory, the population is unaware of the troubles, but as soon as war starts on their own borders, everything is revealed" (21).

The object is to convince the Athenians that Philip is neither a really formidable enemy nor an ally whom they should trust, that he has nothing to recommend him but an unbroken series of successes, his good fortune, his *tyche* which has preserved him from the setback that might lead to his total collapse. No one despises the favour of Fortune, "which counts so much in human affairs," but "I would choose the *tyche* of Athens, if we are willing to do our duty, rather than the *tyche* of Philip. I can see many more claims to the favour of the gods in you than in him" (22). The favour of Fortune and of the gods has to be earned, as everyone knows; they will not help anyone who does not bestir himself; but if a man of despicable character has won the favour of Fortune by his vigorous spirit, how can Athens fail to win even greater favour? This final conclusion Demosthenes leaves his hearers to draw for themselves. He is hoping that shame and pride will goad them into action.

By explaining Philip's weakness and denouncing his moral character, he has prepared the way for the appeals that he made in the *First Philippic*. These appeals have acquired much greater force since he has told them that their opponent is not really formidable—if only they will change their attitude. He finishes with a more specific appeal—they must not blame others until they are in control of the situation themselves (27). It is no wonder that commanders and men avoid the enemies they are sent out to fight, and seek out more profitable "private wars" (28). The excuses must be removed, the men must be paid, and "you must become your own masters again" (30). This means paying taxes and serving on campaigns themselves; it also means not letting certain politicians "dictate what they want as though they were tyrants". The Assembly must listen to all speakers and choose the best proposal that is put before it. The speech finishes where the *First Olynthiac* started.

With the *Third Olynthiac* Demosthenes makes a fresh start. He takes more trouble than before to explain the situation and the great opportunity that is offered to the Athenians. After a brief introduction, in which he gives the impression that other speakers are being more bellicose, but less realistic than he is, he begins the narrative which he says is necessary if they are to understand the problem that faces them:

"You will remember when the news arrived, two or rather three years ago, in Maimakterion [November 351], that Philip was laying siege to Heraion Teichos, in Thrace; and after much discussion and uproar you voted that we should get forty triremes to sea, that citizens up to the age of forty-five should embark on them, and that we should pay an *eisphora* of sixty talents" (4).

It was not until next summer, however, that Charidemus was sent out, with ten triremes (but no troops) and five talents; a report came that Philip was sick, another that he was dead, and the expedition came to nothing, as there seemed to be no point in it any longer: "And yet this *was* the time. If we had sent help with enthusiasm then, as we voted to do, Philip would not be troubling us now that he has recovered. We cannot change the past, of course; but now another opportunity for armed intervention has arisen, and the reason that I reminded you of past events was to make sure that you would not make the same mistake again" (5–6).

There is not a word about Philip's series of aggressions or his dishonesty, nothing is said even about his difficulties; all that matters is to make it clear that his attack on Olynthus opens up a new opportunity for Athens to intervene. It is taken for granted that no one will dispute the conclusion; help must be sent, but: "How is it to be done, tell us that" (10). And so he tells them that they should set up a legislative committee (*nomothetae*), which will be empowered to repeal certain laws that are doing harm: "I mean, in plain language, laws about the Theoric Fund and some of the laws about military service" (11). He says no progress can be made until this is done. A direct proposal to divert the Theoric Fund to military purposes would expose the speaker to prosecution (it is possible that Apollodorus had already been prosecuted for making such a proposal).[27] And he tells them, at some length (11–13), that no one can be expected to propose "what is best," if the threat of a *graphe paranomon* hangs over him. The way must be made clear so that the law about the Theoric Fund can be repealed.

He does not linger too long on such dangerous ground, but passes on to safer and more familiar themes—the need for effective action (which is in their power) as well as mere resolutions, Philip's *hybris*, the opportunity given them by his latest acts of aggression. But he comes back to the Theoric Fund, telling them that the money is there to pay for the expedition (20). We should like to be told how much money there really was in the fund, but as before he soon shies away from the dangerous subject and appeals to their pride and patriotism: "Men who snatched up their arms

27 Cf. Dem. 59.3–5, Pickard-Cambridge, Demosthenes, 201, Cloché, Démosthènes, 86–87.

and marched forth against the Corinthians and Megarians[28] cannot allow Philip to rob Greek cities of their liberty because they lack money to pay the expenses of an expedition." (20). He deplores the decadence of the present age, when Athenians have become the tame playthings of politicians (31), who shut them up in the city and dole out to them the payments on which they live. Even free speech has been destroyed: "By Demeter, I should not be surprised if a more severe punishment were given me for speaking to you like this than to the men who have created this situation; you no longer have the right to speak freely on all subjects; yes, I am surprised that the privilege has been granted to me now" (32).

He has found the occasion to remind them of his courage in speaking out boldly and, as before, he finds a suitable simile to make them understand the treatment they are enduring at the hands of politicians; the relief-payments that they receive are like the invalid foods that physicians give their patients, enough to keep them alive, but not to give them strength (33). Instead of letting politicians treat them like paupers, they should look upon military service as a privilege, and recover their pride by doing something to earn their payments: "I am asking you to do for yourselves what you respect other people for doing, and not to relinquish the honourable position which your ancestors won in many splendid struggles and handed on to you" (36).

If the logic of this appeal were fully worked out, it would run: "Recover your self-respect and claim your privilege of fighting for your country, so that you can check Philip's progress and defend the freedom of Greece, responding to the call for help that Olynthus gives you." It is the reverse argument to the appeal of the *First Philippic*: "Philip is threatening the freedom of Greece and you must check him and you can; and it can be paid for; you must serve and be proud to uphold the best traditions of Athens."

In all these speeches, it would be easier for us to decide how well or badly he is advising the Athenians if he had given us more detailed information about military and financial matters. It seems that, as in the law courts, he thinks he has a better chance of achieving his object by appeals to character; and he therefore appeals to the undesirable character of Philip and his political opponents and the patriotic character of his audience, which he claims to share with them. When narrative is introduced, it is in order to illustrate Philip's character and aims and to contrast the present weakness of Athens with the true Athenian character which their history reveals. The strength of these speeches is that one cannot reply to them without appearing to contradict the unquestionable

28 In defence of the sacred territory of the Orgas. Cf. p. 122 above.

principles that they set forth, and they are composed with too much technical skill to be ridiculed or pushed aside. We should understand the course of Athenian politics in these years far better if we knew more about the arguments with which Eubulus and Aeschines and Philocrates supported their points of view.[29] Demosthenes tells us that they appealed to "the traditions of our ancestors," just as he did. But what were the arguments that won the decisions for them?

The thirteenth oration Περὶ Συντάξεως (*On Financial Organization*), though perhaps never delivered, was evidently designed for a meeting of the Assembly in 350 or 349.[30] The opening sentence shows that the subject for discussion was the use of available resources (περὶ τοῦ παρόντος ἀργυρίου) including the Theoric Fund. The speech does not reveal to us the details of finance and taxation that we might have hoped to find in it. But it is no surprise when Demosthenes insists in the opening paragraphs that distribution of money should not be discussed apart from matters of military organization (3). He reminds them of the recommendations that he had made in the *First Philippic*.[31]

Although he never mentions Philip or any of the troubles in the North, some of the arguments of the *Olynthiacs* make their first appearance here. There are some passages that correspond almost word for word,[32] and he has not spoken for long before telling the Assembly that a military force consisting only of mercenaries is useless, that the money available should be used to pay citizens for service in the field, and with a force that is properly "their own" they can do what is needed, instead of merely bringing generals to trial in the courts (4—5); and that they failed in their responsibilities when they did nothing to stop the overthrow of democracy in Mitylene and Rhodes (8).

He attacks the politicians who oppose him, jeering at their obsession with the two-obol distribution from the Theoric Fund and their absurd alarms of revolution, when they think that a theft of public money must be part of some anti-democratic plot (14).[33] He quotes what they say about him: "He comes forward when it suits him, and fills our ears with

29 Cf. G. L. Cawkwell, "The Defence of Olynthus," CQ 12 (1962), 122—40, and "Eubulus," JHS 83 (1963), 47—67.
30 See p. 122 above.
31 See pp. 124—25 and note 13 above.
32 13.20 corresponds to 2.29, 13.15—31 to 3.23—32. Cf. also 13.23—24 with 23.199—200.
33 It is easy to believe that politicians sometimes sought publicity and popularity by raising an alarm about "spies" or "traitors," and an attempt to protect an unfortunate victim of such a "scare" might damage a man's reputation. Cf. the story told in 18.132—44, which may show Aeschines standing up for a suspected traitor's civil rights (though of course Demosthenes does not represent Aeschines' behaviour in that light).

words disparaging the present and praising our ancestors; before he has finished he has carried us off our feet and made us swell with pride" (12). Demosthenes does not deny the accuracy of the description,[34] but says they have forgotten how to listen to a speaker who gives them "the best advice," and that "anyone who wants to help the city must begin by curing your ears" (13). As in the *Olynthiacs* he complains that they are letting politicians become their masters, letting an orator with his own general and his private army of three hundred men become stronger than the democracy.[35] This is the kind of anti-democratic conspiracy that he wants them to resist, and a comparison follows with "the days of our ancestors," when true freedom prevailed (21). Men have lost their pride in Athenian citizenship; how can they have any pride of spirit, if the politicians will not let them do anything of importance? "The pride that men have in themselves is limited by the occupations that they pursue" (25).[36]

This very proper sentiment reappears in the *Third Olynthiac* (3.32), but there it is the conclusion which follows the comparison of old and new, and it prepares the way for a final exhortation to the Athenians to change their habits and act in a way worthy of themselves. In this speech it is the prelude to this comparison—a development of the comparison which has preceded; here the gnomic sentiment precedes the comparison (13.25–31), in the later speech it follows it (3.25–32). Rather than ask which is the better arrangement, it is more useful to notice the different logical contexts in the two speeches. In the *Third Olynthiac* Demosthenes complains that the politicians are concerned only with "pleasing the people", and the Assembly is rebuked for accepting what gives them temporary gratification; here he is censuring the politicians for their excessive power and representing the Assembly not only as morally weak but as politically powerless. And instead of leading up to a definite proposal or a plea for decisive action, as in the *Third Olynthiac*, he is content with a more innocuous demand, that the demos recover its powers, so that it can act in a worthy manner and not betray its friends (34–35). In the earlier speech the argument leads from the people's loss of pride to their loss of power, in the later from loss of power to loss of pride. The latter

---

34 But he does defend his use of the "high style:" εἰ δέ τῳ δοκῶ μείζους ἢ κατ' ἐμαυτὸν λέγειν λόγους, αὐτὸ τοῦτ' ὀρθῶς αὐτῶν ἔχει· τὸν γὰρ ὑπὲρ τηλικαύ- της πόλεως ῥηθησόμενον λόγον καὶ τοιούτων πραγμάτων παντὸς ἑνὸς τοῦ λέγον- τος ἀεὶ μείζω φαίνεσθαι δεῖ (13.18).

35 νυνὶ δὲ πολιτεύεσθε κατὰ συμμορίας· ῥήτωρ ἡγεμών, καὶ στρατηγὸς ὑπὸ τούτῳ, καὶ οἱ βοησόμενοι μεθ' ἑκατέρων τριακόσιοι (13.20).

36 ὁποῖ' ἄττα γὰρ ἂν τἀπιτηδεύματα τῶν ἀνθρώπων ᾖ, τοιοῦτον ἀνάγκη καὶ τὸ φρόνημ' ἔχειν (13.25).

sequence is better suited to a speech which is to end with a plea for positive action.

Demosthenes uses the same arguments in different speeches; he seems unwilling to abandon an argument that he has used once, but when he uses it a second time he may arrange the sequence of thought differently. One must also notice how little specific information he provides, though one might think the Assembly would welcome more precise detail. Although he fulminates against other politicians, he offers very little specific criticism of what they have actually done. As in the courts, he does not wish to present "facts" that do not strengthen his case. He evidently believes he should leave it to his opponents to explain, if they can, how the unfortunate series of incidents occurred—Amphipolis, Pydna, Potidaea, Methone. He must think that they will do their case more harm by their attempts at explanation than he can by giving his version. It is our loss that he has not given us more narrative; and we may suspect that his judgment was wrong, that he could have made the danger in the North clearer if he had permitted himself to tell the story in greater detail. Despite all his denunciations of Philip's character, he did not succeed in persuading the Athenians to take speedy or decisive action or in teaching them how to avoid being outplayed by Philip.

Chapter IV

iii. Third Group

On the Peace, Second Philippic

We have no text of any address of Demosthenes to the Assembly in the years between 349 and 346 (though the quarrel with Meidias will have kept him in the public eye), and only two speeches from the next four years—*On the Peace*, in 346, after the Peace of Philocrates had been signed, and the *Second Philippic* in 344 or early 343. In his prosecution of Aeschines, in 343, he shows that he has not lost his fighting spirit, but in 346 he is much less aggressive than in the *Olynthiacs*. He is less optimistic, more cautious, more willing to recognize difficulties, and when he introduces himself in *On the Peace* he seems uncertain of his reception, much more apologetic;[1] it is as though he had exchanged the rôle of prosecutor for that of defendant. He says he has a plan of action, but does not present it,[2] and though he denounces the corrupt ways of politicians,[3] he seems more immediately concerned to assure the Athenians that he is incorrupt himself and to justify the advice that he gave them in former years (which they rejected).

He tells them how he advised against giving any support to Plutarchus in Euboea (and was almost torn apart by men who persuaded them "to make such great mistakes in return for small benefits") and reminds them how foolish they were to trust the actor Neoptolemus (7). He recalls how "certain persons" assured them that Philip, though apparently pro-Theban, would not harm the Phocians, whom the Athenians had supported against Thebes in the Sacred War; they said he had promised to weaken

---

1 Some ancient critics, who expected Demosthenes to be consistent in his outlook, regarded "On the Peace" as a spurious oration. The scholiast writes: τινὲς δὲ ἐνόθευσαν τοῦτον τὸν λόγον, ὡς ἀνομοίαν ἔχοντος ὑπόθεσιν τῆς γνώμης αὐτοῦ, οὐ προσσχόντες ἀκριβῶς τῷ σκοπῷ τοῦ ῥήτορος. ἐπειδὴ γὰρ δοκεῖ ὑπὲρ Φιλίππου λέγειν, ὃ οὐδεπώποτε ὤφθη ποιήσας, ᾠήθησαν εἶναι αὐτοῦ τὸν λόγον ἀλλότριον.

2 Blass comments (Att. Bered. III, 343): "D. sagt nicht ein Wort darüber, wie das durch den Frieden und nach dem Frieden verlorene wiederzugewinnen sei, und die Annahme ist daher unausweichlich, daß dies Prooemium von Haus aus mit dieser Rede nichts zu thun hat, wenngleich kaum ein andrer als D. selbst es derselben vorgesetzt haben kann." It is just as easy to believe that Demosthenes knows exactly what he is doing in making a promise that he does not fulfil; what he means, surely, is that they will, in time, be able to recover their losses, if they are not over-hasty. Cf. Jaeger, Demosthenes, 157–62.

3 His denunciation is mild compared with what he had said in the "Third Olynthiac" (cf. section ii above, pp. 134–35).

Thebes, to restore Thespiae and Plataea, and to let Athens have Oropus and Euboea in place of Amphipolis. In fact Philip did what the Thebans wanted; he dismantled the Phocian cities and robbed them of their political existence. In *On the Embassy* Demosthenes will blame Aeschines for deceiving the Athenians over these supposed "promises," but here he is content to defend himself by insisting that he warned them—"I said that I thought the speaker was talking nonsense" (10)—and to proclaim his own integrity: "I am not corrupt in the judgments that I form, no one can point to any profit that I have made out of my policy" (12). And he uses a shrewd comparison to explain what corruption means: "When you bring in money on one side of a question, it is like putting an extra weight in the scale; it adds weight to the argument and tips the scale in its favour; but the man who does it will never again be capable of honest or correct reasoning" (12).[4]

Times have changed since 349, and Demosthenes makes his points soberly and briefly. The time for fighting Philip has past, the opportunity was missed; Athens cannot feel any pride or satisfaction in the peace, but it would be foolish to break it after the losses they have suffered (13). Philip, by supporting Thebes and the other defenders of Delphi against the Phocians, has emerged as the champion of the Delphic Amphictyony and created an Amphictyonic group; they must not provoke this group to a quarrel or attack Philip without its support. But he also tells them that their position is not really dangerous; no aggressive move, whether by Athens or against Athens, will receive much support in any quarter, because no one wants to increase the power of anyone else; and the Thebans will not attack Athens, because they know that, if they gain any advantage by their attack, the real winner will be Philip (13—17).

This is the same technique that he used in the *Olynthiacs*, warning them of a danger and then telling them that it is more apparent than real. He warns them against provoking this co-called Amphictyonic convention "to the point where they will feel themselves obliged or entitled to make war in common against us" (14). But instead of telling them what might be "the basis for war in common against us,"[5] he talks about issues which

4 Though not so often quoted as the passage about the "body politic" and the "structure of politics" (2.9—10) or the comparison of the Athenians with unwise borrowers (1.15), this picture of a corrupt politician as a man who puts extra weight on one side of a scale is a striking one.

5 A πρόφασις κοινοῦ πολέμου is a "justification" for war in common. In "On the Symmories" Demosthenes had spoken of the need for ensuring that the ἀρχή of a war will be just (13.3), and it will never be "just" to start a war ("fire the first shot") unless the πρόφασις is "just." For the political meaning of πρόφασις, in Demosthenes as well as in Thucydides, see L. Pearson, "Prophasis and Aitia," TAPA 83 (1952), 205—23, and "Prophasis. A Clarification," TAPA 103 (1972), 381—94.

the group would not think serious enough to justify their intervention; no one would support Philip against the Athenians if they went to war with him on the issue of Amphipolis, nor would anyone support Thebes against Athens in a quarrel over Oropus. As in earlier years, he has to be careful not to appear pro-Theban; the Thebans, he tells them, are no friends of Athens, but "no matter how stupid one may suppose them to be, they know perfectly well that, if they get into a war with us, they will have all the troubles and a certain third party will sit waiting to pick up the winnings" (15).

The real danger, which he wants them to recognize, is not unlike that of which he warned them in *On the Symmories*. Athens cannot expect support from her supposed allies unless their interest is directly involved, and if the Athenians are not careful they may find themselves isolated without any support at all. But in the years since 354 he has learnt how to make his warnings more palatable. Instead of telling them how they might find themselves drawn into a major war, he mentions some possible minor conflicts, none of which is likely to "escalate" into a major war. They might find themselves fighting the anti-Spartan group in the Peloponnese if they seemed to be drawing too close to Sparta, the Thebans might fight them if support were given to their exiles, the Thessalians if Phocian exiles were protected, Philip if his Amphictyonic status were threatened (18–19). These powers might unite in a common war against Athens only if each of them was provoked individually, and if they failed to realize how unlikely any of them were to obtain their desired object. In the past they had not always realized when they were merely serving Philip's purpose, and the real danger was that they had not learnt their lesson (23).

This contradicts his earlier statement—that they all knew very well that Philip would be the real winner in any war. But this is the message that he has to give, and he seems to show how reluctantly he has reached his conclusion by the indirect method of argument he has employed. In *On the Symmories* he was careful to say at the beginning that he was no friend of Persia; here he waits until the end before pointing out that he is no friend of Philip and does not believe in "appeasement" or "peace at any price:" "Must we submit in cowardly fashion to every demand that is made of us? No, what I think is that we must do nothing unworthy of ourselves, that we must avoid war and let everyone see that we are reasonable and talk reasonably" (24). Some concessions may have to be made to avoid provoking the Amphictyonic group into a war for the sake of "the shadow at Delphi", περὶ τῆς ἐν Δελφοῖς σκίας (25). The danger is that these people may think they are being called upon to protect the integrity of Delphi.

Demosthenes must have known that the Assembly in 346 was unlikely to favour any action that might provoke Philip, but he states his opinion firmly in case anyone should think he is so foolish as to want some aggressive move. He has no need to point out the military strength of Philip; it is his diplomatic victory that he wants to be understood.

In the next two years Philip gives the Athenians many reasons to complain about his violation of the peace terms, and in the *Second Philippic*[6] Demosthenes thinks the time has come to tell them that complaints are not enough; it is no use "saying the right things" if they do not accomplish any of "the necessary things."[7] He is preparing himself now for the full-scale attack on Aeschines in *On the Embassy*, an attack which had to be postponed when Aeschines discredited his witness Timarchus by exposing his disreputable past. He is now sharply critical of the men whom he considers responsible for the peace of 346 and (as in the *Olynthiacs*) he accuses speakers of being frightened to say anything that may displease the Assembly (3).

Using the familiar *logos-ergon* antithesis, he says that the skilfully devised "just arguments" of the Athenians have not stopped Philip; if they excel in words, it seems that he excels in deeds (4). And he takes on once again the task of proving that Philip is the enemy of Athens, starting a narrative which is designed to show them what sort of man Philip is:

"Over what areas did Philip acquire power immediately after the peace? Over Thermopylae and Phocis. Yes, and what use did he make of his power? He chose to do what suited the Thebans, not what Athens would have wanted. And why? Because he was watching his opportunities to increase his possessions and get everything in his hands; he was not thinking in terms of peace or order or any kind of just settlement. And he noted quite correctly that in the face of your city and your character there was no offer he could make, nothing he could do, which would persuade you to betray any of the other Greeks to him for the sake of your own private gain; he saw that you had some regard for what was just and were unwilling to suffer the disgrace of doing anything so dishonourable, that you foresaw the inevitable consequences, and if he attempted any move of this kind you would oppose him just as strongly as if you were at war with him. But the Thebans, he thought (and events proved

6 In the archonship of Lyciscus, 344–43, according to Dion. Hal. Ad Amm. 1.70. The precise occasion cannot be established.
7 In "On the Peace" he wanted it to be apparent to everyone that they were saying τὰ δίκαια (5.24), but now he says: ἀεὶ τοὺς ὑπὲρ ἡμῶν λόγους καὶ δικαίους καὶ φιλανθρώπους ὁρῶ φαινομένους καὶ λέγειν μὲν ἅπαντας ἀεὶ τὰ δέοντα δοκοῦντας τοὺς κατηγοροῦντας Φιλίππου, γιγνόμενον δ' οὐδέν, ὡς ἔπος εἰπεῖν, τῶν δεόντων (6.1).

him right), would let him do whatever he wanted in return for what he gave them; far from making difficulties or standing in his way he thought they would even join him in a military expedition, if he asked them; and now he has formed the same opinion about the Messenians and Argives, and is offering them help. There is no higher compliment he could pay you, men of Athens" (7–9).

This is much more frightening than anything he said in *On the Peace*. He tells them now that Philip is actually at work forming anti-Athenian groups and taking advantage of the moral weakness and gullibility of people like the Thebans and Argives; he must know how different the Athenians are, since it was his own ancestor, King Alexander, who discovered that they could not be bribed, "when they were given the chance to rule over the rest of the Greeks if they would submit to the Persian king" (11). This time the appeal to their pride and integrity should not only rouse them to resistance, but should make them understand that Philip knows their true character; he must know that he cannot control Greece unless he controls Athens, and he is trying to use the Thebans and Argives to help him, as Xerxes did.

Demosthenes does not marshal evidence in any systematic attempt to prove the very doubtful thesis that Philip is working on such a clearly defined plan of imperialism;[8] instead of disentangling fact from rumour, he treats Philip like a guilty defendant, inviting his hearers to assume that he is acting from criminal motives: "Everything that he does, if you look at it in the right way, shows that his whole policy is directed against Athens. And in a way this has been forced upon him. Just consider. He wants to establish an empire, and he realizes that you are the only people who can stop him" (16–17).

He deals in summary fashion with objectors who think they know better, who say Philip is helping the Thebans because they have a "juster"

---

8 Demosthenes has been taken very seriously to task for using this kind of language about Philip. Cf., e.g., E. Meyer, "Isokrates' Brief an Philipp und die zweite Philippika," SB. Berlin 1909, ph. hist. Kl., p. 769, n.1. He takes it as certain "daß die Darstellung aller dieser Vorgänge bei Demosthenes durch und durch verfälscht ist und daß Philipp gar nicht daran gedacht hat, Athen anzugreifen, sondern im Gegentheil sich sehr ernstlich bemüht hat, mit ihr in ein gutes Verhältnis zu kommen und daher den Frieden peinlich beobachtet hat." Pickard-Cambridge, "Demosthenes," 308–09, thinks the "Second Philippic" was "based on a false premiss," but adds: "But that Philip was scheming for the ultimate overthrow of Athens, and deceiving her with offers of friendship until the convenient moment came, was a perfectly possible inference from the facts before the orator, viewed in the light of Philip's past dealings with other peoples." It is far from certain that many members of the so-called "pro-Macedonian" party felt the same confidence in Philip that Isocrates expressed in his letter.

cause than the Athenians (13), and with others who say that he has made concessions to the Thebans against his will and is really suspicious of them (14). He is not concerned, as in the *Olynthiacs*, to explain Philip's difficulties or the uncertain basis on which his power rests. He prefers to tell the Athenians quite dogmatically what must be in Philip's mind: "He is on his guard, watching you, building up opposition to you by cultivating some of the Thebans and those among the Peloponnesians who sympathize with the Thebans" (18).

Instead of castigating the Athenians for their weakness and lack of foresight, as he did in the *Olynthiacs*, Demosthenes now flatters them by telling them what a high regard Philip has for them. He has not said a word yet about military action. He wants to tell them first about the diplomatic efforts that have been made to counter Philip's moves, especially in the Peloponnese, how he himself and others have tried to warn the anti-Spartan group against accepting Philip's offers, how, for example, he told the Messenians that "in seeking to avoid a war you may find that you have acquired a master" (24–25). But he admits that such diplomatic representations have only a small chance of success. The Athenians will have to act on their own account; they must consider by themselves what action they should take (28).[9]

The action which he calls for, though not with much confidence (ἦν μὲν οὖν δίκαιον), in the next sentence, is neither diplomatic nor military: "The right thing, men of Athens, would be to summon before you the men who made the promises by which you were induced to make the peace" (28). He means, of course, Philocrates and Aeschines, whom he cannot mention by name in the Assembly. He is preparing his way for the

---

9 περὶ μὲν δὴ τῶν ὑμῖν πρακτέων καθ᾽ ὑμᾶς αὐτοὺς ὕστερον βουλεύσεσθε, ἂν σωφρονῆτε· ἃ δὲ νῦν ἀποκρινάμενοι τὰ δέοντ᾽ ἂν εἴητ᾽ ἐψηφισμένοι, ταῦτ᾽ ἤδη λέξω (28).
These words make one think that a foreign delegation is present in the Assembly, and that it will be considered how to reply to their message after it has withdrawn. In the *hypothesis* to the speech Libanius, citing as his authority the "Philippic Histories" (of Theopompus or Anaximenes?), says Philip had sent an embassy complaining of slanders that the Athenians were spreading about him and that Argos and Messene had sent delegates at the same time complaining that Athens was too friendly in her relations with Sparta. It has also been thought that Sparta sent an embassy, asking for Athenian help in countering Philip's friends in the Peloponnese, though there is no direct evidence of its presence. The difficulty of maintaining the right balance between the two groups in the Peloponnese was already noticed in "On the Peace" (5.18, cf. p. 140 above), and the problem that Demosthenes faces is still the same one. His language is not calculated to soothe the ruffled feelings of a foreign delegation, and unless something has been lost ₁rom the text he has no further suggestions to make about improving diplomatic relations. Cf. G. M. Calhoun, "Demosthenes' Second Philippic," TAPA 64 (1933), 1–17, Jaeger, "Demosthenes," 164–65.

prosecution of Aeschines. The epilogue to the *Second Philippic* serves as an introduction to the speech *On the Embassy*. He is no more ready now to make a formal motion or to set forth a plan of action than in *On the Peace*, and his attack on Aeschines offers him a convenient way of escape from the unanswerable question into which his argument has led him. Logically his argument demands that Athens should renew the war against Philip and renounce the peace. But he cannot recommend such a course of action yet.

Chapter IV

iv. Fourth Group:

On the Chersonese, Third Philippic, Fourth Philippic

In the spring of 342, when Demosthenes delivers *On the Chersonese*,[1] things are different. He does not recommend caution any more, does not express fear that a rash move may unite Philip's allies in a war against Athens. A mercenary force, commanded by the Athenian Diopeithes, is in the Chersonese to reinforce the efforts of the Athenian cleruchs.[2] Two years earlier Demosthenes, as well as other politicians, would have considered its presence there a dangerous provocation. Now it can be explained that Athens is not officially declaring herself ready to fight Philip, that her intentions are entirely peaceful, because Diopeithes' activities can be disowned and he can be ordered to withdraw. But the pretence of peace has given way to something more like "cold war," and this can be seen from the very beginning of the speech.

Demosthenes has very little patience with the scrupulous people who think that Diopeithes' force is behaving aggressively and should be withdrawn. He insists that it is Philip who is offering the provocation—or do people think that "he is not doing the city any harm and not making war" so long as he keeps his hands off Attica and the Piraeus? He says that the efforts of Diopeithes "to defend the Thracians" are part of the necessary resistance to Philip's advance, and it is folly to withdraw a force which is on the scene of action: "You know quite well that nothing has contributed so much to Philip's success as his ability to be first on the scene of action ... whereas we wait until the news arrives that something is going on, and then start our confused preparations" (11).

The argument is familiar. No new expeditionary force is needed this time, but the Athenians must realize what will happen if Diopeithes' men are withdrawn. Byzantium will be rendered helpless against Philip's attack. This is a city which must not be allowed to fall into his hands, and they

---

1 Dion. Hal. Ad Amm. 10, puts it in the archonship of Sosigenes (342–41).
2 In the "Letter of Philip" 3 Diopeithes is accused of taking the initiative in invading Thracian territory and of various acts of violence. Whatever the truth may be about the authorship of the letter, its object is to show the attitude that Philip adopted or might have adopted. It is not necessary to believe that its statements are strictly accurate. But Cardia may have had good reason for objecting to Diopeithes' high-handed methods. Cf. the *hypothesis* to 8.

must see the opportunities they are creating for him: "Suppose he comes to Chalcis and Megara, just as he came to Oreus not so long ago. Do you think it is better to fight him *here* and let the war reach Attica or make difficulties for him *there*?" (18). This is a return to the language of 349.[3]

Equally familiar is the complaint that Athenians are refusing to pay property taxes or go out on service themselves. And they are keeping Diopeithes so short of money that he has to find his own ways of raising it. He is exacting protection money ("favours," εὔνοιαι) from the maritime allies as the price of protecting their shipping. Instead of censuring him for this irregular practice, they should commend him for the work he has done with so little support from Athens. Politicians have found it convenient to let them think they can cure their troubles by punishing their commanders, but they must learn once again how to use their power properly: "Politicians should accustom you to be gentle and merciful in meetings of the Assembly, because here you are settling issues with members of your own number and between yourselves and your allies; but it is in your preparations for war that you should show yourselves terrible and severe, because then you are preparing to settle the issue with your opponents and enemies" (33).

As in earlier speeches Demosthenes wants the Athenians to change their attitude, instead of making things easy for Philip and disheartening their allies by their perversity. He reminds them that Philip is just as dangerous to those who try to help him as to those who resist him (the experience of Olynthus made that plain enough),[4] and "he cannot let Athenian freedom sit waiting for the opportunity to attack him" (42). He tells them that Philip has definite plans for establishing an empire, and that he would not be making such an effort to add Thrace to his dominions if it were not the first step in a much larger scheme of conquest (44–45).[5] The Athenians must therefore see the necessity of establishing a standing military force, so that they can fight him on level terms (47).

---

3 Cf. 4.50, 1.25.
4 In 18.47–48 Philip's treatment of collaborators is worked up in a notable passage: "No one has the traitor's interest at heart when he hands out money . . . Lasthenes was called 'friend' only until he betrayed Olynthus, Timolaus only until he betrayed Thebes, Eudicus and Simos of Larissa only until they put Thessaly in Philip's hands. Since then the whole world is full of traitors who found themselves cast out and scorned, treated in the worst possible way." Demosthenes is not yet ready to use such strong language.
5 "Who will believe that Philip is suffering the tortures of the damned in the Thracian winter (ἐν τῷ βαράθρῳ χειμάζειν) just for the sake of the wheat and barley in storage there?" (8.45). The bodily pain and injury that Philip was prepared to endure "for the sake of empire and dominion" is also worked up in 18.67.

Rearmament may be expensive and troublesome, but the alternatives are much worse.

The time has come now to appeal to their pride. Suppose they had the word of a god to assure them that Philip would not attack them if they kept quiet and let him conquer the world. Would they accept such a bargain? He would rather die than suggest it. Or will they tell him that they are ready to take action "when the necessity arises?" He answers with an indignant outburst which recalls the *First Philippic*: "The necessity, which one might call the free man's necessity, has not only risen but has long since past" (51). No "necessity" can drive a free man harder than shame at what has happened; are they waiting to be threatened with blows and mutilation, as though they were slaves?

The next step is to show that the alternative to resistance is not only shameful but impossible—there is no hope that they can persuade Philip to keep the peace. Orators serve no purpose by comparing the hardships of war with the blessings of peace; they should compare the hard sacrifices of war with the terrible alternatives that face Athenians if they refuse to be parted from their money.

One after another the arguments from earlier speeches reappear, and Demosthenes seems to have no difficulty in adapting them to the new circumstances. As in the *Olynthiacs* he turns an apparent difficulty into an opportunity. It is supposed that Diopeithes' aggressiveness has made their position in the Chersonese awkward; instead of punishing him (as they had so often punished commanders in former years, when they forced them to neglect their proper tasks) they should make good use of the army he has at his disposal—and strengthen it. Philip is not actually threatening an attack on any ally, but he will certainly attack Byzantium if they give him the chance. His φιλοπραγμοσύνη now appears in the guise of imperial ambition, his feverish activity has an identifiable purpose, which cannot be realized unless he destroys Athens.

Philip's character and intelligence play a large part in the argument —his *hybris* (62), his constant deceit of those who trust him, his autocratic methods, his recognition that he cannot treat Athens like other Greek cities. He cannot allow Athens to preserve its political freedom, but he knows how to take advantage of its tradition of free speech: "Ours is the only city in which a man is permitted to speak freely in the interests of the enemy" (63). The attack on Athenian politicians who are doing Philip's work for him becomes fiercer than ever before; and he contrasts himself with these so-called "fearless" politicians who are willing "to sacrifice what matters most to Athens if only they can win acclaim for one day" (71).

Demosthenes presents his case in such a way that a politician who tries to answer it can be charged with helping Philip or attempting to degrade or betray Athens. This makes it possible for him to turn his heaviest guns on his Athenian opponents. Now that the Athenians are in deadly peril, he tells them, they must recognize that the politicians who betrayed them deserve to be beaten to death: "It is impossible to overcome the enemies outside the city, until you punish the enemies who are within the city" (61).

References to past events are brief, and there is no attempt at narrative. It is taken for granted that people will understand quick remarks about a variety of places. Also notably lacking are the solemn *paradeigmata* in appeals to Athenian pride and tradition. The only *paradeigma* comes late in the speech, when Demosthenes is answering the charge that he is offering the Athenians "mere words." He reminds them how important an orator's task is by recalling the vigorous speech which Timotheus made urging the Athenians to chase the Thebans out of Euboea: "It was Timotheus who made the speech, and you who took action; it was the two parties together that accomplished the task" (75).

A special feature of this speech is the extensive use of snatches of dialogue. He had started this practice in the *First Philippic* and he used it occasionally (but not very often) in the private orations, as in *Against Pantaenetus*, when the speaker imagines himself having an altercation with the defendant. There are also some good examples in *Against Meidias*.[6] There are no examples in the first group of speeches before the Assembly, two or more in each speech of the second group, one in *On the Peace* and one in the *Second Philippic*.[7] But in *On the Chersonese* they are more numerous, with the result that the speech takes on a more dramatic character and seems to demand a more histrionic style of delivery.

He dramatizes the people's refusal to face unpleasant facts by imagining himself in a dialogue with them:

"Suppose Diopeithes' army is dissolved, what shall we do if Philip attacks the Chersonese?"

"We shall of course put Diopeithes on trial."

"And what good will that do?"

---

6 21.48, 136, 202—04 (a particularly good passage). Cf. also 22.8; 37.52; 39.30. There is a good example in 32.15—16, but the authorship of the speech is in doubt (see above, Chapter II, pp. 52—55). It might be unwise for a speech-writer to give his client passages of dialogue, unless he were sure of his ability to handle them effectively. Demon, the speaker of 32, was probably an experienced speaker. Apollodorus, a thoroughly experienced speaker, was fond of using dialogue, cf. 50.26—28, 34—39, 48—49; 52.8—11; 53.10—12; 59.82.

7 4.10—11, 25, 66; 13.12, 14; 1.16, 19; 3.10, 19, 22, 34; 5.24; 6.13.

"Well, we could go out ourselves from here to defend the place."

"And suppose contrary winds make it impossible?"

"Oh, but he won't make the attack."

"And who is to guarantee that?" (17).

In another passage he tries to make them see what people must think of their policy elsewhere in Greece:

"Suppose the Greeks were to demand an account from you of the opportunities you have let slip through sheer apathy, suppose they asked you: 'Men of Athens, is it not true that you are constantly sending us delegations, telling us that Philip is plotting against us and all the Hellenes, and that we must watch out for him, and so on?' You would have to agree that this was so, and say, 'Yes'. 'Well then, you miserable people, the man has been detained for ten whole months by sickness and winter and occupied by warfare all the time, so that he cannot return home, but you never liberated Euboea or recovered any of your possessions; you were at home and perfectly healthy' (this is supposing they would say people behaving like you were healthy!) 'with nothing to do, and he established two tyrants in Euboea, setting up one in a fortified position directly across from Attica, the other facing Sciathus. If you did nothing else, you might have dislodged them from these positions, but you didn't. Without any question, you have stood aside to make way for him, you have made it plain that even if he dies ten times over you won't make a move. Why bother us, then, with these delegations in which you find fault with us?' What reply shall we make if they speak like that, what shall we be able to say? Nothing, so far as I can see" (35–37).

There are also dialogues in which he faces his opponents and critics,[8] and in these dialogues he is constantly saying he is "astonished" at what goes on (just as, in forensic speeches, he gives his clients plenty of opportunity to express their "amazement" at their opponents' shamelessness).[9]

On the Chersonese has been greatly admired by some critics, but it will disappoint readers who have been expecting more specific proposals, now that he has prepared the way for them. It would be easier for us to see how well he met the real needs of the moment if we had the text of other speeches given at the same meeting of the Assembly, or if we knew more about other speeches of his own, to which he makes reference in various passages in *On the Embassy* and *On the Crown*. He was of course particularly proud of the speech that he made in 339 in the critical meeting of the Assembly after the news reached Athens that Philip was at

8 See especially 68–71.
9 Preuss, "Index Demosthenicus," records over thirty examples of $\theta\alpha\upsilon\mu\acute{\alpha}\zeta\omega$ in the first person singular.

Elatea. He tells us, in *On the Crown* (18.188), that his words "caused the danger that threatened the city to pass like a cloud," and this time he certainly made clear and specific proposals to meet the emergency.

The speech seems to have followed some of his familiar methods of argument. According to his own summary (18.173–80) he found fault with those who exaggerated the immediate peril, claiming to know Philip's intentions better than they did. Philip's object, he said, was to make a show of military might, so as to encourage his friends in Thebes and overawe his enemies there; Athens must support the anti-Macedonian party in Thebes, or else all Thebans would be united by Philip in a movement against Athens. It is the same kind of warning that he gave in *On the Peace* and the *Second Philippic*, that a false move might drive their potential allies into Philip's arms, and he wants simultaneous military and diplomatic moves which should keep Thebes on their side. This time when he asks the question, "What do I say that we should do?" (18.177), no one could call his answer vague or cowardly. He says that his proposals met with universal approval, that there was not a single dissenting voice when they were put to the vote.

We have to rely on the *Third* and *Fourth Philippics* if we want to trace his progress towards this final achievement. What new ways does he discover of presenting his point of view? The *Third Philippic* begins in familiar style—nothing is being done to stop Philip, who is flagrantly violating the peace, because politicians are concerned only with preserving their popularity or prosecuting their rivals and the Assembly is content to be diverted by them from doing its proper work (2–4). But he says things can still be put right and he repeats a sentiment that he had used at the beginning of the *First Philippic* (4.2): "What is worst about the past is best if one looks towards the future; our present plight is the result of having done nothing right; but if things were like this after we had done all the right things, there would not be even any hope of improvement" (9.5).

Any discussion of the *Third Philippic* must distinguish between the "longer" and "shorter" versions of the speech. A number of passages are omitted by the tenth century manuscript S (and in manuscripts descended from it), but added by a later hand in its margin, since they were preserved in other manuscripts. These passages can be omitted without spoiling the coherence of the argument, and the question therefore arises whether they are genuine. And if they are (which is likely enough, since they are in good Demosthenic style and manner), did Demosthenes include them in his address to the Assembly or not?[10]

10 Cf. J. E. Sandys, "Demosthenes, On the Peace, Second Philippic, On the Cher-

The question is unanswerable, but we should notice the different form which the argument takes if certain passages are excluded. In section 5, after the protest about Athenian inactivity, Demosthenes says: "It is your lethargy that Philip has conquered, the city is not beaten, you have not even made a move." And if we omit sections 6 and 7, as S does, the argument of 8 follows naturally: "If we can keep peace and if it is really in our power (ἐφ' ἡμῖν) to do so, well and good; but if Philip is really making war, while pretending to keep peace, we must take action; we may pretend it is peace, as he does, but to think it is really peace is pure madness" (8—9).

Section 6 follows equally well after 5, beginning with the same kind of conditional clause: "If we could all agree that we are at war with Philip (if corrupt politicians did not make it impossible for us to take action) . . ." But in 7 the text breaks off in the middle of a sentence: "If it is within our power to decide between peace and war," εἰ ἐφ' ἡμῖν ἐστι τὸ βουλεύεσθαι περὶ τοῦ πότερον εἰρήνην ἄγειν ἢ πολεμεῖν δεῖ . . . It is difficult to see how this sentence can be completed so as to link up with the beginning of 8, but it is quite easy to find the link with the beginning of 9, for example:[11]

"If we could admit that we were at war and were not being stopped by corrupt politicians, all would be easy; but if (or rather "since," as is often the real meaning of εἰ) it is still in our power (ἐφ' ἡμῖν) to make the decision, let us face the facts; only a madman would say that we are at peace."

It is possible, therefore, that 6 and 7 offer an alternative to 8, that Demosthenes' own text contained both versions and he did not decide until the last moment which was the better. His willingness to experiment with alternatives was noticed earlier in this chapter, when it was shown that the speech *On Financial Organization* contained several passages which appear in the *Olynthiacs* in slightly different form and in a different context.[12] In this case the text of the *Olynthiacs* revealed what his decision was (and it inclines us to believe that *On Financial Organization* was never delivered), but the situation in the *Fourth Philippic* (which appears to "borrow" passages from *On the Chersonese*) does not admit of such a simple solution. Instead of asking which is the "better" of two alternative

sonesus, and Third Philippic" (London 1900), lix — lxvii; M. Croiset (ed. Budé), Harangues II 90—91.

11 Sandys, op. cit. (see previous note), p. lxv, would complete the sentence in 7 with φημ' ἔγωγ' εἰρήνην ἄγειν ἡμᾶς δεῶ, as in 8 immediately after ἵν' ἐντεῦθεν ἄρξωμαι. Various solutions are possible. Sandys lists earlier literature on p. lxxii.

12 Cf. above p. 122, and for the use of arguments in different order in the "First Philippic" and the "Third Olynthiac," p. 134.

versions (or how Demosthenes chose between them), it is preferable to remember his tendency to rearrange the order of his argument when he uses it a second time (as has been illustrated earlier in this chapter).[13]

Since Demosthenes wants to convince the Athenians finally that Philip is their enemy and is fighting a war against them, he combines argument with narrative in the manner of his forensic speeches. He describes the deceptive approach that Philip used towards the Phocians, the Thessalians, and the people of Oreus, and then asks: "Do you suppose he will adopt a different method in dealing with you, present you with an open declaration of war, while you can still be deceived by the pretence of peace?" (13). He explains what else Philip is doing besides conducting a campaign in Thrace—trying to control Megara, to set up puppet tyrants in Euboea, and to support the anti-Spartan group in the Peloponnese — and invites them to see the consequences if all these schemes of Philip are successful. And with this picture drawn for them to see, he has reason to hope they will agree with him when he asks for immediate military intervention in the Chersonese and at Byzantium (20).[14]

He goes on to strengthen his case with some effective *amplificatio*, which is designed to increase their indignation and at the same time lessen their fear or admiration of Philip. The failure to stop Philip is the more disgraceful because he is not even a Greek, "and not even a barbarian who might be proud of his place of origin, but a miserable Macedonian, from a country where in former days you could not even buy a slave that was worth anything" (31). In the past an attack on liberty by any Greek state has met with a quick resistance from other Greek states, but now there is no comparable reaction when a miserable Macedonian attacks them. Speakers in the courts often contrast their own or their friends' tolerance with the violence and *hybris* of their adversaries, and this is the pattern of the present argument, except that the tolerance of the Greeks in face of Philip's *hybris* is not praiseworthy but shameful.

Demosthenes gives some carefully chosen examples of Philip's *hybris*; when he could not be present himself to preside over the Pythian festival, he sent slaves to take his place (32); he gave instructions to the Thessalians about the right way to govern their country, and sent his representatives to set up tyrants in Euboea (33). And why are such things allowed to

---

13 Cf. especially pp. 136—37 above.
14 He does not discuss the strategic importance of Byzantium or offer any details in his narrative of what has happened there, because this had been done by other speakers, καὶ τοσοῦτόν γ' ἀφέστηκα τῶν ἄλλων, ὦ ἄνδρες Ἀθηναῖοι, ὥστ' οὐδὲ δοκεῖ μοι περὶ Χερρονήσου νῦν σκοπεῖν οὐδὲ Βυζαντίου ... (19), one of the rare occasions when he takes advantage of the help given by previous speakers.

happen, which would have been unthinkable in former days? Demosthenes has the answer ready:

"There was an element in the national character, men of Athens, which has been lost now, something which rose above the wealth of Persia and kept Hellas free and never suffered defeat in any battle on land or sea, the loss of which has ruined everything and upset the whole world for us. What do I mean? I mean that everyone used to loathe the men who took money from the would-be conquerors or destroyers of Hellas" (36–37).

And the severe resolution passed against Arthmius of Zelea, "because he brought the gold of the Persians into the Peloponnese", is quoted to illustrate the integrity of former days, when "barbarians trembled before the power of the Greeks, instead of Greeks before barbarians" (42–43).

This appeal to national pride is particularly well-timed and the preparation for it has been more careful than in any previous speech; this is one of the reasons why he is able to sustain its intensity so long, from 36 to 45.[15]

When he finally decides to break the tension, he does so with a single word, saying there is a "silly" ($\varepsilon\dot{\upsilon}\dot{\eta}\theta\eta\varsigma$) story circulating to the effect that Philip is not yet as strong as the Spartans were during the time of their hegemony, when "our city kept them at bay" (47). Demosthenes has often protested before against this familiar objection that the time is not yet ripe for intervention,[16] but now his reply is more carefully reasoned. He points out that methods of warfare have changed: "It is not because he has a hoplite phalanx that we hear of Philip going wherever he wants, but because he has light-armed troops, cavalry, bowmen, mercenaries, and so on. And when he attacks a city that is unhealthy within itself, when no one comes out to defend his own city, through lack of trust, that is when he is able to bring up his machinery and start besieging the place. I need not point out that he makes no distinction between winter and summer" (49–50).

Demosthenes himself had used the *paradeigma* of Spartan power in the *First Philippic*, reminding the Athenians how boldly they had resisted

15 It is arguable that the appeal is more effective in the "shorter" version, that the orator's task is rendered more difficult if the passages omitted in S are included. For example, the parenthetic remarks in 41, which offer formal justification for the resolution about Arthmius, interrupt the intensity of the appeal. And in 32 the additional details which explain Philip's powers at the Pythian festival do not help to illustrate his *hybris*.

16 The "Olynthiacs" constantly emphasize the need of not letting the opportunity pass and the evil results of hesitation in the past, e.g., 1.8–13; they also point out that if Philip is not checked in the North, he will be able to attack Attica (1.25). In 4.10 the objection is met by an appeal to the pride which should drive a free man to take action. Here the argument is of a different kind.

Sparta despite the heavy odds against them and that "nothing need frighten you if you are on your guard" (4.3). Now he rejects the *paradeigma* as irrelevant and misleading. Philip must be fought with different weapons, attacked in his own country, which offers many opportunities for doing him severe damage, and a pitched battle must be avoided;[17] and they must use their wits as well as weapons of war, and remember that they cannot overcome their enemies until they punish the men in Athens who are serving the enemy's interest (53).

He reinforces this familiar warning by reminding them what happened at Olynthus, Eretria, and Oreus, with new details and names that he has never mentioned before. The Olynthians were persuaded by Philip's agents to expel Apollonides, (56) and at Eretria, after the people had been induced to expel the loyal party, Philip sent Hipponicus and a thousand mercenaries, pulled down the walls of Porthmus, and established three tyrants in power—Hipparchus, Automedon, and Cleitarchus (58). At Oreus the protests of Euphraeus only landed him in prison, and no one else dared utter a word of warning until the enemy's army was seen approaching the walls; Euphraeus killed himself and his supporters were killed or exiled (61–62).

The lesson is more frightening than ever before. The Athenians must not wait until they "make the final reckoning and discover that there is nothing more to be done" (65). Delay may be fatal: "While the ship is still sound, no matter whether it is large or small, that is the time when sailor and steersman and every man in his turn must do his best, and see to it that no one, deliberately or otherwise, capsizes the vessel; once it sinks beneath the waves, no efforts are of any use" (69).

Demosthenes is sparing in his use of imagery, and usually explains the comparison that he is making;[18] but the ship of state is a familiar enough image to need no explanation.

At the close of the speech the Athenians are urged to make preparations for war and to send out embassies to other parts of Greece to explain their actions.[19] Demosthenes has not said much before about the value of embassies, but now he pays tribute to the good work done by "the admirable Polyeuctus and Hegesippus and others" (as well as himself)

---

17 εἰς δ' ἀγῶνα ἄμεινον ἡμῶν ἤσκηται (8.52). No such direct statement has been made before. One might compare it with the earlier naïveté of 14.9: ἐγὼ δ', ὦ ἄνδρες 'Αθηναῖοι, νομίζω τὸν μὲν πόλεμον τὸν πρὸς βασιλέα χαλεπὸν τῇ πόλει, τὸν δ' ἀγῶνα τὸν ἐκ τοῦ πολέμου ῥᾴδιον ἂν συμβῆναι, i.e., war needs triremes and money, but battles need brave men, and that is where Athens has the advantage.

18 Cf. above pp. 130–34.

19 The "longer" version specifies embassies to the Peloponnese, to Rhodes, to Chios, to the King (71).

in tours of the Peloponnese (72). The conclusions and proposals are the same as usual.

The special interest of the *Third Philippic* lies not so much in its conclusions or its emotional appeals, as in the skill with which the various arguments are manipulated. Demosthenes never remains in one position of attack for long, but moves round his various positions, strengthening each one in turn as he comes to it. Before he makes any formal proposals, he wants it to appear that only a traitor could propose anything different. He uses the evidence of events with careful economy, not wasting time with unnecessary complexities or piling up one detail after another; his brief narratives are perfectly tailored to make the particular point that he wants to establish. Each emotional outburst is carefully motivated by descriptive passages which precede it. It is the timing of these appeals rather than any special art in their writing that we must admire.

There is not much that need be said about the *Fourth Philippic*. Earlier critics thought they could detect errors of historical fact which would prove it a forgery, but their suspicions are not justified; and every paragraph is well written, with thought and phrasing quite characteristic of Demosthenes. But the lack of design and unity in the speech makes it very difficult to believe that he could have delivered it or wanted anyone to read it in the form in which it has been preserved.[20] It contains long passages which are almost, but not quite, identical with passages in *On the Chersonese*, not conclusively better or worse because of the differences. There are, however, ways in which these apparent "borrowings" can be accounted for, and this is not the most serious problem which the speech presents. The real trouble is that it cannot be regarded as a finished composition; the various parts of the speech are not combined, and there is no clear line of argument such as we expect to find in a Demosthenic oration.

Didymus and Dionysius of Halicarnassus seem ready enough to accept the speech as one of the *Philippics*, and Didymus is prepared to date it in the summer of 341.[21] But one cannot properly give any precise "date of composition" to an unfinished work, since different parts may have been written at different times and not be fully reconciled with each

---

20 This was the view of Blass, Att. Bered. III 384—92 and Weil, "Les harangues de Démosthène," 357—66. It has not been upset by the commentary of Didymus, which was not known to them. Cf. Croiset, Harangues (ed. Budé) II 112—19.

21 This must be what Didymus means by his apparent doubt whether to date it in the archonship of Nicomachus (341—40) or Sosigenes (342—41), col. I 29—30, II 2—3, i.e. before or after the end of the Athenian calendar year in midsummer 341. Cf. A. Koerte, "Zu Didymos' Demosthenes-Commentar, I. Die vierte Philippika," Rh. Mus. 60 (1905), 388—410. He prefers the earlier alternative.

other. If the text represents "work in progress" (or "work abandoned") its presence in the Demosthenic corpus has to be explained. A number of "spurious" speeches were included in the corpus from early times, and one possible explanation is that various papers were found in the orator's house after his death and treated as his own work—perhaps because it was in the interest of "publishers" to claim them as genuine compositions.[22] The papers may have included copies of speeches by contemporaries and also rough drafts and fragments; and it has been suggested that the *Fourth Philippic* is the result of an editorial attempt to combine various scraps that were found on his desk or in his cupboard.[23] The hypothesis cannot be proved, but it is quite an attractive one.

The text, as we have it, does not suggest that the occasion of the speech was different from that of *On the Chersonese* or the *Third Philippic*. The opening paragraphs present some of the themes of the *Third Philippic* (10.8—10 correspond to 9.11—13), and there follows a passage which corresponds almost word for word to 8.38—45. The argument here is that Philip will be forced to destroy the democratic government of Athens, if he is to become master of all Greece. But whereas in *On the Chersonese* the way is carefully prepared for this warning, here it is introduced quite abruptly. Likewise in 31 it is suggested that Athens should seek help from the Persian king; if this is a serious proposal, it needs to be made with care; but it is made quite abruptly, and then dropped in favour of a discussion of the Theoric Fund (35—45), without any logical connection between the two themes, followed by a digression on the great traditions of Athens.

These abrupt and unmotivated transitions are quite uncharacteristic of Demosthenes, whose best work is marked by careful timing and motivation. This is particularly true of his appeals to pride and his emotional outbursts; his climacteric arguments are motivated with quite remarkable

22 Cf. Jaeger, "Demosthenes," 38—39, and L. Pearson, "Apollodorus, the eleventh Attic orator," in The Classical Tradition, Studies in Honor of Harry Caplan (Ithaca 1966), 350.

23 Cf. Weil, "Les harangues," 362—66, Croiset, "Harangues" (ed. Budé) II 118—19. It has been argued that the passages which appear in similar form here and in "On the Chersonese," were first written as they appear here, and that "On the Chersonese" represents a final revision. For this view and variations of it see C. D. Adams, "Speeches VIII and X of the Demosthenic Corpus," CP 33 (1938), 129—44; P. Treves, "La composition de la 3me Philippique," REA 42 (1940), 354—64; and S. G. Daitz, "The Relationship of the De Chersoneso and the Philippica Quarta of Demosthenes," CP 52 (1957), 145—60.
No purpose is served by suggesting that the speech was designed not for delivery but for circulation as a political pamphlet. Why should it be less carefully composed if intended to be read than if intended for delivery? Cf. P. Wendland, Göttingische gelehrte Anzeigen 1906, 362—64.

skill. There is no such master touch in the *Fourth Philippic*. Indeed the thoughtful composition of the other speeches can be recognized all the more clearly in comparison with the lack of coherence here. There is good writing in many parts of the *Fourth Philippic*, but no critic, ancient or modern, has ever maintained that it is a good speech. It is a disappointing end to the series of *Philippics*, which should really be completed with the fighting speech of 339, that Demosthenes describes in *On the Crown* (173–80) and which he himself evidently regarded as his finest effort.

Chapter V

Attack and Defence. The Contest with Aeschines

i. The Embassy

Demosthenes first opened proceedings against Aeschines in 346, charging him with misconduct on the embassy which had negotiated the peace with Philip. Aeschines countered by bringing suit against Timarchus, who was cooperating with Demosthenes in the prosecution, charging that he had plied the trade of a male prostitute and was therefore breaking the law by taking any part in public life; he won his case, discredited the man completely, and Demosthenes had to drop his suit for the time being. But two years later Philocrates, the other leading member of the embassy, went into exile rather than face prosecution by Hyperides,[1] and Demosthenes seized the opportunity to re-open the case.[2] He could tell the jury now that Aeschines had always been afraid of a fair trial, and that was the reason why he had thought it necessary to attack Timarchus: "Before he came into court to render an account of his actions, he removed one of the men who were calling him to account, and he is going round threatening others" (2).

As on other occasions Demosthenes begins his case by pointing out what kind of man the defendant is, a man who has no scruples about using dishonest methods to eliminate opponents or bring pressure on members of the jury. He makes his point by a series of contrasts. He invites the jury to compare the unworthy behaviour of Aeschines with the conduct that is expected of an ambassador and to bear in mind what are the responsibilities of an ambassador, for which he can be called to account: "For his report, in the first place; then for the recommendations that he makes; and thirdly for the instructions that you gave him; in addition there is the matter of the time taken up by his mission; and finally you will want to know whether or not he has shown himself open to offers of money in carrying out his various tasks" (4).

Demosthenes promises to prove that "there was not a word of truth in the reports that Aeschines made and that he prevented the people from

1 Cf. Aesch. 2.6; 3.79, and Dinarchus, Dem. 28, Hyperides, Euxen. col. 39.
2 He does not pretend, however, that his task is easy, since lawsuits are dependent on καιροί as well as πράγματα (19.3).

hearing the truth from me; that the course which he recommended was the exact contrary, in every respect, to what was needed; that he let time pass, in which the city lost its chance to achieve many important results; and that he was paid for all this, just like Philocrates" (8).

He also wants everyone to notice the contrast between Aeschines' earlier activities and his later career. In earlier days he had been a vigorous opponent of Philip, and in his speech to the Ten Thousand at Megalopolis he had warned the Arcadians of Philip's methods (10); he is expected to refer to this "fine long speech" in his defence; Demosthenes hopes to destroy any credit that he can claim for it by contrasting it with his later behaviour.[3]

Demosthenes says that at one time he had full confidence in Aeschines' integrity: "Until we returned from the first embassy, I for one, men of Athens, had no notion that he had sold himself" (13). On the day that they returned from this embassy (the first of three missions of Philip) Aeschines made a "short and reasonable speech," but next day, in the Assembly, there was a great change. The people seemed ready to accept the treaty proposal that the various allies of Athens wanted, after Demosthenes had supported it in a speech:

"You were ready to accept this proposal and would not listen to a word from the despicable Philocrates. But Aeschines stood up to address you and supported Philocrates in a speech for which he deserves to die many deaths, saying you must not think about your ancestors or listen to people who spoke of trophies and battles at sea, urging you to vote formally that you would not help any Greeks who had not helped you in the past" (15–16).

This account may be grossly unfair, and Aeschines will do his best to show that it is.[4] But Demosthenes does not linger on it; he describes next what happened in the Boule, after they returned from the second embassy, the purpose of which was to obtain Philip's signature and his sworn acceptance of the treaty:

3 Aeschines retorts that Demosthenes is in no position to complain of inconsistency or lack of firmness, αὐτὸς ὢν ἀνδραποδώδης καὶ μόνον οὐκ ἐστιγμένος αὐτόμολος (2.79), and he explains carefully how plans for organizing resistance to Philip had to give way to plans for peace. His argument is perfectly sound, but the jury might accept Demosthenes' interpretation, if they were first convinced that Aeschines lacked integrity.

4 Aeschines gives an entirely reasonable account of this speech and the circumstances in which it was delivered (2.75–77), but pays little attention to Demosthenes' praise of his speech on the previous day (63) and calls witnesses to prove that Demosthenes' account of these two meetings of the Assembly is quite inaccurate (63–67). Each orator uses the same "facts" to prove a different point.

"I came forward and denounced these two men, telling the whole truth . . . I described the speeches which this man made, at the time when you were arranging the peace, and the situation into which they had brought the city. I urged you not to abandon what could still be saved . . ." (18).

He has not yet given any account of what happened on the second embassy. He wants first to describe his own attempt to save the situation, to save the Phocians and keep control of Thermopylae, in contrast with the monstrous confidence trick that Aeschines plays on the Assembly, when it meets and he is the first speaker:

"He refrained from giving any report of what was done on the embassy, said nothing about what had happened in the Boule, said nothing to dispute what I said there. But he made a speech which put before you such astonishing gains and advantages, that he had you all in the hollow of his hand" (ὥσθ᾿ ἅπαντας ὑμᾶς λαβὼν ᾤχετο, 19).

According to this account Aeschines said he had persuaded Philip to adopt every item that Athens wanted, to be severe towards the Thebans and to spare the Phocians; all the Athenians had to do was to sit quietly at home until they heard the good news that Thespiae and Plataea were being re-established as cities and that the Thebans, not the Phocians, were being made to restore to Apollo's temple in Delphi all the wealth that it had lost; Philip had been convinced that it was the Thebans, not the Phocians, who were really guilty (21). The speech met with a tremendous reception, and when Demosthenes got up to say he knew nothing of all this that they were saying, "they stood on either side of me, this man and Philocrates, shouting and pushing me off the platform, and finally jeering at me; and you laughed, and would not listen to me or believe anything different from what he told you" (23).

If the jury will believe that Aeschines made all these misleading predictions and that this is a fair and accurate account of his "report" to the Assembly,[5] Demosthenes has won his case already, before even start-

---

5 It cannot in fact be an accurate account. Cf. G. L. Cawkwell, "Aeschines and the ruin of Phocis," REG 75 (1962), 453–59. He notes with surprise how little "disquiet at Demosthenes' account" there has been among modern historians, although if the Athenians found they had been misled by Aeschines' speech, as Demosthenes tells the story, "it is inconceivable that he could have escaped trial and condemnation" in 346. He suggests, therefore, that when the Assembly met (on the 16th of Scirophorion) the Athenians must have already known that no military action could save Phocis, and that Aeschines was merely consoling them with the hope that Philip's hostility to the Thebans would prevent him from attacking the Phocians; even if Demosthenes protested, as he says he did in "On the Peace" (10), that such hopes were vain, it would still be true that Aeschines was not guilty of misleading the Athenians "in any serious sense." But if this is what happened, why has not Aeschines said so?

ing his narrative. He wants them to notice how suddenly Aeschines has come to trust Philip; if everything turned out exactly the opposite to what he predicted, it must be because "he sold the truth for money" (28). These are the points that he hopes they will keep in mind when his more detailed narrative begins.[6] It will be a long time before Aeschines has the chance to meet these accusations, and when his turn comes to speak, the damage may be past repairing.

Instead of "telling the whole story from the beginning," Demosthenes insists on the disastrous results of this embassy which Aeschines and Philocrates pretended had been so brilliantly successful. So as to make sure that he will not be held responsible himself for the disaster of Phocis, he produces formal evidence of his protest in the Boule (he does not call witnesses to support his account of the scene in the Assembly); he says his innocence is proved because he denounced the others, "but all the guilty person had to do was to keep quiet and follow the tactics of obstruction" (33). And when the news arrives that Philip is actually at Thermopylae, Aeschines calms the fears of the Athenians and makes sure that they do not listen to the protests of Demosthenes or anyone else (35).

There is still no direct evidence of guilt, and poor judgment might seem to be a more likely explanation than treachery. But sceptical jurors may be persuaded by a document which is presented to them under the guise of evidence. This is a letter of Philip to the Athenians which seems to clear Aeschines of some of the charges against him, because Philip admits that he himself prevented the ambassadors from carrying out some of their tasks, though he says nothing about any of the famous "promises." The letter seems to help Aeschines without incriminating Philip—surely the jury must see that Aeschines wrote the letter for Philip to sign (38),[7] and that he was responsible for its failure to mention the vigorous efforts of Demosthenes to ransom prisoners of war! (40).[8] Demosthenes

6 Cf. Weil, Plaidoyers politiques, 222: "Après avoir fait ainsi entrer dans l'esprit des juges l'idée de la trahison d'Eschine, Démosthène aborde le récit du voyage et du séjour à Pella. C'est là qu'il parle des entrevues sécrets, des présents offerts et acceptés. Il ne peut fournir la preuve de ces faits, mais les esprits prévenus contre Eschine par tout qui précède trouveront ces faits probables, presque nécessaires. L'argumentation sert en quelque sorte à établir ce qui aurait dû être le point de départ de toute l'accusation; les fondations de l'édifice ne soutiennent pas les constructions supérieures, mais y sont, au contraire, suspendues."

7 This seems like a rather wild accusation, but it must have alarmed Aeschines, who took some trouble to show that it was absurd (2.124—29). He is careful to offer the evidence of his fellow ambassadors that he never went to Philip on the night when he was supposed to have written it.

8 Aeschines will, in fact, try to belittle and ridicule these efforts, with his story of Demosthenes' servants carrying two bedrolls, one of which, so he said, contained a

makes good use of this letter, pointing out its lack of cordiality in contrast with previous letters of Philip, so that it is left to Aeschines to reassure the Athenians by his confident declarations. If Philip had really intended to carry out these so-called promises, the only way to do it would have been to say nothing about them in advance—is it possible that Aeschines frustrated Philip's excellent intentions by revealing them to the Assembly? The alternative is hardly meant to be taken seriously.

A more important document is now produced, the resolution of Philocrates which the Assembly passed despite the protests of Demosthenes. Close association with Philocrates may be taken as one more sign of Aeschines' guilt,[9] and Demosthenes is careful to show that he was not on good terms with Philocrates himself; that is why he reports the gibe of Philocrates in the Assembly: "It is no wonder that Demosthenes and I see things differently, since he drinks water and I drink wine" (46). He has already described how Aeschines supported the resolution of Philocrates, and he may expect him to defend it as a proper resolution. Thanks to the optimistic and reassuring report of Aeschines the Assembly permitted Philocrates to add a clause saying "if the Phocians fail to hand over the temple to the Amphictyons, the Athenians will take measures against the persons who prevent this being done" (49). Demosthenes argues that since the only Amphictyons present in the North were the Thebans and Thessalians, this clause surrendered the Phocians to their enemies—it was the clearest act of betrayal! Aeschines will reply that the Athenians could still have sent out a military force, and that Demosthenes prevented it, despite an actual invitation from Philip that they should do so;[10] but Demosthenes can reply that it was already too late to accomplish anything by interference. He appeals to the calendar to show that each event follows in sequence as each piece of news reaches its destination. Aeschines does not attempt to refute this argument directly.[11] Though it may not be strictly accurate in all its detail, it is put together with great skill and probably could not be destroyed without a greater display of ingenuity than a jury would tolerate.

talent in cash, "a sum barely enough to ransom a single man of any substance" (2.99–100).

9 Aeschines in his turn will take pains to show how much support Demosthenes gave to Philocrates in the early days of the peace negotiations; when Philocrates was brought into court on a *graphe paranomon*, "it was Demosthenes he asked to speak in his defence, not me" (2.14).

10 2.137–39. Cf. the comment of Cloché, Démosthènes, 116–17.

11 Aeschines' account of these critical days (2.140–43), though totally different, because it concerns itself with different incidents, does not in fact contradict Demosthenes' story.

The dreadful consequences of such treachery have yet to be described, and Demosthenes describes the desolate Phocian countryside which he saw on his journey to Delphi, "houses pulled down, city-walls dismantled, no sign of any young men in the fields, just a few women and children and pitiful old men" (65). The Phocians had saved Athens from slavery in 404, when the Thebans wanted to enslave the city, and this is what Aeschines and Philocrates allow to happen to them: "I believe that our ancestors, if they heard of it, would think it no sin to stone these men to death with their own hands" (66).

The full depth of their guilt is emphasized with some cleverly contrived *amplificatio*. These corrupt men, whom Philip needed to do his work for him, turned out to be even more corrupt than necessary! (68). Unlike Macedonians, who were not free men and would not have to face the free citizens of a city that stands for freedom, "they were your duly appointed ambassadors and undertook to deceive you, with whom they would be spending the rest of their lives" (69).

"Shameless" is the word that describes this kind of man: "And I am told that he will sink to such a depth of shamelessness as to blame the Spartans and the Phocians and Hegesippus" (72).[12] It is quickly shown that the Spartans are not to blame; they saw what Philip's real intentions were as soon as he came to Thermopylae; and when Philip realized that they would not help him, "he sent Aeschines to mislead you." He did not want the Athenians to discover that he was working for the Thebans; they might make things difficult for him by sending aid to the Phocians (77). As for the Phocians, however reprehensible their conduct in the past, they gave Philip no cause to change his mind if he had really intended to save them. Aeschines will say that no Phocian has made any complaint against him.[13] Of course not; they are too miserable and too badly frightened to raise their voices in accusation against anyone (80—81).

The Phocians had been the buffer between Philip and the Thebans, they had controlled Thermopylae and blocked Philip's path, preventing any move on his part against Attica or Euboea or the Peloponnese. Aeschines may think he is appealing to Athenian religious scruples and placating the Thebans by insisting on the "impiety" of the Phocians, but when he told the Assembly that Philip was going to save them, he was playing on anti-Theban feeling in Athens and widening the breach be-

---

12 Cf. Aesch. 2.131—35. It is not necessary that Demosthenes should have heard the actual words of Aeschines before introducing this anticipation; this "anticipation" might have been already in the spoken version of the speech, though there are places where real anticipation would be unlikely. Cf. A. P. Dorjahn, "Anticipation of arguments in Athenian oratory," TAPA 66 (1935), 274—95.

13 Aesch. 2.142—43.

tween Athens and Thebes, just what Philip wanted him to do: "How could a man show greater *hybris* towards you?" (85).

Hybris and shamelessness make the portrait look more familiar. But the good reputation of Aeschines cannot be destroyed by unsupported statements about his character. It will take a skilful narrative to reveal his character and convince members of the jury that they were wrong to respect him. Hardly anything has been said yet about his general character or his past life, which might explain his treasonable conduct. The tactics that were used against Meidias and Androtion are not suitable here.

Two more documents are presented in evidence to show how far the situation deteriorated over the years (thanks to Aeschines and Philocrates)—the resolution of 353, when Philip's path was successfully blocked at Thermopylae, and the resolution voted in 346 after the invasion of Phocis, "when you brought women and children in from the country and decided to celebrate the festival of the Heracleia inside the city" (86). Demosthenes can rest his voice while the texts are read out, and then he is ready for a further outburst about the irrelevancy to be expected of Aeschines in his defence. He will probably talk about the blessings of peace and the opportunities that it gave Athens for rearmament and financial recovery (though it gave Philip much greater advantages): "This godforsaken little clerk will try to defend himself as though he were being accused of making peace" (95). It is the incompetent generals, who mismanaged the war, who should be thanked for the peace.

If nothing worse than incompetence can be proved against Aeschines, the jury should let him go free; but this is not a very generous offer, because Demosthenes will not let him say that he was misled or deceived by Philip's promises. Since he has never uttered a word of complaint against Philip, it is clear that he is Philip's "loyal hired hand" and deserves to die three deaths (110). Demosthenes appeals to the evidence of "the facts"—"No one can say that they are influenced or partial towards one side or the other" (120). When a Thessalian delegation asked the Athenians to approve Philip's appointment as an Amphictyonic member, Aeschines actually supported the request (111–13), and he has never tried to prove his innocence by disassociating himself from Philocrates or complaining of Philocrates' ill-gotten wealth: "He is given the chance to clear himself and he refuses it" (118).

These "facts," even if accurately reported, prove nothing except a preference for avoiding unnecessary fuss and useless bluster; there was really nothing Athens could have done to prevent Philip's appointment to the Amphictyonic council. But by using them as "indications" (*semeia*) Demosthenes is building up a circumstantial case which it will not be easy to answer. More "facts" follow. A third embassy was sent to Philip, "on the basis of the hopes" raised by Aeschines' report. Demosthenes refused to go, but Aeschines accepted the appointment and would have gone, except that "these men held a consultation to decide whom they should leave behind in Athens" (122). A physician was found to make a sworn statement that Aeschines was not well enough to go, and his brother was appointed in his place. It is taken for granted that he is left behind to keep an eye on Demosthenes, in case he urges the Assembly "to pass some of the measures that were needed to save the Phocians" (123).

For all we know, Aeschines may have been genuinely ill, but Demosthenes gives the jury no time to think. He assaults their emotions with a piece of dramatic description, reminding them how the news of the Phocian disaster reached Athens:

"Five or six days later, after the Phocians were destroyed and Aeschines had completed the task for which he was being paid (it was just a job for him, like any other), after Dercylidas had turned back from Chalcis and brought you the news of the ruin of Phocis when you were met in Assembly at Piraeus, you were of course deeply shocked to hear of the disaster and distressed at what had happened to them, and you voted to bring in the women and children from the country, to prepare the defence posts and fortify the Piraeus, and to celebrate the Heracleia inside the walls of the city. And in the midst of all this turmoil and confusion our wise and clever friend here, with the beautiful voice, without any authorization from Boule or Assembly, set off on his embassy to join the man who was responsible for all these disasters, not worrying at all about the sworn statement that he was a sick man or that someone else had been chosen to take his place or that the law prescribes the death penalty for actions of this kind. He never thought how shocking it was that he had previously reported a price put on his head by the Thebans and now, with the Thebans in control of Phocis as well as all Boeotia, he walks right into the middle of Thebes and the Theban camp. He was so completely beside himself, so totally taken up with the thought of the pay he had earned, that he dismissed all other thoughts from his mind or chose to ignore them—and left Athens" (125—27).

Demosthenes knows that Aeschines will say he went to Thebes in a final desperate effort to save the situation,[14] but if the jurors are already convinced that he is a traitor, they may refuse to listen to him. He rejects indignantly the thought that it might be politically prudent for the

---

14 Aeschines describes his work on the third embassy in 2.139—42. He dismisses as ridiculous the charge that his presence on this embassy was unauthorized, and says a Phocian delegation will testify that he saved many lives. He cannot deny that he was present at the victory celebrations in Thebes (though he does deny that he made himself conspicuous, 2.162).

Athenians to spare Philip's friend; they would do better to win Philip's respect by punishing him, as in former days they won the respect of the Persian king by putting Timagoras to death, letting the king know that he accomplished nothing by giving him forty talents.

The first part of the speech finishes with a contrast between the recently acquired wealth of Aeschines and Philocrates (the reward of treason, evidently) and the losses that Athens has suffered. Demosthenes has been preparing the way for his principal narrative section, the narrative of the second embassy, and he has been following the same kind of procedure as in the speech *Against Meidias*. There he began by recounting Meidias' assault on him at the festival (21.13–18), a recognized, admitted act of violence, just as here he begins with Aeschines' report after the second embassy and goes on to mention other incidents which can be taken as "signs" that he was working in Philip's interest. In both speeches he wants the jury to know something about the defendant's character and purpose before offering a more detailed narrative. He takes for granted that everyone is familiar with the unpleasant and violent character of Meidias, his *hybris* and *aselgeia* (21.1). The portrait of Aeschines has to be built up more gradually.

Finally the account of the second embassy begins (149). The task of the embassy is to obtain Philip's sworn agreement as soon as possible and not give him the chance to make further aggressive moves before he is bound by his oath to keep the peace. Demosthenes explains how, before they left Athens, he insisted that they must sail to the Hellespont at once and not give Philip time to win control of that area (150). He explained also the importance of maintaining the Phocians in control of Thermopylae, and once Philip had taken the oath "if he did not carry out his part of the agreement, you could close his markets and, by a blockade, keep him short of money and materials; he would be the slave to the terms of the treaty, not you" (153).

Accordingly, the Boule adopted his motion that "the ambassadors should set out as soon as possible and Proxenos, the strategos, should take them to the area where he knew Philip was to be found" (154). They set off, but their speed was very slow:

"We met Proxenos at Oreus, but they would not take the chance to sail and carry out their orders; instead they travelled by a roundabout route (ἐπορεύοντο κύκλῳ), so that it took us thirty-one days to reach Macedonia. Meanwhile Philip got possession of Doriscus, of Thrace, the fortress area, and Hieron Teichos, while I protested vigorously and constantly. First I said plainly what I thought, then I tried to explain to them what they seemed not to understand, finally I abandoned all pretence and denounced them as corrupt and abominable traitors. It was Aeschines who opposed me and stood out against what I kept on saying and what had been recognized in your resolution" (155–57).

Just as earlier in his speech he began with Aeschines' report to the Assembly, so now he begins with an undeniable fact that needs explanation — that it took them thirty-one days to reach Macedonia. Why did it take them so long? Aeschines says they spent the time administering the oath to Philip's allies. No, says Demosthenes; none of these allies took the oath until much later, "in the inn at Pherae" (158), when Philip's army was already on its way into Greece; and this delay was part of Philip's plan; he did not want his allies to be bound by any oath "to the Athenians and their allies" until it was too late to protest against his march into Phocis; he did not want his allies to see the text of the agreement which (unless he could alter it) included Phocis in the alliance.

Quite evidently, if Aeschines and Philocrates had been in Philip's pay, they would have done their best to avoid any early approach to his allies. Demosthenes says they "did what he wanted of them with every mark of exaggerated respect" (160), but he has no way of proving his accusation. He has not been able to induce other members of the embassy to testify against Aeschines.[15] And the documents which he cites prove nothing (162). So he tries to make up for his lack of evidence by pointing out some contrasts. On the first embassy they pushed on through hostile territory, without waiting for the herald who was being sent to guarantee their safe passage (and there was no special need for haste then); now, with no fear of danger to delay them, they dawdled (163–64). And while Demosthenes spent large sums of money ransoming prisoners of war, as witnesses will testify, they took all the money that Philip offered them. He has no course no evidence of these "gifts," but relies on his skill as a narrator:

"This was Philip's way of testing us all. To each of us he sent a special messenger with a gift, a large sum of money, men of Athens. And when a certain person refused the gift (I have no need to name myself as that person, since my behaviour and the facts make it clear), he thought we would be foolish enough to accept a gift made 'in common.' He thought it would protect the individuals who had sold themselves if we all had a share, on a small scale, in a 'common gift.' And when I raised objections, they divided what would have been my share. I asked Philip to use the money for the benefit of prisoners of war. It was hardly decent for

15 He says bravely "you will know in a moment how well this pleased the rest of us" (157), but adds that he does not want anyone "to be under any compulsion to-day to show himself an honest man." Aeschines, on the other hand, goes to some trouble to explain how Demosthenes antagonized his companions on the journey (2.97–98).

him to expose these two and say that this man and that man had the money. He could not avoid the expense, and so he agreed to do what I asked, but put it off, saying he would send the men home in time for the Panathenaea" (167—68).[16]

And what did Aeschines and Philocrates do in return for these gifts? They contrived, says Demosthenes, to exclude Phocis and Cersobleptes and Halos from the treaty, contrary to the agreement that had been drawn up in Athens, they tried to alter the text of the resolution that gave the embassy its instructions, they added Cardia to the list of Philip's allies, they prevented Demosthenes from writing to Athens and sent a letter themselves which was full of lies. Aeschines even accused Demosthenes of promising Philip to organize an anti-democratic coup in Athens; but it was Aeschines, not Demosthenes, who paid all those private visits to Philip (and these visits are confirmed by witnesses). It is left to the jury to imagine "what these men must have done when they were in close touch with their paymaster" (177). Proof of Aeschines' treachery may be lacking, but the opportunity and the temptation were certainly present.

Instead of looking vainly for proof Demosthenes reminds the Athenians (as he did before) of the losses that they suffered and recalls how severely in the past they used to punish politicians who caused much less serious damage to the city. In former years, when policy had been more carefully designed and the Assembly was less negligent, the risk of damage was less; but now "the places that could have been saved were lost because he insisted on travelling by the land route, and what could have been saved by telling the truth was lost by his lies" (181). He also reminds them that in a democracy, where autocratic methods do not prevail, it is a matter of vital importance not to waste time: "After everything else, once a decision is made, and it seems to be the right decision, time has to be allowed for the incompetence of 'the Many,' while they provide the necessary material, so that the decisions can be put into effect. The man who steals time at these moments is not merely stealing time, he is actually taking away the power of action from the people" (186).

This double comparison, between present and past and between democracy and autocracy, shows Demosthenes' rhetorical ingenuity at its best. Cicero imitates his manner and method in an even more complex combination of comparisons in the Second Philippic (6.13—7.18).

Demosthenes never misses an opportunity to turn what his opponent says against himself — especially what he may say by way of defence or

16 Apollophanes is produced as a witness (168), but we are not told what he said; if he merely corroborated the account of the conversation with Philip about ransoming prisoners, his evidence proves nothing.

counter-attack. Aeschines is expected to say that Demosthenes obstructed Philip's friendly intentions. Demosthenes meets this charge by saying Philip had no such intentions, and claims to prove his point by offering one more letter of Philip in evidence. But Aeschines will also, no doubt, complain that he is being disloyal to his fellow-ambassadors and will cry out, in his theatrical manner: "Where is the salt, where is the table that we shared, where are the libations that we poured together?" (189).

Demosthenes first meets this charge quite simply, when he says that sharing a table with others has never released a man from the obligation to denounce their misdeeds. But this is not all. He asks permission to tell a story "which has nothing to do with the embassy" (192). Philip, he says, was generous towards the daughters of a man who had killed his own brother, freeing them from captivity, at the request of the actor Satyrus, and providing dowries for them, since their father was dead. Aeschines, by contrast, behaved despicably towards a " respectable free-born lady" (196) who had been taken prisoner at Olynthus. She was brought into a drinking party, and the drunken guests demanded that she sing for them; when she refused, Aeschines and Phrynon called in a slave to beat her with a whip, and "she might have been killed" if another guest (whom Demosthenes claims as his informant) had not taken her away. How can a man "who has behaviour of this sort on his conscience" appeal to "good manners" or "decent feelings?" Will he have the effrontery to look you in the eye and proceed to tell you about his 'splendid career' in that gorgeous voice of his? The thought chokes me" (199).

Aeschines will of course deny that there is a word of truth in the story, and we may well believe him,[17] but Demosthenes insists that it is told in many different places, and he pushes his advantage home. He reminds the jury of the disreputable religious ceremonies in which Aeschines assisted his mother, "rolling about on the floor with drunkards, and a mere boy was all he was," and the wretched living he made as a clerk and an actor of minor parts; and this was the man who brought a morals charge against Timarchus (199—200). What else but a pack of lies can they expect from such a person?

This massive personal attack, in the worst of taste by modern standards, is not mere wanton abuse, but has a definite purpose. It is

17 Aeschines is at first content to say that the jury rejected the story at once "on the basis of my decently conducted life" (2.4). Later he produces the story that Demosthenes approached a certain Aristophanes of Olynthus, offering him money to say that the lady was his wife (152—54). According to the scholiast, a demonstration of protest was organized by Eubulus at this point in the speech. Blass, Att. Bered. III 358, notes how much effort Aeschines made to refute the story and draws the quite unnecessary conclusion that it may have been true.

meant to suggest to the jury that the crime of treason is not altogether surprising in such a man, if they bear in mind that behind the facade of his fine words and imposing presence there lies a fundamentally unsound character, which has not been helped by an unfortunate upbringing. This is dangerous and carefully contrived slander.

He tells the jury once again how he spoke up in every meeting of the Assembly to denounce their treachery[18] (in case Aeschines is foolish enough to say that Demosthenes is equally guilty) and they could say nothing in reply, "because it is truth that is strong and the guilty conscience that is weak. This is what paralyses the tongue, gags the mouth, chokes a man and makes him silent" (208).

After using all the resources of rhetoric with such alarming skill it is appropriate to say that rhetoric is of little importance in a case like this, that all argument on his part is merely subsidiary to "what they know already." And in two long breathless sentences he tells them what it is that everyone already knows:

"If all the promises that they made to you have been fulfilled since peace was made, if you admit that you were so hopelessly spineless and weak that, though the city was not threatened by any invasion by land or blockade by sea or any other serious danger, at a time when you could buy grain at a good price and were, generally, just as prosperous as you are now, knowing what was going to happen, with adequate warning from these men that your allies were going to be ruined and the Thebans were going be made strong, that Philip was going to seize the Thracian territory and set up bases in Euboea from which he could attack you — if, knowing that everything that has happened was going to happen, you then made peace and made it gladly, you may acquit Aeschines; do not add to your shame by committing perjury, because if this is the true situation he is not guilty of any offence against you, and I am out of my mind, acting like a madman in prosecuting him.

"But if what has happened is the very reverse of this, if they held out many attractive prospects to you, saying that Philip was devoted to Athens, would save the Phocians and curb the *hybris* of the Thebans, that he would give you even greater favours than he promised at the time of the Amphipolis incident if he could have peace, that he would restore Euboea to you and Oropus — if this is what they said and what they promised, and if all their promises were false, if they have made fools of

---

18 We have the actual record of his protests in the Assembly (but without mention of any names) in "On the Peace" (5.10) and the "Second Philippic," αἰσθόμενος φενακιζομένην τὴν πόλιν, προὔλεγον καὶ διεμαρτυρόμην καὶ οὐκ εἴων προέσθαι Πύλας οὐδὲ Φωκέας (6.29).

you and practically robbed you of Attica itself, then condemn Aeschines, do not add to the outrageous treatment you have suffered (I don't know what else to call it) and for which these men have been paid; do not bring the curse of perjury on yourselves" (218–20).

The whole case against Aeschines is contained in these two sentences, which are written with great care and which only an orator with perfect control of his technique could hope to deliver effectively. Aeschines is told that he cannot hope to be acquitted unless he gives a creditable explanation of his report to the Assembly. And if he somehow convinces the jury that he gave warning of Philip's real intentions, he will be asking them to face a most unlikely and humiliating "fact" – that Athens behaved weakly and dishonourably. Demosthenes defies the jury to accept this alternative.

He insists further on the gravity of the disaster and the enormity of Aeschines' guilt, and points out that he has no motive for making false accusations. If he wanted money, it would be much easier to obtain it from Philip than to make Aeschines pay for his silence. He complains that the Athenians seem not to know who their true friends are or to "love their friends and hate their enemies," as Philip does; this, it seems, is something that an autocratic ruler does more effectively than a democratic state; this must be the reason why they show no respect for a man who spends his own money in obtaining freedom for prisoners of war and acquit men who take bribes and betray the city and its allies. They must restore respect for integrity and true values in Athens by condemning Aeschines, who took advantage of their uncertainty in judgment to ruin the imprudent but innocent Timarchus, but took no steps to prosecute Phrynon, who sent his own son to Philip to "live a life of shame" (227–33).

The emotional outbursts in this speech are never prolonged, and Demosthenes eases the tension by recalling something which "had almost escaped his notice". Aeschines, he says, will probably try to confuse the issue by saying: "He actually praised us, he gave a dinner for Philip's ambassadors," without mentioning that this was on the return from the first embassy, before there was any indication of criminal conduct.[19] Then

---

19 Aeschines does not say exactly on what occasion Demosthenes entertained the Macedonian ambassadors (2.111), but he says quite specifically that Demosthenes praised his fellow ambassadors and proposed that they be invited to dinner in the Prytaneum "on the return from the second embassy" (ἥκων ἀπὸ τῆς ὑστέρας πρεσβείας, 2.121). This particular protest of Demosthenes, it seems, must be a later addition to the speech, when revised for publication, because, as Weil says in his note on the passage (Plaidoyers politiques): "Toute la sagacité de Démosthène n'eût pas suffi pour prévoir cette rouerie." And Aeschines could hardly have made such a misleading statement if Demosthenes had previously given warning of it. Cf.

he renews his solemn appeal, telling the jurors that "the gods will know when a man has given a vote contrary to justice," and they must "trust the gods in the hope of a fair future for themselves and their children," rather than acquit a defendant who has condemned himself out of his own mouth, and look for gratitude from him.

The warning against loving false friends has reached its proper conclusion, and he breaks the tension again by trying to make Aeschines look ridiculous. He quoted lines from Hesiod and Euripides when prosecuting Timarchus[20] — did he not see that these verses could be used against himself better than against Timarchus? Demosthenes decides that the time has come to show that Aeschines is as stupid as he is dishonest,[21] and that his pretensions to learning are absurd. Ex-actor though he is, and though he has played the part of Creon in Sophocles' *Antigone*, he has disregarded Creon's famous lines in that play: "He 'saw disaster striding towards the city' but gave no warning of it, he took no thought that 'the ship of state sail bravely on its way,' but overturned it and did his best to see that it fell into enemy hands."

Not only is Aeschines represented as stupid, so that no reasonable explanation need be offered for his unaccountable behaviour, he is also said to mask his cruel and heartless nature with his dignified manner and beautiful voice; and when he displayed righteous indignation, in his prosecution of Timarchus, he overacted the part, like the third-rate actor that he was, with his excessively "stagy" manner, imitating the pose of the statue of Solon when he offered it as an example of *sophrosyne*, Solon with his hand enfolded in his gown: "It isn't when you are speaking that you need to keep your hand inside your gown, but when you are on an embassy. You are the man who went round with your hand stretched out, palm upward, and disgraced your countrymen, and now you put on this display of righteousness here. You think that because you have practised how to deliver a few wretched little speeches you can escape paying the penalty for your misdeeds" (255).

Spengel, "Die Dispositio der demosthenischen Rede περὶ παραπρεσβείας," Rh. Mus. 16 (1861), 556. If this "anticipation" is removed from the text, there is only a very brief interval between the preceding emotional outburst and the equally emotional appeal that follows (the same appeal in different form). The interval between the two appeals may be thought an improvement in the design of the speech, but (for all we know) the original version may have included a passage which has been replaced by this "anticipation."

20 1.128–29, 151–53.

21 This is not the first time that Aeschines has been ridiculed for his stupidity. In 72 his preposterous lies are represented as an insult to the intelligence of the jury— "one would think he was being tried in some other court, and not by you who are fully conversant with the facts."

Demosthenes is able to break off and take a well-earned rest after this tremendous climax by asking the clerk to read out an extract from Solon's verses. When he speaks again, he takes his cue from Solon's declaration that it is the gods who save the city; there can be no better time than the present to condemn Aeschines and stop the plague of corruption and treachery that has broken out all over Greece. He holds out the terrible example of the Olynthians, "those unfortunate people whose disaster is due to nothing so much as to this kind of thing" (263). And he contrasts the strength of Athens in former days with its present weakness, since it became not only safe but respectable to receive bribes: "When Lasthenes roofed his house with lumber from Macedonia, when Euthycrates (without paying anything) was able to maintain a large herd of cattle and someone else was supplied with sheep, someone else with horses," and the public apparently respected them for it (265).

The tone of the passage will be familiar from the political orations, but there is more detail now in this description of corruption in high places. The contrast between past and present is developed further by recalling the famous sentences on Arthmius of Zelea and Callias (271–73), and the sentences of death or exile passed on other less well-known men because they took money when serving on an embassy. Some of them were condemned despite good service to the city in earlier life. Aeschines cannot claim any such distinguished service (or distinguished ancestors), but even if he could, he cut himself off from making any appeal for pity by his savagery in prosecuting Timarchus, when he warned the jury against pitying the poor man's elderly mother or small children. As usual, Aeschines' words are turned against him; he had argued that the condemnation of Timarchus should have a salutary effect on young people, and as though he had forgotten to mention it before, Demosthenes picks this moment to reveal the "real reason" why Aeschines attacked Timarchus — it was because he had proposed the death penalty for anyone who was found supplying Philip with arms or naval equipment: "Upwards flows the stream to-day and all talk of harlotry is reversed" (287). This parody of the famous chorus in Euripides' *Medea*[22] is one more attempt to make Aeschines' verse quotations and heavy moralizing look ridiculous.

All Aeschines' credits are turned against him. He has a powerful defender in Eubulus; Demosthenes pretends to turn angrily on Eubulus and asks him what he means by helping men who are in Philip's pay, after he has denounced Philocrates and his peace and called down curses on

22 ἄνω ποταμῶν ἱερῶν χωροῦσι παγαί
καὶ δίκα καὶ πάντα πάλιν στρέφεται (Med. 410–11),
parodied by Demosthenes: ἀλλὰ δῆτ᾽ ἄνω ποταμῶν ἐν ἐκείνῃ τῇ ἡμέρᾳ πάντες οἱ περὶ πορνείας ἐρρύησαν λόγοι.

Philip's head: "I don't want anyone to be saved or ruined just because a certain person wishes it" (296). The imaginary altercation helps Demosthenes find his way back to the argument with which his speech began, the contrast between Aeschines' earlier career and his later treachery. He quotes some extracts from Aeschines' speech to the Arcadians at Megalopolis, which he mentioned earlier; in that speech Aeschines had called Philip "a barbarian and a demon of destruction" and described his horror when he met a procession of women and children marching southward — spoils of war from Olynthus, a gift of Philip to one of his supporters; now he calls Philip "the best type of Hellene and a lover of Athens" (308) and is on friendly terms with Philocrates, "who brought free women of Olynthus here for the white slave market" (309).

The series of contrasts and comparisons goes on further, and the long outburst of indignation makes great demands on the orator's skill and strength. But he wants to end on a note of ridicule:

"Before he did the city all this harm, he used to admit that he had worked as a clerk, admitted his gratitude to the people for electing him, and behaved like a modest man; but now that he has done all this damage, he raises his eyebrows and is up in arms at once if anyone speaks of 'Aeschines the ex-clerk,' and complains that this is abusive language. We see him marching acros the Agora with a gown that reaches his ankles, keeping pace with Pythocles' stride, and he puffs out his cheeks, letting you know that he is one of Philip's best friends and enjoys his hospitality, one of the men who would like to be free of the democracy" (314).

A final brief narrative and commentary is needed to explain how Philip planned his coup and why he needed a man like Aeschines. His difficulty was that the Phocians blocked his path at Thermopylae; unless he allied himself with them against the Thebans the Athenians would not let him through the pass; but he could not make them his allies without breaking his promises to the Thessalians. The only solution was to make the Athenians think he was siding with the Phocians; he had to find someone who would deceive the Athenians and save him from discredit (320). He had to make sure that the Athenian ships would not interfere at Thermopylae, and when Demosthenes tried to slip away and bring warning to Athens, he stopped him. He is pictured talking to himself:

"It will be announced by the Athenian envoys that the Phocians will be left unharmed. People may distrust me, but they will believe them and so put themselves in my hands. Then we shall send for the Athenians to come here; they must think that they are getting everything they want, so that they will vote no resolution to stop me. The report of the embassy and its promises will be such that they will not stir a finger in Athens, no matter what happens" (324).

The story fits together perfectly. The familiar sequel is told again briefly, with a few fresh details to give it new life; and the conclusion is made to appear inevitable: "It is because of these men and their accept-ance of Philip's bribes that we have lost everything" (335).

Demosthenes is far from proving that Aeschines is guilty of treason, but if he did not actually convince the jury, he certainly disturbed them and frightened Aeschines very severely. His arguments are sometimes logically weak and his lack of direct evidence makes his case weak in law. The art of the speech consists in concealing his legal and logical diffi-culties.

Critics in antiquity, who wanted to explain why the verdict went against Demosthenes, felt it necessary to conclude that it was not a good speech. Applying the conventional rules of rhetoric, they found the com-position faulty, complained of repetition and lack of organization, and thought that the speech might have been improved (and some passages omitted altogether) if Demosthenes had revised his manuscript with greater care.[23]

Modern criticisn is more willing to pardon the neglect of rhetorical conventions. An earlier generation of scholars was prepared to believe that some passages were misplaced and some transitional passages lost alto-gether, but Blass[24] and his successors have little sympathy with such efforts to improve the text or with a pedantic approach which applies the rules in a narrow, unimaginative style of criticism. The art and originality of *On the Embassy* will certainly not be recognized by readers whose sole criterion is conformity with rules of composition. It is more profitable to observe how ingeniously narrative is blended with argument, refutation with *paradeigma*, ridicule with appeals to patriotic sentiment, and how easily the orator moves from one style to another without any appearance of incongruity or incoherence. It may be granted that Demosthenes has overstated his case, ethically and logically. It is very doubtful if he could have presented it in a more convincing manner if he had confined himself within a narrow set of rules.

We can judge the effectiveness of the speech best by reading the reply of Aeschines, which was certainly revised for publication and was designed to show the larger Athenian public how ill-founded the accusa-tion was. He speaks of his fear that the jury will be misled by the cleverly contrived and malicious contrasts that Demosthenes presented to them,

23 Our information about these criticisms comes from Photius, Bibliotheca, Codex 265.
24 Att. Bered. III 362—63.

and trusts they will pay more attention to his good record than to slanderous accusations. (4—5). He describes the first embassy in detail, hoping to
show Demosthenes in an unpleasant light as a man who prosecutes a fellow
ambassador out of purely malicious motives, and he contradicts him on
various points of detail. As the jury were warned, he did not refuse the
invitation to recall and describe his own speeches, and he took trouble to
explain and justify his address to the Assembly after the first embassy,
which Demosthenes thought so deplorable (57—64).[25]

Before dealing with the principal accusations, which relate to his
conduct on the second embassy, he prepares the way with a carefully
planned and savage attack on the character of Demosthenes, hinting that he
was lucky not to have been prosecuted on the same charges as
Timarchus.[26] He says also that Demosthenes had been an unreasonable
and inconsistent opponent of the peace negotiations and behaved in an
offensive and ridiculous manner on the journey to Macedonia (98—107).
It was not so easy to disprove his own responsibility for the delays of the
second embassy and the disaster of Phocis. Demosthenes did not describe
their conference with Philip, since it would not help his case, but
Aeschines gives a full account, supported by the evidence of witnesses,
describing Demosthenes' speech as well as his own. His real defence is that
nothing, in his opinion, could have stopped Philip from doing what he was
determined to do (118), and "I reported to you what I saw as I saw it, and
what I heard as I heard it" (81).

He objects very strongly to Demosthenes' account of his "misleading
report" to the Assembly, but he does not describe the speech himself. It is
evident that he was not proud of it, and knew that he had been wrong in
his predictions;[27] he wanted to make his error seem excusable by saying it
was shared by the majority of responsible people at the time. His error
does not prove him a traitor, and we must suppose that his reputation

---

25 Here, and in "Against Ctesiphon" (3.67—68), he insists that Demosthenes was
    wrong in saying foreign ambassadors were present on this occasion (16); his com-
    plaint is that Demosthenes did not wait for the envoys from other cities to arrive
    before rushing through the arrangements for peace; in "On the Crown" Demos-
    thenes modifies what he had said—he says there were no diplomatic missions
    outstanding (18.23). For an attempt to disentangle the confusion see G. L. Cawk-
    well, "Aeschines and the Peace of Philocrates," REG 73 (1960), 416—38.
26 Cf. notably 2.68 and 148.
27 Cawkwell (see p. 160, note 5 above) thinks it must have been possible to contradict
    Demosthenes' account of this "misleading report," but cannot explain why
    Aeschines did not do so. Pickard-Cambridge, Demosthenes 280—82, calls his
    defence against this charge "unconvincing." Weil, more decisively, says it is equi-
    valent to admitting "la credulité, l'aveuglement, l'incapacité," and adds: "Je suis
    du nombre de ceux qui ne croient pas à l'innocence d'Eschine," Plaidoyers poli-
    tiques, 220—21.

stood high enough to protect him from being found guilty (it was only by a narrow margin that he escaped).[28] We can also understand why both speakers thought it was necessary to blacken each other's character; this was a case in which the *ethos* of each speaker provided the decisive argument for or against him.[29]

In *On the Embassy*, as in some of his political speeches, Demosthenes faced a task that was too difficult. It was not possible to prove the guilt of Aeschines, and we may admit, in the circumstances, that it was right that he should fail. It remains to see how much he learned from his failure and how he succeeded in the second round of his contest with Aeschines.

28 Plut. Dem. 15. Some ancient critics maintained that neither speech was ever delivered. For the evidence and good reasons for rejecting it see Weil, Plaidoyers politiques, 234–36. Cf. also the brief note of G. Mathieu, Plaidoyers politiques III 19, n.4, and Blass, Att. Bered. III 351–52.

29 Aeschines says so in almost so many words, when he says the jury will pay more attention to the careers of Demosthenes and himself than to their arguments, μᾶλλον προσέχουσι τοῖς βίοις ἡμῶν ἢ τοῖς λόγοις (2.150). Cicero follows in their footsteps when he makes violent attacks on the character of Antony and Verres, in order to make the specific accusations more plausible. And in his defence of Flaccus he remarks that the accuser has taken up the main accusations only after attacking the defendant's private life, "cum adulescentiam notaris, cum reliquum tempus aetatis turpitudinis maculis consperseris" (Pro Flacco 2.5).

One way to defend oneself against such attacks was to ask influential friends to testify in one's favour, but it might be unwise to suggest that one is relying on their influence (cf. Dem. 32.31). Aeschines, certainly, is careful to be modest in introducing his *synegoroi*, who include Eubulus and Phocion (2.184).

Chapter V

The Contest with Aeschines

II. The Crown

Aeschines' final attempt to discredit Demosthenes by his prosecution of Ctesiphon was made in 330. Early in 336 Ctesiphon had proposed in the Boule that a crown be given to Demosthenes in appreciation of his services to Athens, a proposal that was technically illegal for two reasons; Demosthenes was still holding public office and had not yet submitted to his audit, and it was contrary to rule to ask that the crown be presented in the theatre.[1] The Boule approved the motion without question, but when it came before the Assembly Aeschines declared under oath that it was contrary to law and it was not put to the vote.[2] He did not proceed, however, with a *graphe paranomon* against Ctesiphon; the shock of Philip's assassination and the startling events that followed caused too much confusion and uncertainty in Athens to encourage that kind of lawsuit, and he did not take up the case again until 330, when the political climate may have seemed more favourable to an attack on Demosthenes. After the defeat of Sparta at Megalopolis the memory of their failure at Chaeronea may have become less bitter to the Athenians, their inability to resist Macedonia and their error in attempting it more difficult to deny. By suing Ctesiphon Aeschines would be bringing Demosthenes into court as the man responsible for their error; if καιροί were as important as πράγματα, this might be the right time.[3]

A jury may not think a technical irregularity serious enough to justify a verdict that will ban Ctesiphon from public life, and Aeschines will have to do more than prove him technically guilty. He will also not achieve his purpose unless he establishes that Demosthenes is totally unworthy of such an honour, is a man of questionable integrity, and has

---

1 Aeschines presents quite adequate evidence of the law in support of his accusation (3.9—48), and the texts of fourth-century inscriptions which record the voting of crowns to Athenian citizens regularly contain the proviso "when he has submitted to audit" (ἐπειδὰν τὰς εὐθύνας δῷ). Cf. SIG³ 227, 281, 299.
2 This is the sequence of events presented in each of the two *hypotheseis* to "On the Crown", and nothing that Aeschines or Demosthenes says contradicts it. Cf. e.g. Dem. 18.9 and 118.
3 Cf. 19.3 and above p. 158, n. 2. On the apparent καιρός of 330 cf. Pickard-Cambridge, Demosthenes, 428—32.

"misled" the people. But if he handles the case right, he hopes to obtain his revenge, to ruin Demosthenes as well as Ctesiphon. He has to persuade the jury that unless Ctesiphon is found guilty, the real culprit, Demosthenes, will go unpunished. And he has twenty-five years of Demosthenes' career at his disposal to use as evidence that the man who called him a traitor in 343 is the real traitor himself.[4]

The parallel with *On the Embassy* is easy to see. Demosthenes will not be able to refute the technical charges against Ctesiphon, just as Aeschines could not escape his unfortunate "misleading report" to the Assembly; Aeschines will say that Ctesiphon in praising Demosthenes told outright lies, such as a guilty man needs to protect him; and he will want to make Demosthenes responsible for the defeat of Chaeronea, as Demosthenes blamed him for the disaster of Phocis.

Demosthenes in his turn will want to make the technical offence of Ctesiphon appear illusory or trifling, but failure to do this effectively will not necessarily be fatal. If he can contrast his own career with that of Aeschines to his own advantage and build up a convincing picture of loyal service to Athens, he can make it appear that a verdict against Ctesiphon is an insult to national tradition. The jury must be persuaded that they cannot punish Ctesiphon for his wish to honour a great patriot. It is a tremendous challenge, the greatest challenge that Demosthenes has ever faced in court, and his magnificent response to it has caused the speech to be regarded not only as a masterpiece of oratory, but a triumphant declaration of the ideals of a free people.[5]

Aeschines insists (or pretends to insist) that it is the first duty of the jury to enforce the law, not to concern themselves with the character of Demosthenes: "I did not begin by describing the personal life of Demos-

---

4 It has been argued by D. J. Ochs, "Demosthenes' Use of Argument," in: Demosthenes, On the Crown, A Critical Case Study, ed. J. J. Murphy (New York 1967), 162—63, that Aeschines would have done better to confine himself to the legal issues and that "only his hatred for Demosthenes and a near psychotic desire for revenge could have motivated his subsequent assault." It is rash to think that one understands the situation better than Aeschines, especially since the record of Attic oratory shows litigants generally reluctant to rely on the letter of the law alone. It is probably nearer the truth to say that Aeschines himself lacked the capacity to handle the political issues successfully. Cf. R. Chevallier, "L'art oratoire de Démosthène dans le discours sur la couronne," Bull. de L'Assoc. Budé (1960), 202: "Eschine avait bien vu la véritable question, mais n'avait pas suffisamment d'envergure pour la traiter."

5 This special quality of the speech has been appreciated by many writers, even by Demosthenes' severest critics. Cf. e.g. Blass, Att. Bered. III 436; Pickard-Cambridge, Demosthenes, 437—45; Cloché, Démosthènes, 259—64; G. Kennedy, The Art of Persuasion in Greece, 231—36; M. Croiset, Les idées morales dans l'éloquence de Démosthène (Montpellier 1875), 173.

thenes or by recounting any of his crimes against the city (though they are numerous enough), but first of all I explained how the laws forbade the crowning of persons who were still subject to audit" (3.202–03). He therefore defies Demosthenes to deny the "fact" of Ctesiphon's guilt. But just as he himself had escaped a verdict of guilty by a narrative which revealed a career of public service (a narrative of events not always strictly relevant to the case), so now he expects Demosthenes to follow similar tactics and tells the jury they must not tolerate such dodging of the issue. Demosthenes answers by protesting that his adversary has no right to tell the jury the right way to listen to his defence, that the laws allow each speaker to choose the manner and the order in which he states his case, and they must listen impartially to both sides (1–2).

It is no surprise that Demosthenes begins by comparing his position with that of the prosecutor, who does not stand to lose so much if he fails in the case or risk giving offence by praising his own achievements. He knows of course that the jury will listen to him with full attention, but he flatters them by telling them how much their good will means (and always has meant) to him.[6] He prays to the gods that the verdict will further the good name of the city and conform with the private conscience of each of them (8). The exact meaning of this prayer will not be entirely clear until he reaches the closing section of his speech, but his introduction is dignified and careful.[7] He has adopted a personal approach to the jury that only an adept and self-confident politician would dare attempt; and he does his best to take advantage of the good relation that he hopes he has established:

"If you believe that I am the kind of person he represented me to be (and I have lived my whole life among you), do not let me open my mouth. No, not even if all my political achievements have been admirable, but rise to your feet and find me guilty this minute. If, on the other hand, you have always supposed me to be a better man than Aeschines (and of a better family), if you believe that I and the members of my family are no worse than any decent citizen (I don't want to be boastful), then don't trust the other things he tells you, since it is clear that his whole account must be misleading. Continue to show me the good will that you have always shown me in many hearings throughout my career. Though you are

6 A similar approach is used by Lysias, "Against Eratosthenes."
7 Demosthenes means that his policy, in the time of crisis, helped Athens to maintain her good name. A man who says this is not being humble and unsure of himself, and it is surprising that Quintilian should think so: "In illo pro Ctesiphonte timido summissoque principio" (11.3.97). Blass, apparently paraphrasing Quintilian, makes a subtle correction, "würdevoll zugleich und bescheiden auftretend," Att. Bered. III 420.

a perverse and malicious person, Aeschines, you have shown yourself naive and simple (κακοήθης δ' ὤν, Αἰσχύνη, τοῦτο παντελῶς εὔηθες ᾠήθης) in your expectation that I would neglect the treatment of my political career and turn my attention to the abusive slanders that you have uttered" (10–11).

Like Demosthenes in *On the Embassy* Aeschines had hoped that a distorted picture of his opponent's character might turn the scale in his favour, and this is Demosthenes' defiant answer—Aeschines' method shows that he is as stupid as he is nasty. The stupidity of Aeschines is thus taken for granted from the very start of his speech.

The next stage is to complain of his indirect attack, suing Ctesiphon when other legal methods of prosecuting directly were open to him. Demosthenes tries to argue that such perversity shows the lack of any real basis for the accusations, but he must know that his conclusion does not follow logically,[8] and he soon abandons this form of argument, and turns to his first narrative section, to describe what things were like in 355, when the Phocian War started—"not that I was to blame for the situation, since I had not yet entered public life" (18). He gives a magnificent description of the unhappy state of Greece:

"Athenian feeling supported Phocis, though you could hardly approve of what the Phocians were doing, and you were ready to rejoice at any troubles the Thebans might suffer; your bitterness against them was neither unjust nor unreasonable, since they had exploited their success at Leuctra quite outrageously. The Peloponnese, moreover, was torn in two by strife, with the anti-Spartan faction not strong enough to ruin Sparta and the faction that had formerly owed its power to Sparta no longer in control in the various cities. The result was that here, as everywhere, there was conflict, with no decision in sight, and great confusion" (18).

---

8 There is a series of contrasts. The accusations are exceedingly serious, but the attack is spiteful and personal, in defiance of democratic tradition (οὔτε πολιτικὸν οὔτε δίκαιον). In his present attack Aeschines was voluble and dramatic (ἡλίκα νῦν ἐτραγῴδει καὶ διεξῄει, 13), but in the past, when all kinds of legal means were open to him, he was silent. His present attack might be understandable if he had attempted direct legal prosecution in the past, but he refused it and now "we find him many years later putting on this theatrical display of jeering and abusive accusation" (τοσούτοις ὕστερον χρόνοις αἰτίας καὶ σκώμματα καὶ λοιδορίας συμφορήσας ὑποκρίνεται, 15). His whole accusation is based on personal resentment, but he has no grievance at all against Ctesiphon, whom he threatens with ruin. The argument has shifted; one can forgive a direct attack on a man with whom one has a quarrel; but to attack him indirectly by damaging someone else is totally deplorable.
The conclusion—"and so you can see how false his accusations are" (17), does not follow; despite the valid rhetorical contrasts, the argument has no logical or legal value.

182

Demosthenes resists the temptation to describe Philip's aggression and his progress in the years that follow or his own counter-efforts in the *First Philippic* and the *Olynthiacs*. His immediate concern is to explain why Athens had no choice in 346 except to make peace when Philip offered it (and offered assistance to her enemies). He does not want to claim or disclaim responsibility for events leading up to the peace, though he does take the trouble to contradict Aeschines' statement that he frustrated a plan for peace that might have been shared by "the common council of the Hellenes."[9] He insists that Aeschines' story is complete nonsense (24), and that Aeschines is showing himself a stupid and unscrupulous liar even in his account of these early years.[10]

The story of the second embassy follows, to show "who it was that worked for Philip in the matter of the peace and who worked for you and sought the interests of Athens" (25). He describes the delay on the journey, despite his own insistence on speed and the resolution of the Boule urging them to make haste (he has the text of the resolution read out as in the former trial). He has no new evidence that might justify a reversal of the verdict of 343. He is content to show that Aeschines, in his speech, misrepresented the parts they played, when he said nothing of the resolution of the Boule but ridiculed the politeness of Demosthenes to Philip's envoys in Athens: "And what should I have done? told the superintendent of the theatre not to assign them seats? They would have sat in the two obol seats if I had not made the proposal to give them good seats" (28).[11]

He exaggerates the delays on the embassy to an extent that would not have been possible in 343, saying that they "sat for three whole months in Macedonia" (30),[12] and describes how Philip delayed their

9 3. 58, 61
10 Conventional rhetorical criticism explains Demosthenes' tactics by saying he is using the *status translationis*, shifting the issue from himself to Aeschines. Cf. F. P. Donnelly, S.J., "Rhetorical Commentary to Demosthenes, On the Crown," reprinted in: Demosthenes, On the Crown, A Critical Case Study (see note 4 above), p. 138. One cannot be sure that Demosthenes understood his tactics in these terms. It is more helpful to notice that he regularly prepares the way for answering or establishing charges by characterizing himself or his opponent; and here he does it by narrative. Cf. Chevallier, op. cit. (see note 4 above) p. 203: "La présentation même des faits est déjà interprétation. Ils ont valeur des signes."
11 The Assembly was due to meet in the theatre, and Aeschines describes how Demosthenes "buttered up" the ambassadors, settling them in front seats with cushions and purple rugs, after leading them into the theatre at daybreak: "Then when they left Athens he hired three mule carriages for them and accompanied them on their way as far as Thebes, making the city look ridiculous" (3.76).
12 More accurately it was fifty days altogether, from the time when they left Athens, until they met Philip, including twenty-three on the journey. Cf. 19.57 & 155, and the note of Mathieu in the Budé edition on 18.30.

departure until his own preparations for invading Phocis were complete, and then he "hires this despicable creature to give you the report which resulted in your losing everything" (33). The "report" is described, with some quotations to show the pompous theatrical style affected by Aeschines, and the disastrous events that followed; and, as in *On the Embassy* (19.86), the text of the resolution is read out which called upon the Athenians to bring in their belongings from the country. It is taken for granted that Aeschines is guilty of treachery (nothing is said about the earlier trial) and responsible not only for the ruin of Phocis but the destruction of Thebes, "this man who weeps for the sufferings of the Thebans," thought he "owns property in Boeotia and farms their land." The contrast with himself is not forgotten: "Naturally I am filled with joy; my surrender was demanded immediately by the man who destroyed Thebes" (41).

Demosthenes apologizes for deserting the chronological order of events and returns to the unhappy peace of 346, which the Athenians had to observe, though they knew they had been betrayed, like all the Greeks except "the despicable Thessalians and the thick-skinned Thebans" (42–43). He expects the jury to understand that Philip makes further use of Aeschines and other corrupt politicians in the "cold war" that follows, as he builds up his formidable military machine. He recalls his own constant warnings, but "the cities were sick" (αἱ δὲ πόλεις ἐνόσουν, 45), and people were short-sighted and lazy, thinking that "it couldn't happen here," until the cities lost their freedom and the politicians found that they had indeed "sold themselves" and were regarded with contempt as they deserved (45–46). His description leads him into a perfectly timed digression on the folly of traitors, who think their employers will be grateful and continue to treat them with respect: "This is not what happens at all. Quite the contrary. When the person who is seeking power gains control of the situation, he is also master of those persons who sold him his victory. He knows what contemptible men they are, and now at last he shows his contempt and his lack of faith in them, and rubs their faces in the mud" (προπηλακίζει, 47).

Examples are given from various cities to show that traitors always come to a bad end, homeless and despised. It is because someone fights traitors and saves his city that a city still has something that a traitor can sell; a man like Aeschines can thank his opponents that he is still alive and receiving his pay (49).

This passage marks a turning point in the speech. Demosthenes says he has described these past events in order to cleanse himself of the "stale dregs" of Aeschines' dishonesty, with which Aeschines has drenched him (one can see him, with an expression of disgust on his face, brushing at imaginary stains on his gown). But his real purpose in this first narrative section (17–52) is to blacken Aeschines' character before he sets out to answer the real charges.[13] It is high time, one might think, "to speak about the actual indictment" (53), but he brushes aside the technical charges against Ctesiphon, saying that Ctesiphon praised him for "doing and saying what is best for the city," and his task, therefore, is to show "whether I am worthy of the crown and the public citation, and also to explain the laws which determine the legality of the proposal" (58). And without any serious attempt at legal argument he returns to describe the situation as it was "when I began to take part in public life" (60):

"Everywhere in Greece, not just in certain cities but everywhere, it happened that a crop of traitors had sprung up (corrupt and god-forsaken men) larger than anyone can remember appearing before. Philip took these men as his partners and co-workers. The Greeks were already on sufficiently bad terms with each other, but he made things even worse, deceiving some, making offers to others, corrupting others in every imaginable way, and he divided us into numerous camps, though we all had one interest in common—to prevent the increase of his power" (61).

Earlier Greek literature offers nothing quite like this sketch or the comparable sketch of the situation in 355 that is given in the earlier narrative (17–20).[14] Whether accurate history or not, it suits his purpose perfectly. He wants to show that Philip is taking advantage of all that was worst in Greek politics and making it difficult for honest men to enlighten their short-sighted countrymen. And the implication is clear that anyone who appeased Philip, or accepted his help in obtaining some temporary advantage for his city, must have known that he was helping to humiliate his own city and to strengthen Philip's hand:

"Which course was Athens to follow, Aeschines, was it to abandon its pride and worth, to put itself on a level with Thessalians and Dolopians and destroy all that its ancestors thought right and valuable? Or, instead of actually doing such a terrible thing, was it to allow this result to follow

13 Quintilian (7.1.2) describes the different procedure of Aeschines and Demosthenes, "cum accusator a iure, quo videbatur potentior, coeperit, patronus omnia paene ante ius posuerit, quibus iudices quaestioni legum praepararet."

14 One might hope to find parallels in Thucydides. Hermocrates, for example (4.59–64), tries (unsuccessfully) to convince the delegates at the conference of Gela that the quarrels between cities in Sicily offer a dangerous opportunity which the Athenians may exploit; it is interesting to speculate what kind of speech Demosthenes might have written for him. Alcibiades (6.18), in his attempt to explain the situation to the Athenians, is not specific enough. Nor does Thucydides tell us as much as we should like to know about the opportunity that Brasidas exploited in Thrace (4.78–80). Cf. R. Chevallier, op. cit. (see note 4 above) p. 205.

which it knew would follow if no one stopped it, which it foresaw well in advance, it seems?" (63).

Either choice, Demosthenes says, would have been equally disastrous, because active co-operators, like the Thessalians, and those who let events take their course, like the Arcadians, Messenians, and Argives, are now worse off than Athens which decided to resist. Philip has always treated his allies just as badly as his opponents (64). It follows that Athens had a clear duty to resist. What other advice could a politician like Demosthenes give, if he had any regard for Athenian tradition?

"What could I propose . . . when I knew very well how my country had always striven for primacy and honour and its good name, how it had spent more money and more lives in the pursuit of its high aims than each one of the other Greek cities had spent on selfish interests, and when I saw that Philip, with whom we were in conflict, in his pursuit of empire and supreme power had lost an eye, broken a collar-bone, suffered wounds in arm and leg, and been prepared to sacrifice any part of his body that fortune might choose to demand of him, if it meant that he could save the rest of it to live a life of honour and dignity?

"No one would dare say, would they, that it befitted a man brought up in Pella (a small obscure place, as it was), to be filled with this great ambition, to let the thought of dominating the Hellenes enter his mind, but that you, Athenians, with reminders before you every day, in everything you heard and saw, of your ancestors' greatness, should have been possessed with the kind of weakness that compelled you to surrender your freedom to Philip without striking a blow? Of course no one would say such a thing" (66—69).

The appeal to Athenian tradition is beautifully timed; the jurors are being told, as in *On the Embassy*, that they are trapped by "the facts."[15] They cannot say it was wrong to resist Philip. But even if they do, they must admit that it was not Demosthenes who proposed the formal moves that led to war, but Eubulus, Aristophon, and Diopeithes (70); and it was Philip, not Athens, that broke the treaty by his new aggressive moves (71). And once it is admitted that Philip is the aggressor, Demosthenes can say boldly:

"When I saw him robbing everyone of freedom, I resisted him, I never stopped warning the people and telling them that they must not give up. And it was he who broke the peace by seizing our ships, it was not Athens, Aeschines" (72).

Once it is admitted that Athens followed the right policy, Demosthenes can speak in greater detail about his part in it during the years

15 Cf. pp. 170—71 above.

preceding the outbreak of war. He supported Athenian diplomatic efforts in the Peloponnese and military intervention in Euboea, when it was necessary to drive out the tyrants that Philip had set up in Oreus and Eretria. Aeschines never raised objections when Demosthenes was honoured with a crown then for his valuable services (83). But he showed his real sympathies by receiving the ambassadors from the Euboean tyrants in his own house when they came to Athens (82). This complaint is just as worthless as Aeschines' complaint of the courtesy Demosthenes showed to Macedonian ambassadors,[16] but anyone who is already prejudiced against Aeschines may take it as one more sign of his willingness to appease Philip by "flattery".

After Philip had been driven out of Eretria "by a policy and decisions which were due to me, though certain persons may burst their lungs screaming to deny it" (87), he tried to win control of the Athenian grain route, and when his allies, the Byzantines, refused to help him, he laid siege to their city. Here again it was Athens, with vigorous support from Demosthenes, so he says (88), that kept Philip out of the Hellespont and rescued Byzantium. Aeschines had argued that the Byzantines, like the Euboeans, had forfeited any right to Athenian assistance,[17] so that it would have been strictly "just" to abandon them. Demosthenes replies that Athenian action in helping them was both "expedient" and "honourable," and in accordance with the best Athenian tradition, and that it increased their prestige enormously to show generosity towards a former not very faithful friend, after Philip had treated his ally so shabbily (93).

The argument offers a splendid illustration of the rhetorical precepts of Aristotle, as it counters the claims of τὸ δίκαιον by appeals to τὸ συμφέρον and τὸ καλόν.[18] Demosthenes takes the opportunity to contrast the Athenian tradition of generosity with the treacherous meanness of Philip and Aeschines by introducing some *paradeigmata* from earlier history. Sixty years previously, when the Spartans were at the height of their power, Athens supported Thebes and Corinth against them despite all the harm that they suffered at their hands in the Decelean War (96). In later years, after Leuctra, they supported Sparta against Thebes, because

16 Cf. p. 182 above.
17 Aeschines makes no such statement in any speech, though Demosthenes says here (95) that he slandered the Euboeans and Byzantines by inventing numerous non-existent acts of hostility they had committed. And previously (19.16) he recalled with horror Aeschines' speech after the first embassy in which he proposed that Athens should never help any Greeks unless they had previously given help to Athens.
18 Aristot. Rhet. I 1358b. τέλος δὲ ... τῷ μὲν συμβουλεύοντι τὸ συμφέρον καὶ βλαβερόν. ὁ μὲν γὰρ προτρέπων ὡς βέλτιον συμβουλεύει, ὁ δὲ ἀποτρέπων ὡς χεῖρον ἀποτρέπει, τὰ δ' ἄλλα πρὸς τοῦτο συμπαραλαμβάνει, ἢ δίκαιον ἢ ἄδικον, ἢ καλὸν ἢ αἰσχρόν.

"you will not bear grudges or try to balance accounts, when there is a threat to liberty or survival" (99). And in a similar spirit Athens defended Euboea against Theban aggression in 357, without taking account of the ill-treatment they had suffered from Euboeans in the past (99). With such models to guide him, how could he leave the Byzantines to their fate and dishonour the city's high ideals? (101).

He had been ἐπιστάτης τοῦ ναυτικοῦ in 340 and made a number of changes in the trierarchic system. He says that, despite attempts by rich people to bribe him and prosecute him,[19] he introduced the new law which divided the burden more fairly between rich and poor and, more important: "It got the ships ready for sea on time" (102).[20] He therefore declares triumphantly: "Just as in domestic affairs I did not prefer the thanks of the rich to the rights of the poor, so in Hellenic affairs I did not think Philip's gifts and hospitality more valuable than the common interest of all the Hellenes" (109).

As though this triumphant conclusion has given him strength, he now announces his intention to speak about the technical charges in the indictment. He begins by trying to exploit the plain man's prejudice against legal arguments: "I don't suppose you can understand them any more than I did, most of them" (111). He may impress some plain men on the jury by his protest that a man cannot be subject to audit for the gifts he has made to the city, but since the law insisted on an audit for all office-holders his protest is legally worthless.[21] He does his best all the same to argue that only a "worthless god-forsaken pedant" (119) like Aeschines would want to enforce such a law. Aeschines (3.34) had cited the law which stated categorically that "in the case of a person crowned by the people, the announcement must be made before the people on the Pnyx, and nowhere else." Demosthenes tries to confuse the issue by citing another statute, the law regulating the award of crowns by demes and phratries (the familiar device of citing an irrelevant document); he argues that a paragraph in this law makes a different rule,[22] but Aeschines shows

---

19 Aeschines himself (3.222) reminds the jury that he accused him of seriously reducing the number of trierarchs. His accusations are repeated by Dinarchus, In Dem. 42.

20 Neither orator tells us much about the administrative details of this trierarchic law. For discussion see Cloché, Démosthènes, 178–80. Later in the speech (312) it is said that Aeschines was paid two talents by the leaders of the symmories to attack the law; they were perhaps able to modify it in some respects.

21 Cf. p. 178, note 1 above. There can hardly be any doubt that Aeschines is right. Cf. Cloché, Démosthènes, 223–24.

22 One cannot trust the wording of the "law" which is included in the manuscripts of the speech at this point and which ends τούτους δ' ἐξεῖναι ἐν θεάτρῳ Διονυσίοις (120). Like other so-called "documents" included in the manuscripts, many of which contain flagrant errors, it has evidently been fabricated on the basis of what

188

carefully that there is no conflict between one law and the other
(3.35—47), and Demosthenes' only hope is to make Aeschines appear
mean and envious for insisting on the letter of the law: "You are so stupid
and imperceptive, Aeschines, that you cannot see the point. The crown
brings the same distinction to the person honoured, no matter where the
announcement is made; but the announcement is made in the theatre for
the benefit of the persons conferring the honour—since foreigners are
present" (120).

Demosthenes pushes the legal difficulties out of the way, as though
only a small-minded pedant like Aeschines would pay attention to them,
and makes this an excuse for a new attack on his character. The attack is
more virulent than anything that has gone before,[23] and he excuses himself (in a quite unconvincing manner) by saying it is prompted by
Aeschines' slanders, "not because I am a lover of foul language" (126). As
in *On the Embassy*[24] he scoffs at the high-flown language of this "miserable little clerk":

"Like an actor in a tragedy, crying out 'O earth and sun and true
worth,' and so on, and appealing to 'Intelligence and Paideia, which teach
us to distinguish right from wrong'—you will have heard him speaking in
this manner. But when did you, you scum of the earth, or your people
have anything to do with 'true worth' or how could you distinguish 'right
and wrong'? No one who really had these qualities would ever speak like
that about them; he would blush to hear anyone else using such expres-
sions. But people who lack them, as you do, and in their crass way claim
to possess them, succeed only in distressing everyone who hears them
speak; you won't make anyone think you have such qualities" (127—28).

As in *On the Embassy* it is suggested that the depravity of Aeschines
is hardly surprising if one remembers his family background—his mother

Demosthenes says in the text. He breaks off without quoting the whole text
himself (121) and Aeschines takes him to task for this (3.35). It is indeed possible
that he interrupted the reading of the clerk so that the precise details would not be
made clear.

The "documents" in "On the Crown" have given rise to much discussion—who was
responsible for fabricating them, at what date, and with what purpose? For a
useful summary of the various questions at issue see G. Mathieu, "Plaidoyers
politiques," IV 17—21. It seems that some, at least, of these "documents" had
found their way into editions in the Augustan age, since they occur in some
papyrus texts of the speech. P. Treves, "Les documents apocryphiques du
Corona," Les études classiques (1940), 138—174, argues that a date in the early
second or late third century B.C. is likely for some of them.

23 This violent denunciation of Aeschines, in the manner of a peroration after the
charges have been formally answered, is often called the "false epilogue." There is
no warning that an extended narrative section will follow. Cf. G. Mathieu, Plaidoyers politiques IV 15, and Blass, Att. Bered. III 425.

24 Cf. above pp. 169—70, 172—73.

Empusa (Miss Filthy Hagg), who worked as a prostitute in a disreputable religious congregation, and his father Tromes (Brother Tremulus), who was a schoolmaster's slave; their more respectable names, Glaucothea and Atrometus, he says, were acquired later when, by some means or other, they obtained Athenian citizenship (127–30).

There is no point in taking Demosthenes to task for offending against modern standards of good taste and good manners, since this kind of slanderous attack was acceptable in Athenian courts and literature has preserved other equally crude examples.[25] However preposterous the charges, there was no doubt the possibility that some of the mud might stick. The orator must have delivered this abusive tirade at a furious speed; the whole section 129 would have to be spoken without a pause for breath, and 130 with only one pause. But the court would be expected to pay closer attention to 131, where it is charged that Aeschines has shown gross ingratitude to the Athenians who gave him citizenship, giving him and his parents the chance to live useful lives, making him a wealthy free man instead of a penniless slave—and he took advantage of the gift without any sense of obligation.

Ingratitude is the basest of faults, and a speaker never misses the chance to denounce it in his opponent.[26] Demosthenes has some examples ready to show how little loyalty or love Aeschines had for Athens. He stood up for the civil rights of that "notorious traitor" Antiphon, who came to Athens after promising that he would set the shipyards on fire; he might have saved the man from the punishment he deserved (objecting to his summary arrest!) if Demosthenes had not intervened and had him brought before the Assembly (132–33). And as a result of this incident (so Demosthenes says) the Areopagus removed Aeschines from the appointment he had received to represent Athens in an inquiry into the administration of the sanctuary on Delos and replaced him by Hyperides—"not a single vote was cast in his favour." Witnesses are called to testify to the change in the appointment (135); there is no proof that Demosthenes has given the true reason for it.

Two more examples are given of Aeschines playing the part of a traitor. He spoke in favour of Python of Byzantium, Philip's emissary, thus "bearing witness against his native land, and false witness too." And he was found "entering the house of Thrason in company with the spy Anaxinus" (136–37). By telling tales of his supposed treachery in earlier

25 Cicero in his "Philippics" thinks it worth while to say many equally slanderous and malicious things about Antony. Cf. also pp. 197–98 below, and Chapter III above pp. 80–81.
26 Cf. Chapter III above, pp. 88, 103–04.

years Demosthenes has prepared the way very shrewdly for his account of the incidents of 340 and 339, "when Philip was on his march towards Attica, when there was no longer any doubt what was happening, when war had started" (139). What can Aeschines say about his part in public affairs during this period?

The narrative that follows contains the most famous and most highly admired passages in the speech, and it is the most critical part of the speech for Demosthenes. Now that the war with Philip breaks out again, he has to show that he reaches his greatest height as a political leader, while Aeschines degenerates into a pitiable grotesque figure, a "miserable gobbler of tragic verses" who cannot point to anything he did that helped the city (139). He asks the blessing of the gods and goddesses that protect the land of Attica and of Apollo of Delphi as he tells his story; he needs their blessing and their help to make his story convincing; he must tell it very carefully, to make the jury understand how cleverly everything was arranged by Aeschines and Philip.

Just as in *On the Embassy*, he explains Philip's problem;[27] he cannot make headway in his war against Athens without help from Thebes and Thessaly; he must set the Thebans and Thessalians at odds with the Athenians so that they will let him pass through their country. He needs to produce a situation in which they will want him to command their joint forces—in a war that involves the Amphictyons, for example;[28] and if it is an Athenian who stirs up the trouble that creates such a war, no one will suspect that he had a hand in it: "And this is exactly how things turned out. How did he manage it? He hired Aeschines" (148—49).

Aeschines now becomes the central figure in the narrative. He is appointed *pylagoros* to represent Athens at the *Pylaea* (the Amphictyonic meeting) at Delphi.[29] As Demosthenes tells the tale, it is his chance to do Philip's work:

27 Cf. above pp. 174—75.
28 Demosthenes does not think it necessary to explain how and why Philip will be able to use the affairs of the Amphictyonic council for his own purposes. He expects every member of the jury to remember how the seats on the council formerly held by the Phocians were given to Philip, in return for the part he played in defeating them in 346. The Thessalians held the majority of votes on the council, and the Athenians are afraid that Philip, whose military machine is far more powerful than any other, may gain an overwhelming influence in the council if he is supported by the Thessalian bloc, while posing as a defender of religion and piety.
    For further detail and explanation see Pickard-Cambridge, Demosthenes, 171—76, 286—89; Busolt-Swoboda, Griechische Staatskunde, II 1292—96; H. W. Parke and D. Wormell, The Delphic Oracle I (1956), 100—02, 224—37.
29 A *pylagoros* was a delegate from a city, sent to represent its interests at a *Pylaea* (the meetings were held alternately at Thermopylae and Delphi). The members of the council are called *hieromnemones*.

"Looking neither to right nor left, he went on to finish the task he had been engaged for. He put together a fine-sounding speech, with a mythological digression to explain how the land of Crisa came to be declared sacred.[30] And since his audience, the *hieromnemones*, had no experience of oratory and no suspicion of what might happen, he persuaded them to vote for a tour of the area that the Amphissans were cultivating. The Amphissans said it was their own land, but he charged it was part of the sacred land" (150—51).

Demosthenes is brief, because Aeschines has already explained the circumstances of the meeting and described with special pride the oration which he delivered there (3.107—122). According to his account, the Locrians of Amphissa wanted to ban the Athenians from the temple at Delphi, because of their support of the "sacrilegious" Phocians in the Sacred War, and were looking for support from the Thebans, who were incensed at an insult they had received from the Athenians—the dedication of some shields in the new temple at Delphi commemorating the Battle of Plataea with the inscription 'Taken from the Medes and the Thebans when they fought against the Hellenes.' The chairman, he says, invited him to speak in reply to the Locrian protests, but he was infuriated by the rude interruption of an ill-mannered Amphissan and retaliated by denouncing the impiety of the Amphissans who were cultivating sacred land.

Demosthenes insists that the Locrians had made no formal complaint against Athens and it was quite unnecessary for Aeschines to speak as he did—he had in fact been engaged by Philip to make this speech, with the object of producing the disastrous results that followed! "The explanation that Aeschines has given you is a pack of lies" (151). Never before has Demosthenes contrived to turn Aeschines' own words (of which he is proud) against himself with such terrifying effect:

"The Amphictyons went on their tour of the area, with him as their guide, and the Locrians made an attack on them; they came near to shooting them all down and they actually laid hands on some of the *hieromnemones*. The immediate consequence was a series of complaints and a declaration of war against the Amphissans. At the beginning Cottyphus took command of a purely Amphictyonic army, but when some of his men never reported for duty, and those who did appear did

---

30 The story would be known to every educated Greek—how Crisa, the gateway to Delphi, had once charged exorbitant prices to the pilgrims and the Amphictyons retaliated by declaring the rich plain the sacred property of Apollo, so that anyone who cultivated it for his own profit would be guilty of gross impiety. Demosthenes takes it as typical of Aeschines that he should explain it all so solemnly and pedantically.

nothing, the next step was to offer the command to Philip at the next Amphictyonic meeting. This was what had been planned from the start by the party of traitors in Thessaly and elsewhere.

"They had good arguments to justify their proposal. The only alternative to making Philip the commander was to levy taxes themselves and pay for mercenary troops, with penalties for those who refused to pay. Never mind the details. They saw to it that Philip was asked to take command. And without any delay he got his army together and was all ready apparently for action in the plain of Crisa; but he waved good-bye to Crisa and the Locrians, and we find him taking possession of Elatea; and if the Thebans had not quickly changed their attitude, when they saw this, and come over to our side, it would have been like a torrent in flood crashing down on our city. As things were, the Thebans blocked the way for the moment. For that we must thank, first of all, the gods for their good will towards us, but so far as any one man deserves gratitude, I am that man" (151—53).

Without contradicting the observable "facts" of Aeschines' version, he has given a new twist and new life to the story by the presumption of Aeschines' treason.[31] The narrative began from Philip's point of view, then shifted to Aeschines; now it is Demosthenes' turn to take the centre of the stage. As usual, he has no more than three characters on the stage at one time.[32] Aeschines and the Amphictyons have played their part; the Thebans now join Philip and Demosthenes. His task now is to show that he deserves the credit for arranging the alliance with Thebes. It can hardly be accidental that he rests his voice, by calling on the clerk to read out some documents,[33] before starting on the most critical passage in the whole speech, the famous dramatic description that begins ἑσπέρα μὲν γὰρ ἦν:

"It was evening when a messenger came to the *prytaneis* with the news that Elatea was in Philip's hands. At once they got up in the middle of their dinner, cleared the people out of the shacks in the Agora and set fire to the wicker screens,[34] while others were busy sending for the

31 He cites some documents, to give the impression that they strengthen his case—the text of the Amphictyonic resolutions and a letter of Philip to his allies in the Peloponnese, in which he declared he was carrying out the wishes of the Amphictyons (and it was Aeschines who made this pretence possible!) (154—58). The actual text of Philip's letter, if we had it, would be a most interesting document.

32 Cf. Chapter II above, p. 50.

33 Two Athenian resolutions, to show that the situation was understood in Athens, and two letters of Philip, to show how hard he was trying to keep Athens and Thebes apart (164—68).

34 Why set fire to these screens? Was it an accident, the result of panic? or was it done deliberately, in order to clear the Agora quickly, or to give a signal to people

strategoi and calling for the trumpeter. The whole city was full of confusion. Next morning, at break of day, the *prytaneis* called a meeting of the Boule in the Chamber, while you were on your way to the Assembly; the whole citizen body was seated on the hill before the Boule finished its business and prepared its draft proposal.

"Then, when the Boule had come into the Assembly, and the *prytaneis* reported the news they had received, after the messenger had been brought forward and made his announcement, the herald put his question: 'Who wishes to address the meeting?' And no one came forward. He repeated his question, but still no one rose to his feet, though all the *strategoi* were there, all the regular speakers, and the city itself was calling for a proposal that would save the city (because when the herald speaks, as the laws command him, we must suppose that this is our city speaking with a common voice).

"Should people who were concerned for the safety of the city have come forward? In that case all of you, every Athenian should have risen to his feet and marched to the bema. Of course all of you were anxious to preserve the safety of the city. Should the wealthiest men have come forward? Then it was up to the three hundred. Or the people who were patriotic as well as rich? Then it was up to the men who had made the large advances of property tax, since it was their wealth and their patriotism that prompted such action. It seems, however, that the occasion and the day called for someone who was not just patriotic and wealthy, but who had followed the course of events from the start, who had reasoned out correctly what motives and purposes Philip had in acting as he did. A man without this knowledge, who had not made a thorough examination of the question, no matter how rich and patriotic he was, would know no better than anyone else what had to be done, would have no special qualification to advise you.

"Now I was the man who came forward on that day. I faced you and told you some things to which I shall ask you to pay special attention now, for two reasons. I want you to know that I was the only speaker, the only politician who did not desert his post in the hour of danger, but was ready to present myself, to speak and make the necessary proposals on your behalf. The other reason for asking you to listen is so that, with the expense of only a little time, you will have a better understanding of politics hereafter" (169–73).

outside the walls that a special emergency had arisen? No precedent for any such signal is known, and it is tempting to dismiss the fire as a mere indication of panic. Cf. the comment of P. Treves in his edition of the speech, "L'Orazione per la Corona" (Milan 1955).

Demosthenes is so proud of the speech he delivered that morning, that we cannot help wondering why no written version of it has been preserved. He told the Athenians they must not encourage Philip's friends in Thebes or discourage the anti-Macedonian party there by any display of coldness or distrust, which might throw them into Philip's arms; he told them they must learn to fear *for* the Thebans, who were nearer to the threat of attack than they were, and proposed they should make a display of military force, marching out to Eleusis, so as to reassure their friends of their support; and he proposed that they should appoint ten ambassadors, who should decide, with the ten *strategoi*, when was the right time to go to Thebes. He says that his proposals were accepted without any opposition and put into effect: "And I carried through right from beginning to end, and devoted myself unreservedly to the perils that beset the city" (179).

He keeps himself in the centre of the stage as his narrative ends, and starts a comparison of himself with Aeschines, which will be developed further after the clerk has read out the text of the resolution that was passed that morning—Aeschines may have acted heroic parts on the stage (at village festivals), but "I did everything that was demanded of a good citizen" (180). He leaves it to the jury to make the comparison between his practical advice, followed by untiring efforts to see that it was carried out, and the elaborate rhetorical display of Aeschines at Delphi. Constantly in his political speeches he had told them that the first, and essential step was to change their attitude;[35] and now he points out how well he succeeded in changing their attitude towards Thebes, "a change from the past when our cities had been at daggers drawn, angry and resentful of one another. This resolution caused the danger that threatened the city at that time to vanish like a cloud" (188).

The contrast between himself and Aeschines is generalized in a gnomic passage about the difference between a counsellor (ὁ σύμβουλος) and a mischievous litigant (ὁ συκοφάντης), but he offers no detailed narrative of the events of autumn and winter leading up to the battle of Chaeronea. He has nothing to gain by describing a national misfortune, unless he wants to make his opponent responsible for it (as he tried to make Aeschines responsible for the ruin of Phocis). It is enough to remind the Athenians that their defeat was a creditable, even a splendid failure, and that the only alternatives would have been ignominious and unworthy of Athens. Like a ship's captain, he cannot be blamed for the loss of his ship, if he has taken the measures that might have saved it (194): "Do not

---

35 Cf. e.g. Chapter IV above, pp. 123, 128.

consider it an indictable offence on my part if Philip succeeded in winning the battle" (193).

And what right, he asks, has Aeschines to find fault? He never offered any alternative to the policy that was carried out, but now he is taking advantage of the misfortune that has struck down the Hellenes, using it for his own purpose—such a man deserves to die, not to find fault (197—98). And what alternative was there to the policy of resistance?

"With what kind of gaze could we now look at visitors to our city, if things had turned out as they have and Philip had become sovereign master of us all, but the fight to prevent this had been fought not by ourselves but by others, even though in former days the city had never chosen inglorious safety in preference to risking everything in the defence of honour?" (201).[36]

The appeal to tradition follows inevitably, and it gives the inescapable answer: "No one has ever been able to persuade the city to throw in its lot with the strong who were against the right and to accept a life of safe subservience" (203). In the days of Themistocles Athenians decided that life was not worth living, unless they kept their country free; the jury cannot think that the spirit of freedom has died or find fault with a man who played his part in defending it:

"When Aeschines finds fault with everything and bids you be angry with me as the man who brought terror and peril to the city, the honour that he is trying to take from me is only shortlived honour, but he is robbing the city of immortal fame. If you decide that my policy was wrong and pass sentence against me, you will make it appear that you were struck down by your own mistake, not by the unkindness of fate. But it cannot be that you were wrong, men of Athens, in taking up the struggle in defence of the safety and freedom of all. No, I call to witness the men who first faced the enemy at Marathon, who stood in the ranks at Plataea and served in the ships at Salamis and Artemisium, and all of those who lie buried in public graves, brave men all of them, all honoured alike by the city, Aeschines, not only those who won a victory, and rightly so honoured, because all of them did their duty as brave men, and the destiny that they met was that which the god had allotted to them" (207—08).

---

36 Cf. "On the Embassy" 218—19 (pp.170—71 above): "If, knowing that everything that has happened was going to happen, you then made peace and made it gladly, you may acquit Aeschines." The argument is worked out differently, but the technique is similar. In his earlier appeal to tradition in "On the Crown" (63—69, pp. 185—86 above), it is argued that co-operation with Philip would have been disastrous as well as dishonourable.

Taking advantage of this tremendous climax, Demosthenes reminds the jury that they must judge a man's service to Athens by the high standards that were set by their ancestors. Aeschines may talk of "trophies and deeds of long ago," but "all that you wanted was to rob me of the respect and good will of my countrymen—you miserable bookworm!" (209). With the thought before them that the "spirit" (φρόνημα) of Athens has other standards besides those of victory and success, they are well prepared for the final stage of the narrative—"when we arrived in Thebes, and found Philip's ambassadors there, our friends fearful, his friends confident" (211). He tells his story soberly; it was he who countered Philip's supporters, when they tried to incite Thebes against Athens, but he does not describe his speech or explain how he persuaded the Thebans to ask Athens for help (213—14).

What was Aeschines doing in those days, when the Thebans showed a splendid trust in their new allies by opening the gates of their city to the Athenian army and the Athenians justified this trust by their "justice and *sophrosyne*" as well as by their bravery "in the battle by the river and the winter battle" (216)? The question is left unanswered, but in describing his own efforts Demosthenes drops the pose of modesty and says he did more than many distinguished politicians of the past ever did, because he took complete responsibility for all his varied activities, persuading himself ("perhaps it was foolish, but I had persuaded myself") that he could do anything as well as anyone else: "And so, whatever was to be done, I was ready at my post" (221).

He points out that he was honoured with a crown for his activities in that winter and spring and that the attempt to block the proposal was a complete failure. He is trying to show that "the facts" refute Aeschines— while Aeschines prefers to ignore "facts" and sneers at his platform mannerisms, as though the destiny of Greece were affected "because I used this expression instead of that or waved my hand in this direction rather than the other" (232).[37] He gives more details of what he did in those critical days, building up the field force that was to fight Philip and winning new allies for Athens. He dismisses impatiently the criticism of Aeschines that he should have driven a harder bargain with these allies and made them pay their full share of the costs; he reminds Aeschines that if Athenian terms had been too hard, Philip was always ready to offer a better bargain; Aeschines would have been the first to complain if the allies had taken Philip's offer and deserted the Athenian cause. He says Aeschines is like a physician who goes to his patient's funeral and tells everyone what the dead man should have done to save his life, though he

37 Cf. Aesch. 3.166—67.

made no such helpful suggestions when the man was alive (243). And he challenges Aeschines to point to any instance in which he failed in his duties as a counsellor:

"And what are those duties? To see developments as they start, to anticipate them and give warning to others. That I did. Also to minimize delays and postponements of decisions, the hazards from ignorance and rivalry and similar troubles that beset all constitutional governments, to transform them so as to produce concord and good will and readiness to do the right thing. All this I did, and no one will ever find that I fell short on that score" (246).

He claims to have passed the test which Aeschines failed so dismally as an ambassador (19.4). He has fulfilled all his responsibilities. He cannot be held responsible for Philip's victory in the field, but does his best to show that military defeat was balanced by a moral victory:

"When it comes to being defeated or not being defeated by money, the victory is mine. Just as the buyer conquers the receiver, if he succeeds in buying him, so he who refuses the money has conquered the buyer. So far as it lay with me, the city was unbeaten" (247).

He says that his work "after the battle" was enthusiastically welcomed and appreciated, and all the wild accusations that were made against him failed. This is the end of the narrative, but he has a few more details to add before the comparison between himself and Aeschines is complete.

He complains once more of Aeschines' carping criticism (βασκανία, 252) and his remarks about the τύχη of Demosthenes, the ill-fortune that seemed to doom all his efforts to failure.[38] This is the signal for another personal attack on his opponent, just as graceless and offensive as before. He compares the "fortune" of Aeschines with his own—the miserable youth and upbringing of Aeschines, while Demosthenes went to the proper schools and met his civic obligations as choregus and trierarch. He must know the danger of speaking like this and says it is stupid to reproach anyone for being poor (256). A modern reader can hardly avoid thinking he is guilty of crass snobbery, but his object, as in the earlier attack, is to ridicule the pretentiousness of Aeschines, to explain his dishonesty and his cowardice in public life as the inevitable result of his unfortunate "background"; he waited to take advantage of other people's misfortunes, as might be expected of a man who always went in fear of being beaten for some petty dishonesty: "But when misfortune hit everyone else, you grew bold; and now you have become a public figure, everyone looks at you" (263).

---

38 Cf. Aesch. 3.115, 157.

Mercilessly Demosthenes insists on the difference between himself and Aeschines and traces it right through their lives:

"You taught in a school, I was a pupil; you worked as a clerk, I attended the Assembly; you acted minor parts, I was in the audience; you were hissed off the stage, I hissed; you helped the enemy, I worked for Athens" (265). The difference is made to appear consistent, and the elaborate comparison leads to the final conclusion that Demothenes, throughout his life, as individual and politician, has observed the standards of an honourable man and a good citizen, a καλὸς κἀγαθὸς πολίτης (278), by his scrupulous honesty in word and deed and devotion to the cause he thinks is right, by his generosity and regard for his fellow men as well as his courage in adversity, by his refusal to turn the misfortunes of others to his own advantage, by using his talents and opportunities for the benefit of Athens rather than for himself. And by all these standards Aeschines has failed.

Even a reader who feels that the high moral tone sometimes rings rather hollow must admit that he makes the fine-sounding phrases of Aeschines seem more hollow still. All the "facts" that have been revealed are designed to show that Aeschines is totally insincere and could not possibly have won Philip's respect except as his paid agent. As in *On the Embassy* Demosthenes takes for granted (quite unfairly) that he ran to Philip "after the disaster" to feather his own nest. Aeschines of course says he went to Philip in order to conciliate him, to prevent him from taking extreme measures against Athens—just as in 346. The politician who conciliates the conqueror (and does so by saying he admires him) is not often respected by his countrymen, even if he does them a useful service. Demosthenes knows that Aeschines cannot answer his insults effectively, unless he is prepared to sacrifice a large share of his dignity and to tell the Athenians that they had to choose between dignity and survival.

Demosthenes makes no such sacrifice; he denies that he lost the respect of his countrymen when they lost the battle; he was chosen to deliver the funeral oration in honour of the men who fell, and he tells the jury now, in moving language, that the relatives of the fallen never looked upon him as tainted by bloodguilt; they thought he shared with them the loss they had suffered, "as the man to whom it mattered more than anyone else that those who died should have been saved and been victorious" (288). Once again he tries to describe his services to Athens, comparing himself this time not only with Aeschines, but with other "loathsome men" in various cities whom he considers responsible for Philip's victory, "each one responsible for cutting off the limbs of his native city" (296): "In none of the counsels that I gave did I weight the scale (as you did) so that it fell on the side that favoured me personally,[39] but I spoke from an upright, a just, an uncorrupted heart. In the greatest actions that our age has seen I took the lead. That is why I claim honour and respect" (298). He refuses to admit that the Athenian cause was hopeless: "If there had been one man like me in each of the Greek cities to play the part that I played here, even if Thessaly had produced one man and Arcadia one man with my spirit, none of the Greeks, this side or the other side of Thermopylae, would have suffered their present fate" (304).

In the final comparison with Aeschines Demosthenes asks to be judged in terms of loyalty and good will (*eunoia*). He is ready to stand comparison with any living politician, and challenges Aeschines to find anyone who showed greater *eunoia* towards Athens than he did—when all strove to win good will by giving what they thought was the best advice to the city; and after the defeat when the city no longer needed advisers, but men who would carry out the conqueror's wishes and flatter his vanity— "all of you were ready for action then, Aeschines, in your splendour, and I was powerless—but I showed greater *eunoia* to my fellow countrymen than you did" (320). Among all the trials that followed, "when my surrender was demanded, when people tried to bring me before the Amphictyonic court, with threats and offers assailing me, with these abominable men let loose on me like wild beasts, I never betrayed my *eunoia* towards Athens" (322). This is the final contrast, between his own faithful loyalty and unbroken *eunoia* towards Athens and the lack of *eunoia* in Aeschines and the "Philippizers." It has been a long elaborate contrast, with many repetitions, but the theme of *eunoia* serves to bring it all together.

---

39 Cf. "On Peace" 12 (Chapter IV above, p. 139) for the notion that money puts an extra weight in the scale.

Index

WITHDRAWN